Peter B. Doeringer

Michael J. Piore

Internal Labor Markets

and

Manpower Analysis

Internal Labor Markets and Manpower Analysis

Internal Labor Markets
and Manpower Analysis

With a New Introduction

Peter B. Doeringer
Boston University

Michael J. Piore
Massachusetts Institute of Technology

M. E. Sharpe, Inc.
Armonk, New York
London, England

To John T. Dunlop

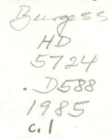

Available in the United Kingdom and Europe from M. E. Sharpe Publishers, 3 Henrietta Street, London WC2E 8LU

Library of Congress Cataloging in Publication Data

Doeringer, Peter B.
    Internal labor markets and manpower analysis.

    Reprint. Originally published: Lexington, Mass.: Heath, 1971. With new introd.
    Includes bibliographical references and index.
    1. Labor supply—United States. 2. Personnel management—United States.
3. Labor supply—United States—Effect of technological innovations on.
I. Piore, Michael J.   II. Title.
HD5724.D588   1985   331.12'0973   85-2063
ISBN 0-87332-351-3
ISBN 0-87332-332-7 (pbk.)

This report was prepared for the Manpower Administration, U.S. Department of Labor, under research grant number 81-23-66-22, authorized by Title I of the Manpower Development and Training Act. Since contractors performing research under government sponsorship are encouraged to express their own judgment freely, the report does not necessarily represent the Department's official opinion or policy. Moreover, the contractor is solely responsible for the factual accuracy of all material developed in the report.

Printed in the United States of America

Contents

Tables

Illustrations

Preface

In this volume we have elaborated the theme of the *internal labor market* that we first developed in our doctoral dissertations completed at Harvard in 1966. This theme of analysis has been reshaped considerably as a result of our subsequent research and advisory activities and by countless discussions and seminars.

We are indebted to an unusually large number of persons who have contributed to our research: to the many managers and union officials who generously devoted their time, and the resources of their organizations, to this study; to members of government and private agencies with whom we have worked in various capacities; and to our friends, associates, and wives who have commented on the project at various stages. In particular, we are grateful to John T. Dunlop who, as teacher and colleague, provided the guidance and challenge necessary to the formation of many of our concepts.

We have been the beneficiaries of considerable assistance in the preparation of the manuscript. Penny Feldman, David Gordon, and Michael Reich provided much of the research underlying our discussion of the disadvantaged labor force in Chapter 8. Christine Bishop and James Zeanah were responsible for computer programming. Helen Blumen helped to document many of our references. June MacArthur edited the manuscript. Virginia Sullivan, Karen Garrett, Jean Neal, Ann Ringle, and Adrienne Collier typed the numerous drafts and revisions.

We wish to acknowledge the kind permission which a number of journals granted to reprint portions of articles published previously: Michael J. Piore, "The Impact of the Labor Market Upon the Design and Selection of Productive Techniques Within the Manufacturing Plant," *The Quarterly Journal of Economics,* vol. LXXXII, no. 4 (November 1968), pp. 602-620; Michael J. Piore, "On-the-Job Training and Adjustment to Technological Change," *The Journal of Human Resources,* vol. III, no. 4 (Fall 1968), pp. 435-449; Peter B. Doeringer, "Determinants of the Structure of Industrial Type Internal Labor Markets," *Industrial and Labor Relations Review,* vol. 20, no. 2 (January 1967), pp. 206-220; and Peter B. Doeringer, "Manpower Programs for Ghetto Labor Markets," *Proceedings of the 21st Annual Winter Meeting of the Industrial Relations Research Association* (1968), pp. 257-267.

Finally, we acknowledge the financial assistance of the U.S. Department of Labor which made this study possible. Much of the study was supported by the Manpower Administration, U.S. Department of Labor, under research contract number 81-23-66-22, as authorized by Title I of the Manpower Development and Training Act. Scholars performing research under such government sponsorship are encouraged to express their own judgment freely. The study does not necessarily represent the Department's official opinion or policy, and we are solely responsible for the factual accuracy of all material presented here.

P.B.D.   M.J.P.
Cambridge, Mass.
November 1970

Introduction

Internal Labor Markets and Manpower
Analysis: A Second Look

This text was originally published in 1971. It has found a wide audience among managers, government officials, and union officers, as well as among students and scholars. In preparing to reissue it at this time, we considered revising the text to incorporate subsequent research findings and to make it more relevant to contemporary policy issues. But we realized that in many respects the book in its original form has come to lead a life of its own.

It has found a much wider audience both in the academic community and in the operating parts of our society than we had initially sought to address. And we ourselves have lost a clear sense of what kind of revision would be most useful to the many different groups among whom the book has found appeal. Instead of a complete revision, therefore, we have decided to preserve the original text and to address, in this new introduction, what we see as the principal limitations of that text today.

The book appears to play two related but distinct roles and to appeal to two audiences. First, it has provided a description of a number of institutional features of the U.S. labor market. As such, it has been used as a guide or map for managers, policy-makers, and economic analysts who need to know how employment and training decisions are actually made at the workplace. The first part of this introduction is designed to show how the map has been changed by research discoveries and by events in the period since the book was originally published.

The book, however, also prompted an analytical debate about the origins of the institutions it describes and their significance for the operation of the U.S. economic system. The second part of the introduction reviews that debate and assesses its implications for the institutional structure of the labor market.

Institutional Descriptions

The basic assertion of the book is that there is an institutional structure to labor markets reflected in a sharp distinction between internal and external market arrangements. The internal labor market is defined by an enterprise, or a part of an enterprise, or by a craft or professional community. Entry into such markets is limited to particular jobs or ports of entry. The pricing of labor, and its allocation from the point of entry to other work positions, is governed by administrative rules and customs. These rules and customs differentiate members of the internal labor market from outsiders and accord them rights and privileges which would not otherwise be available. Typically, these ''internal'' rights include certain guarantees of job security, opportunities for career mobility, and equity and due process in treatment at the workplace.

Having introduced this basic distinction, the book then goes on to characterize the principal features of the administrative rules governing internal labor markets in the United States. It focuses on blue-collar jobs in unionized manufacturing firms but also makes broader comparisons with other workplace situations—enterprise procedures in the nonunion sector, craft jobs in such nonmanufacturing industries as construction and longshoring, craft jobs within manufacturing, and lower-level white-collar and managerial employment.

The book also introduces the ''dual labor market'' hypothesis as it relates to internal labor markets. The basis of this hypothesis is that the main features that distinguish internal from external labor markets are characteristic of only a part of the labor market, the *primary* sector.

The remaining employment opportunities lie in the *secondary* sector, where the internal-external distinction is less important. Work in the secondary sector is low paying and associated with menial social status. It also involves little job security or career opportunity. Relations between supervisors and subordinates tend to be direct and personalistic, and are unmediated by rule, custom, or procedural due process. In addition to these characteristics of jobs and work, the secondary sector tends to be associated with the employment of certain social and demographic groups—women, youth, and ethnic and racial minorities.

Of the two concepts, internal labor markets and labor market dualism, it was dualism that initially attracted the most attention. More elaborate segmentation models were proposed which enlarged on the number of segments or tiers in the labor market.[1] Numerous econometric analyses were conducted attempting to prove or disprove the quantitative significance of segmentation.[2] And the segmentation concept found its way into the macroeconomic literature on wages and unemployment.[3] There were also a number of systematic critiques of segmentation hypotheses.[4]

In this book, however, the concept of segmentation and labor market dualism is actually a by-product of the operation of internal labor markets. It was not until later that segmentation was developed as an independent analytical concept.[5] We therefore concentrate here on developments with respect to internal labor markets.

Research Developments

Given the attention it has received in the literature, there has been surprisingly little original research on internal labor markets since 1971. What there is very strongly confirms the widespread existence of internal labor markets historically and in different countries. But in one respect this research is at odds with the spirit of the earlier research in that it suggests a much wider range of variation in internal labor market practices than originally indicated.

International research. One major source of variation has been uncovered through international research on enterprises in different countries using similar technologies and producing similar products. The most extensive group of studies have been those of LEST in Aix-en-Provence, comparing pairs of enterprises in France and Germany[6] carefully matched for product, technology, and plant size, and the studies of Ronald Dore, initially of automobile plants in Japan and Great Britain.[7] These studies all indicate an enormous international diversity, not readily reducible to differences in technology or labor availability, among countries in general, and particularly between the United States and comparable industries abroad.

Virtually every country studied has strong internal labor markets, but the rules associated with entry and exit and with internal labor allocation and pricing tend to be nation-specific. In no other country is reliance on seniority as extensive as it is in the United States and Canada. Moreover, the practices of lay-off, recall, promotion, and demotion along job ladders that are so common in American manufacturing appear to be less prevalent internationally. Indeed, they may be unique to North America, Britain, and some of its previous colonies.

Internal labor markets in most countries, however, provide more *employment security* than does the United States, at least for workers who have been granted regular employment status. Once hired, workers cannot be easily terminated either for disciplinary or economic reasons. While employment security is enhanced, the rights to a particular job or type of work are less clearly defined and often nonexistent for workers in internal labor markets in other countries. As a result, the employer retains much greater flexibility in the internal allocation of labor.[8]

Rules with respect to wage determination also vary widely among countries. Nowhere are the wages within internal labor markets free to vary as would a price in a competitive market. In some countries wages are tied to the job or the work performed; in other countries worker characteristics such as skill, seniority, or need are more important. In still other countries earnings are regularly linked to the performance of the particular firm or even to the performance of an industry.

One result of these varying arrangements is to give a more extensive meaning to what John Dunlop first identified as national systems of industrial relations, nation-specific imprints that are apparent in the rules of internal labor markets.[9] A second result is considerable variation in staffing patterns and wage differentials within similar internal labor markets in different countries. Overall, it appears that internal labor markets lead to wide latitude in the patterns of earnings, employment, and job security among countries.

Internal Labor Markets in the United States

Recent research has also indicated a somewhat wider variation in internal labor market practices within the United States than is indicated in this text. A variety of quantitative studies of plant-level personnel practices, of which the most extensive were conducted by Richard Freeman and James Medoff and their associates, suggest that our book does capture the central tendency of American practice, at least until quite recently.[10] But studies of major nonunion employers[11] and recent changes in industrial relations practices within unionized firms[12] indicate that there is a significant and growing dispersion of prevailing practices across the country.

Recent studies of lower-level white-collar employment have also emphasized the variation in the structure of internal labor markets within a single enterprise.[13] Osterman, for example, argues that the correct unit of analysis is often not the enterprise itself but some subunit, such as a department or even a shop.[14]

The blue-chip nonunion firms tend to resemble more closely the typical German or Japanese firm than the unionized American company. They combine employment guarantees with much looser job rights: often the line between the responsibilities of management and the rank-and-file work force is blurred, and workers participate in decisions which in most U.S. plants would be viewed as managerial prerogatives.

There are even moves in this direction in the unionized sector of manufacturing. Developments along this line have been particularly rapid since 1980. They have been incorporated in the aggressive strategies of union avoidance increasingly pursued by management. They have also been facilitated by the growing willingness on the part of unions and unionized corporations, in response to nonunion competition, to experiment with new practices within their internal labor markets.

Industries, even particular companies which at the beginning of the 1970's were almost entirely unionized, have in the 1980's developed significant nonunion components operating with distinct sets of allocation and pricing rules.[15] Even some union contracts permit significant differences in wage levels, employment, and job guarantees for the same work within a single company. The most well publicized of these is the 1985 postal workers arbitration award, which establishes sharply lower wage scales for new hires. These arrangements seem to preserve the distinction between the internal and external labor market, but the rules governing internally are no longer uniform; and in addition to employment strategies associated with a given rule structure, they open the way for a range of strategies involving the distribution of production across distinct labor markets within the enterprise itself.

Historical research. The last body of institutional research which modifies our earlier picture of internal labor markets is historical.

Again, that research substantiates the existence of a distinction between internal and external labor markets but suggests considerably greater variation in the American institutional structures than was apparent in the 1950's and 1960's. Some of that research[16] emphasizes the continuity of the internal rules structure. But other research[17] suggests that the dominant postwar practice emerged from disenchantment during the Depression of the 1930's with earlier practices developed in the prosperous years of the 1920's—practices that were much closer to current institutions in Japan, Germany, and to those in American, blue-chip nonunion companies.

General findings. Taken together, these recent research materials suggest the following conclusions. First, internal labor markets are a very general phenomenon, both historically and internationally. They are an extremely widespread, and probably a universal, feature of labor market structure of both developed industrial economies and at least of large organizations in developing economies.

Second, the characteristics of the rules and customs governing such markets are not universal. The text contrasts the variation within the United States between blue-collar manufacturing markets and the markets for craft and managerial workers. But there is also considerable international variation in the structure of internal labor markets for similar types of workers.

The U.S. structure for blue-collar workers—in which wages and career opportunities are tied to narrow, carefully defined jobs; promotion opportunities and layoffs are allocated through a system which gives heavy weight to seniority; and in which employees on lay-off retain rights to subsequent recall—is largely an Anglo-Saxon phenomenon. The general tendency internationally is for employers to more or less guarantee both jobs and income within the internal labor market; there are no temporary lay-offs; and severance generally involves substantial payments. Only when such severance payments are made is the employment relationship permanently terminated. Management generally has, in turn, much greater freedom to allocate workers internally, and pay tends to be linked to skill rather than to job content.

Third, the U.S. system, even for blue-collar workers, is of relatively recent origin. In the 1920's major American corporations practiced a form of welfare capitalism known as the American Plan which defined an internal labor market with features rather close to those of the present Germany or Japanese systems. The collapse of the job and wage guarantees in the Great Depression discredited those institutional forms, and the current system grew up in the late 1930's and the Second World War as a substitute. It was closely associated with the rise of industrial unionism. It spread from union to nonunion shops through private emulation and through more direct encouragement by wartime production agencies. The practices of a number of prominent nonunion companies such as IBM and Texas Instruments, which appear, against the background of the system as described in the text, as unique and exceptional, can be interpreted as the vestiges of the earlier pattern of the 1920's.

Finally, under the impact of the economic crises of the last decade, labor and management have been experimenting with a variety of new labor-allocation and wage-determination procedures. These procedures preserve the internal labor market but eliminate many of the postwar rules and customs described in this book. The substitute arrangements are a set of features reminiscent of foreign practices or of U.S. practices of the 1920's. The patterns as described here are still the typical or dominant patterns, but current practice is much more diverse than it was ten years ago and is changing now in a way that it was not then.

The Analytical Issues

The second set of issues raised by *Internal Labor Markets* is analytic: what is the significance of the institutions the book describes? How do they affect the operation of the economy? Where do they come from? What determines their structure and the variation in structure over time and across countries? How do those structures affect public policy goals, and how might they be changed by policy interventions?

The analytic debate has been largely with conventional economic theory. Since conventional economics is essentially a theory about a competitive market economy, the fundamental question in the debate is about whether the internal labor market is consistent with the competitive market model.

The central proposition of the competitive model is that economic activity is governed by the interplay of a large number of relatively small productive units, each trying to maximize its own welfare and competing among themselves for the resources with which to do so. The pressure of competition on the one hand and the desire to maximize profit or personal well-being on the other lead each unit to deploy its resources in the most effective way possible. Within this system wages vary so as to reflect the scarcity of different types of labor and the cost of augmenting their supply through education, migration, and the like. Because wages vary in this way, they transmit to decision-makers in the firm the cost to the society of different types of work, and they ensure that when the firm engages in activities which are most effective from its private point of view, it is operating efficiently from the perspective of the society as a whole.

The book does not directly address the question of whether the institutions it describes are fully consistent with the competitive view of how the economy operates, and the answer implicit in the text is somewhat ambiguous. Several ways in which the institutional material might be incorporated within the main corpus of economic thought are explored. But we believed then—and are even more convinced now— that the existence of the internal labor market is, in terms of neoclassical theory, basically an anomaly.

The conventional theory we were taught did not lead to the anticipation of internal labor markets as originally described. We would not have discovered their existence through the conventional tools and approaches of economic analysis. Even when they became apparent, neither their mode of operation nor their impact on the economy seemed understandable in purely neoclassical terms.

On the whole, the economics profession has also seen the institutions described in this book as a challenge to conventional theory. Various attempts have been made to reconcile several features of internal labor markets—seniority-based job tenure, wage rigidity, and job-based (rather than individualistic) pay determination—with the overall framework of competitive theory. For some economists the key economic features attributed to internal labor markets are only the result of a series of sequential "spot" markets for labor in which the status quo remains relatively stable. Most attempts, however, have sought to invoke some concept of enterprise-specific human capital, often joining it to other concepts such as "implicit contracts" and "idiosyncratic" labor exchange.

Specific human capital. The earliest of these, enterprise specific investments, grows out of Gary Becker's work on human capital.[18] It predates *Internal Labor Markets* and is, to some extent, incorporated in the text. Gary Becker's basic argument is that skill training can be treated as an investment analogous to the purchase of a piece of capital equipment. Workers are willing to pay its cost because they expect to earn higher wages in the future. Occupational wage differentials act as an inducement to workers to develop skills, and the cost of training "explains" the size of the differential.

This mechanism works, however, only if the skills are widely utilized and if employers must compete for skilled workers. If the skills are specific to a particular employer, the skilled worker must accept whatever wage the employer offers or work elsewhere at the unskilled wage. Because there is no guarantee that the offered wage will compensate the worker for the training, there is no incentive for the worker to pay the training cost. If the firm wants trained workers, it must pay for the training. But then the problem is reversed, for there is no guarantee that the worker will remain long enough to repay the employer for the cost of training.

The wage determination rules and employment guarantees of the internal labor market, in this view, become ways of providing a system of incentives to workers and employers to invest in and recoup the benefits of such specific human capital by minimizing turnover. Others have extended this argument to cover a wide range of employment costs—the costs of recruitment or of screening workers, for example, to determine what skills they actually have. These are like an investment in the sense that they are paid out in the hiring process and lost if the employment relationship is terminated.[19]

Implicit contracts. Implicit labor contracts, unlike commercial contracts and collective bargaining agreements, consist of unwritten understandings between workers and employers. The argument for implicit contracts begins with the recognition that shifts in supply and demand can affect future earnings. In a labor market consisting only of general and transferable skills, such shifts would either be anticipated, and therefore incorporated in advance into market prices and investment decisions of workers, or else unanticipated, so that their earnings and employment consequences would be diffused throughout the work force at the time they occurred.

Where there are specific human capital investments shared by both workers and employers, however, unanticipated shifts in labor market conditions could lead to windfall gains or losses for both groups. Because workers are assumed to be risk averse, they are willing to accept a lower rate of pay in exchange for more certain lifetime earnings. Because employers are thought to be better able to diversify their portfolios and relatively less risk averse than workers, there is the potential for an exchange between risk and pay that benefits both parties. As a result, workers enter into employment contracts that provide workers with greater stability of earnings and employment over their lifetimes than they could expect absent such contracts.[20]

These contracts are intended to equate the present expected value of a worker's lifetime productivity against the present expected value of his earnings, minus a payment to the employer for the risk which is transferred from the worker to the employer. Because it is too difficult to anticipate all contingencies that may affect risk, the contracts are "implicit" in that they embody general principles, enforceable through the need to preserve a "reputation" in the labor market, rather than a precisely specified economic contract that is legally enforceable.

A further element in the implicit contract literature stems from the difficulty in measuring effort and productivity. Where it is difficult to monitor worker productivity directly, shirking is always a possibility. Implicit contracts regarding employment, pay, and effort are thought to provide a means of encouraging commitment and discouraging shirking.[21]

The form that the implicit contracts are alleged to take is that embodied in most internal labor markets in the United States. Job guarantees are tied to seniority as a rule of thumb to provide employment protection in proportion to on-the-job training investments. Partial earnings guarantees are provided through rigid wage rates which ensure against wage cutting. Earnings levels are also loosely tied to seniority. This "backloading" of compensation in favor of senior workers gives employers a chance to reward employees who have lived up to their implicit effort bargains and to weed out those who have not before they can acquire significant seniority.

Idiosyncratic exchange. The idiosyncratic exchange literature, principally developed by Oliver Williamson and his colleagues, further extends the arguments about specific training and implicit contracts as explanations of internal labor markets.[22] The key elements of the internal labor market in this literature are: (1) enterprise-specific investments by workers and employers which prevent spot markets and create incentives for "opportunism," the ability to exploit fixed training and information investments through bargaining at the workplace; (2) "transaction" costs within firms resulting from "opportunism," organizational complexity, and the presence of work teams which make individual productivity determinations difficult; and (3) "bounded rationality," the difficulty for the human mind to reduce a complex and highly uncertain world to a manageable set of explicit contingent contracts.

These various considerations are then used to explain various observed features of internal labor markets. Internal labor markets facilitate joint investments in specific skills because they remove the fear of exploitation. The organizational clarity of seniority-based job and earnings guarantees, objective pay structures based on job content, and rigid pay structures constitute an efficient system for encouraging cooperation, thus overcoming "opportunism" within a firm and reducing much of the need for costly bargaining over pay and employment. Finally, they provide opportunities for employers to achieve efficiencies in information by providing low-cost screening of hard-to-observe qualities of a heterogeneous labor force.

Evaluating Neoclassical Reformulations

All of these are continuing lines of research, and they cannot be judged solely on the basis of the results they have produced so far. But our own view is that they are unlikely to provide a solution to the problems raised for analysis by the internal labor market as an institution. They may provide plausible hypotheses about why internal labor markets exist, but they are unlikely to explain how they function. Thus, for example, the Becker-Oi theory of fixed labor cost leaves the wage indeterminate. The employer wants to hold the worker once hired and hence will pay a wage above what the worker can earn elsewhere, but how high that alternative wage need be is unclear. Presumably, the worker can get more by threatening to move elsewhere, and this throws the workers and employers into a bargaining process. To understand the wage structure, one needs a theory of the bargaining process. The notion of specific training may explain how you get into this predicament but not how you get out.

The problem with the information and idiosyncratic exchange typology is potentially more serious still. Williamson, for example, is preoccupied by the question of efficiency. He seeks to show that the internal labor market is in some sense an optimal arrangement. But his list of characteristics is so long and their definitions so vague, that they become tautological explanations. For example, what exactly is "bounded rationality" beside something which creates internal labor markets? This problem becomes especially acute given the variation in the rules governing internal labor markets over time and across countries. Are the bounds on rationality different in Japan than in the United States? Is exchange more *idiosyncratic*? The terms have not been defined in a way which would enable one to say.

The institutional variation uncovered by recent research poses a similar problem for implicit contract theory. Take, for example, the perception of risk. It is possible that a precise definition of what is meant by risk could be developed in a way that was not tautological. But if such a definition of risk were to explain the existence of internal labor markets, it would have to do so in a way that could be objectively related to systematic differences among workers and employers in different countries, to distinctions among internal labor markets within a single industry in particular countries, and to different historical periods of internal labor market development. Because of the importance of national culture, workplace and work group, and institutional "history" in the formulation of the internal labor markets, we doubt that implicit contracts could provide such an explanation while remaining consistent with neoclassical economic theories which are, by construction, ahistorical and individualistic.

These various attempts to explain the characteristics of internal labor markets in terms of efficiency and competition can essentially be read as an admission that the labor market is suffused with idiosyncratic employment relationships that contradict the universalism of neoclassical theory. Each of the neoclassical reformulations of labor market theory accepts the proposition that enterprise-specific factors are central to the operation of certain types of employment situations. Each starts with the recognition that price-auction arrangements with wage flexibility do not apply to major portions of the labor market and that wage rigidity and long-tenure of employment need somehow to be explained.

Once it is conceded that "ordinary" competition is not a sufficient explanation of labor market operations, the reformulations seek a plausible set of metaphors—enterprise-specific investments, high transaction costs, differential risk aversion, and so forth—which are derived from the neoclassical vocabulary and which could reconcile apparently anomalous labor market behavior with conventional considerations of efficiency. This approach, while seeming to preserve the integrity of neoclassical theory, actually highlights the difficulty in extending such theory to situations where the competition for labor has been interrupted and where nonmarket influences can therefore come into play.

Idiosyncratic exchange provides a good illustration of this problem.

In arguing for the efficiency of internal labor markets, Williamson notes that enterprise-specific factors can lead to what he calls "opportunism"—a short-hand term for threats and bargaining power. Internal labor markets become an efficient device for avoiding the continual exercise of power in day-to-day wage setting and employment decisions at the workplace. Efficient mechanisms for dealing with "power," however, are only tenuously related to the concept of efficiency as it is customarily used in economics.

Thus we doubt that any of the major strands of conventional research will prove capable of assimilating the internal labor market into conventional theory in a useful and meaningful way. They seem at best to provide a vocabulary, or a set of metaphors, for talking about internal labor markets in a language drawn from neoclassical economics. They translate the description of internal labor markets, originally presented in the language of labor market actors, into the jargon of economic theory. But they do not provide an explanation of the origins and current operation of the internal labor market. They do not generate a set of testable alternative hypotheses. Nor can they predict how the institutional structures vary among countries or over time.

Because they fail in these respects, they lack what is generally the great strength of neoclassical explanation of economic structures: a normative referent against which to judge existing institutions and to evaluate public policy. Since they are essentially a vocabulary, not a theory, they make it impossible to judge either the efficiency or the distributive consequences of internal allocative arrangements. They also provide no guidelines through which public policy might attempt to move from one set of such arrangements to another.

While the materials in this book do not provide a competing behavioral "theory" of labor market operation, the vocabulary used to describe internal labor market processes does reflect the actual way in which workers, managers, and trade unions perceive wage and employment decisions. To the extent that one is forced to choose among competing metaphors, there is at least an empirical foundation behind those adopted in this book. The language of the actors, moreover, points toward a very different kind of understanding. We cannot claim to have developed that understanding into a theoretical construction with the rigor and coherence of conventional economic theory in the years since the book was written. We can, however, identify much more clearly now than we could then the characteristics which the development would take. These are briefly outlined in the following section.

Internal Labor Markets and Organic Social Groups: An Alternative Approach

In our view, the accumulated body of research about internal labor markets—their origins, processes, and objectives—suggests that they are not best understood as variants on the general model of the neoclassical firm. Instead, they represent a fundamental departure from conventional theory and provide a basis for formulating a general theory of economic behavior which departs significantly from all major strands of conventional theoretical research.

In particular, we do not believe that internal labor markets can be understood in terms of a theory which starts with individuals as the basic unit of analysis. The actual process through which internal labor markets emerge and evolve over time clearly involves the formation and interaction of cohesive social groups. This is true in the workplace, where the work group interacts with management on the shop floor in a process which both generates rules and customs and sanctions violations of them. It is also true of the political processes and the legal framework within which internal labor markets are formulated and operate.

The institutional structures of internal labor markets are sometimes the product of formal negotiations between organized groups such as trade unions and business firms. But the alternative to such negotiations is not the interaction of individuals in a market process. Rather it is the interplay of formal and informal groups exerting various kinds of social pressures. These pressures range from the ridicule or ostracism of recalcitrant members to threats of physical violence and economic sanctions through strikes, slowdowns, and industrial sabotage.

To be sure, neoclassical economics has not ignored the issue of work groups. It has, however, chosen to describe these groups in a manner which negates their social characteristics and treats them as an extension of the conventional model of consumer behavior.[23] Individuals are thought to come together to form group alliances and act in consort because it maximizes their individual economic welfare.

Even the apparent exceptions, which purport to acknowledge features of groups which distinguish them from individuals, fail to escape the essentially individualistic character of the theoretical framework. Olson and others, for example, have recognized that production may be organized around work "teams" and that groups may be formed to deal with "collective goods," indivisible benefits available to all workers which cannot be subdivided or allocated according to the individual's contribution to their creation.[24] Such a treatment of groups, however, attributes their existence to the need to solve a "technical" problem of efficiently allocating benefits to individual workers in a situation where "individualistic" behavior remains the cornerstone of the theory. The idea that there might be group behaviors—solidarity and collective goals, concern with the distribution of benefits *relative to other workers in the group* instead of distribution *relative to individual productivity*, kinship and friendship obligations, political factions, and concern with fairness and legitimacy—which are irrelevant to individuals *except as they are members of groups* is not a part of these theories.

Moreover, the existence of groups and the consequences of their behavior are always being implicitly compared to a market solution in which individual members are continually testing the costs and benefits derived from participation in the group against those which would be available to them on the external, competitive labor market. Workers are therefore seen as being mobile at will between working as part of a group in an internal labor market and working in a more individualistic situation such as is thought to characterize the external labor market. Group arrangements which preclude such competitive mobility are seen either as imposing "transactions" costs which disrupt perfectly competitive outcomes or as introducing inefficient monopoly influences into the labor market, as in the case of trade unions.

Because groups are studied in relationship to a standard of market efficiency in terms of pricing and utilization of resources in basically individualistic markets, the questions which conventional theory asks about the behavior of groups is limited. When different types of labor contracts are compared, for example, they are judged according to the degree to which they promote economic "optimality" while neglecting their distributional consequences (which may be of paramount importance to the group). Similarly, the conventional literature fails to recognize that the economic relationships within the group, and between one group and another, may be a manifestation of *social* needs being met by the group that are so fundamental to human existence that society could not function in the individualistic mode which underlies traditional standards of optimality.[25]

Social Systems and the Production Process

We prefer to think of work groups as organic entities that are formed naturally as part of the production process. They are not simply aggregations of individuals nor can they be dismantled, either conceptually or institutionally, into their constituent individuals. The real distinction facing workers is a choice among different group structures, not between group and individualistic labor markets. Understanding labor markets dominated by groups requires an analytical understanding of the processes through which such groups arise and evolve.

To do this, one needs to move away from the research techniques and models of neoclassical economics toward other social science disciplines, particularly sociology and economic anthropology. These disciplines do not, to be sure, provide a full scale understanding of group structures comparable to the understanding which neoclassical theory provides of a market economy composed of autonomous individuals. They do, however, provide certain insights into the evolution of the social structures associated with the internal labor market and into why internal labor market factors may provide the explanation to certain perplexing problems posed by conventional theory.

One such problem is "bounded rationality" and other constructs which have been used to describe constraints on individual maximization. In contrast to neoclassical assumptions about individual behavior, and the way in which neoclassical theorists have posed the issue of constraints on rational decision-making, anthropological or sociological frameworks argue that purposive human activity can only take place within a social context. Human activity requires a framework for thought, goal setting, and communication, and such frameworks are preeminently social.[26]

A Structural Framework

The most compelling example of such a framework is language. Human activity presupposes language as a means of communication. Language, in general, becomes the property of large social groups known as "cultures," and smaller groups or "subcultures" develop specific meanings and usages of language which become their property. The attempt of social groups to develop and preserve their languages can clearly have economic significance, but it also has much broader implications for the existence of its members. It affects not only their ability to obtain an economic livelihood: it affects their ability to function at all, it defines their sense of self, and it links the individual sense of self to that of the group.*

The knowledge involved in the ability to function effectively at work is comparable to language. The process through which work knowledge is passed on from one generation of workers to another through informal on-the-job training, and the way in which it evolves through time, is much closer to the process through which language is developed and communicated than it is to an engineering production function. To the extent that knowledge is like a language, it is not a bound on rationality but a prerequisite to rationality itself. Thus, to continue with this analogy, one might have a choice between organizing a shop so that production workers and managers spoke the same language or spoke essentially different languages, but one could not have a workplace in which no language was spoken at all. The notion that the economy could be broken into autonomous units communicating only through the marketplace is equivalent to the notion of a world with no real language.

This conception of productive knowledge as being like language, a property inherent in groups rather than in individuals, is a much more radical departure from neoclassical thinking than it may at first appear.

*One can, of course, construct a neoclassical model of language. A group of individuals could develop a language in order to facilitate economic exchange and maximize their welfare. On its face, however, this approach has very limited plausibility. It undoubtedly explains the diffusion of second languages: English is widely studied because of its commercial utility. But it could not explain the origin of language itself. How would people have thought about the problem of economic organization without a language in which to frame the question? How would they have begun to communicate with each other, to enter into negotiations and frame the agreement which such a contract theory of language seems to imply? And if languages are selected for their commercial value, why do so many languages persist? Why do people continue to teach their children at home Dutch or Creole or Swiss-German, when they themselves speak English, French, and German at work and will subsequently send their children to learn those languages at school so that the children can speak them at work as well? Clearly there are processes and motivations that govern language development which are prior to the economic motivation. The economic explanation must either work through these other processes or compete with them.

It is not possible to fully explore this difference in the present context, but we can perhaps suggest what is involved by reference to the nature of linguistic theory.

If linguistic theory were to characterize a language the way economic theory wants to characterize society, language would be defined by a dictionary of words. But linguistic theory is *structural*.[27] What characterizes a language is not the list of words of which it is composed but rather a set of rules which determine both what words are possible and the grammatical structures which dictate how they are put together to compose meaning. To be sure, languages expand or contract by adding new words and losing old ones. But linguistic theory tends to focus on the more enduring structural forms in which more marginal changes take place. Thus shifts across languages are discontinuous: they move from one structure to another.

The term "bounded rationality" has a very different meaning in such a theory of social form and structure than it does in conventional economics. Applying the economic concept of bounded rationality to the internal labor market is analogous to saying: "We use a small vocabulary because the human mind is incapable of remembering a large number of words. If we could expand our memory capacity, for example, by using computers, we would not need to economize on language in this way." But a structural theory which suggests an explanation of why there are internal labor markets is likely to be much more akin to an explanation of why some people speak only French and some people speak only English. It is possible to have a large territory in which everybody speaks only one language. It is also possible to have bilingual territories where everybody speaks both French and English. But, given an existing set of linguistic arrangements, the movement to a different set of linguistic arrangements is very difficult.

The reason such movements are difficult is that they involve the absorption of a whole new structure. Structural theories are thus not theories about "bounds" on rationality; they are theories of how the human mind functions. They are theories of rationality itself.[28] A theory which likens the internal labor market to a language community will thus produce explanations in which the internal labor market is not so much a "technical" problem as a manifestation of the nature of the human mind. It is unlikely to suggest that a particular internal market structure is inevitable. But it will suggest the difficulties of the process of transition from one internal labor market structure to another.

An analogous point can be made with respect to theories of risk and uncertainty. In economics, risk is expressed as a probability distribution, and changing perceptions of risk involve shifts in that distribution. But one can ask whether the shifts in the distribution are perceived as a part of a continuous or a discontinuous process.[29]

Take, for example, workers' expectations about unemployment. One theory is that workers' expectations of their unemployment are some weighted average of the unemployment of the people around them. These expectations implicitly change with new information about jobs and unemployment, so that the perception of risk is being continuously revised. But workers might just as well treat the unemployment of those around them as a random event drawn from a relatively fixed probability distribution. They might then rarely change their perception of risk in response to the unemployment of their neighbors, preferring instead to modify their perception only discontinuously in response to some unusual historical occurrence which leads them to believe that the distribution itself has shifted. For example, workers who lived through the Depression are much more likely to identify random downturns in the economy with severe economic insecurity than are those who escaped the Depression.

Given these alternative formulations of how risk is perceived, risk in itself becomes a very limited explanation for anything. If it is perceived so as to permit continuous adjustment, then the institutional rules of the internal labor market will be relatively flexible. They will at most introduce a lag into the response to changing economic circumstances. If risk is perceived discontinuously, an institution that reflects that perception will be extremely rigid. It may well have a profound, independent effect on the operation of the economy. But—and this is a critical question—it is unclear how much that effect has to do with the institution itself and how much has to do with the way the human mind perceives, organizes, and deals with uncertainty and risk.

Legitimacy and Performance

A final example to illustrate how our approach departs from that of conventional theory has to do with the relationship between group behavior and economic performance. The major determinants of economic performance are traditionally argued to be investment in human and physical capital, efficient utilization of resources, and technical progress through innovation. The first two are thought to result from individualistic responses to competitive market conditions; the latter, from a combination of innovation processes distinct from market conditions and from competitively determined investments in research and development. Economic institutions and group considerations play no part in this process, except as research and production may be conducted through teams or as groups may distort market signals.

While we make no claim to being able to demonstrate a relationship between innovation and the character of work groups, we would be surprised if there were no link between the social framework of group behavior and the creative propensity of groups in much the same way that a group's language affects its art and culture. There is, moreover, a growing body of theory and evidence pointing to the relationship between the structure of groups and the productivity of the group, not unlike that posited by theories of "X-efficiency."[30]

For example, the recent research by Freeman and others has argued that unionized workplaces in the United States perform more productively than their nonunion counterparts because of a heightened sense of fairness made possible by grievance procedures and other union rules.[31] A variety of comparative studies of internal labor markets and workplace organization have made similar connections between the institutional rules of the workplace and the microeconomic performance.[32] Add to these the vast number of courses and texts on organizational behavior directed at devising ways of designing and managing business organizations to elicit higher productivity, and one has an impressive array of direct and indirect evidence supporting the importance of work groups in achieving improved economic performance.[33]

We would argue that a key feature of the economic performance of social groups is their sense of "legitimacy." Groups which operate under a set of institutional arrangements that they perceive as legitimate will be productive, whereas those that do not will perform poorly. Unlike concepts such as efficiency or risk, there are no technical measures which can be used to define legitimacy—it is uniquely a social and cultural phenomenon. Work groups, like societies, develop standards of legitimacy. Although it would be inaccurate to say that factors such as competition and efficiency are irrelevant to these standards, they are only part of a larger set of considerations in which social values and distributional concerns within the group are often of greater importance.

Moreover, the presence of legitimacy as a factor affecting economic performance is a bar to the types of flexible institutional design envisaged by conventional economic theory. Legitimacy demands a certain continuity of practice over time, or practices become arbitrary and therefore illegitimate. Similarly, the legitimacy within a group cannot be meaningfully compared with the alternative economic arrangements of the competitive market because the competitive market has no group within which legitimacy could be defined and no institutional memory or machinery to ensure its continuity.

Structuralism, Marginalism, and History

These various examples underscore a final point about how we view the internal labor market as part of a structural theory of labor market operation. Structural theories tend to give considerable weight to history in causal explanations. They do this because they incorporate change as a discontinuous process. Neoclassical economics, by contrast, posits continuous marginal adjustments. This contrast is implicit in the previous example of how risk is perceived.

Similarly, the analogy drawn between social processes at the workplace and language suggests that the events which initially determine the social processes are likely to have effects that persist long after the external market environment has substantially changed. As a result, structural approaches such as ours rely more heavily on historical analysis, whereas the contemporary environment is more important for theories of marginal adjustment.

Theory and Policy

The analytical issues raised here are more complex and technical than the descriptive issues. But they are nonetheless critical to judgments about the significance of those institutions and to the formulation of employment and training policy. This has become most apparent in public policy toward the employment of women and of ethnic and racial minorities.

A central thrust of that policy has been to review the rules and customs which define the internal labor market, determine who is admitted to it, and govern the policies of wage determination and job allocation. The government has determined that many of these rules and customs are discriminatory and has tried to change them in order to promote a more equitable distribution of employment opportunity. The abstract, analytical debate in this area of public policy is about the implications of such government efforts. Unless one understands why such rules and customs exist in the first place, it is impossible to determine what basic forces government is attempting to counteract through its policy. It is also difficult to determine what the costs of its efforts are likely to be in terms both of the efficient operation of the economic system and of the rights and privileges of the individuals who currently hold the privileged employment positions.

If the rules and customs of internal labor markets are simply the expression of competitive market pressures, and the institutional structure plays no independent role, it may be that changes cannot be effected by attacking the rules themselves. Competition will simply shift employment elsewhere to situations beyond the reach of policy, or the rules themselves will be revised so that similar competitive results are achieved in a different way. On the other hand, competitive theory suggests that outcomes could be changed by changing the productive characteristics of individual minority group members through, for example, remedial education and training. The internal labor market rules might then be altered by competitive pressures to reflect the changed availability of productive workers.

If, however, the rules and customs which articulate labor market discrimination are the result of historical processes and reflect a deeply ingrained sense of equity or fairness in the work force, or if they are produced by the operation of social groups to which minorities are barred access, efforts to change them by training or retraining individuals will most likely prove futile. Change could probably be imposed by the law; but if the law is to be respected and effective in a reasonable period of time, it would probably have to be based on an understanding of the factors which generated the rules in the first place and on how perceptions of legitimacy are amended.

For example, equal opportunity in blue-collar employment might have been more successful if it had focused on institutions identified more with safeguarding workers' rights than with the direct sanctions of law. This could have included more emphasis on the right of minority workers to form or join trade unions and the strengthening of union power to negotiate new rule structures, rather than focusing on the rules themselves. Alternatively, public policy might have contemplated a redesign of the American industrial relations system, such as was accomplished during the 1930's, to solve problems of equity in employment. The radical changes in industrial relations modeled after the

Japanese which are now being contemplated to meet competitive pressures from abroad could also have been considered as instruments in the pursuit of other employment and income policies.

A similar dilemma is present in the emerging debate about the relationship between employment structures and macroeconomic performance. An influential school of macroeconomics suggest that wage or employment rigidities are chiefly responsible for the difficulties in obtaining full employment and price stability.[34] It has been argued that U.S. unemployment is aggravated by the fact that the internal labor markets make wages rigid in the face of declining demand for labor, forcing employers to lay off workers instead of cutting labor costs in ways which would lead to an expansion in product demand. A similar argument is made in Europe, and in many developing countries, where wages are not only rigid but where layoffs are often prohibited as well. There it is argued that employment opportunities fail to expand when production increases because employers are afraid that the increased output will not be sustained and the firm will be caught in a downturn with excess labor that it cannot discharge. While both of these arguments involve certain assumptions about macroeconomic theory and structure which are themselves controversial, their implications for economic policy depend on the explanation of the internal labor market to which one subscribes.

If the rules and customs of internal labor markets are imposed by organizations attempting to monopolize employment opportunities and enhance the relative position in the labor market of their individual members, improvements in microeconomic performance might also increase macroeconomic efficiency. If the rules are efficient in the sense that they are an effective response to problems of "bounded rationality" or "risk and uncertainty," as those are understood in neoclassical theories, then microeconomic improvements in wages and employment flexibility may only be purchased at a high cost in terms of macroeconomic growth and efficiency.

If the internal labor market is a natural social phenomenon originating under a particular set of historical circumstances, then there may be other structures which serve similar purposes, which are more conducive to macroeconomic stability and even more acceptable now than they were in the postwar period, when the current internal market structures were put into place. But the transitions from the current structure to the new one would probably have to be negotiated in ways which required the continued presence, even the strengthening, of the trade unions and other economic institutions.

Conclusion

The various points touched on in this new introduction are intended neither to wrap up our intellectual concerns with internal labor markets nor to summarize comprehensively the unfinished research agenda. We have provided an interim report on our thinking—one which is full of improvisations designed to suggest, rather than to resolve, what we see as a pressing need to construct a new theory of labor markets.

Whether this would be a single and comprehensive theory, or a set of theories to be selectively applied, we are not prepared to say at this stage. We do believe, however, that such theory would be more concerned with distribution and growth than with static efficiency. It would be grounded more in historical experience than it would be ahistorical. It would depend on group behavior rather than individualistic behavior. Finally, it would stress the importance of institutions as an independent force in the labor market.

While the neoclassical firm would still have a place in such a theory as a special type of labor market institution, it would exist only as one of many forms of organization. Similarly, internal labor markets as described in this book would be only one variant of a more general phenomenon. That phenomenon would encompass not only internal labor market structures found in other countries but also work groups embedded in families, kinship groupings, and many types of informal associations of workers.

Hand in hand with such an institutional theory, we would hope to see new ways of approaching labor market policies with respect to training, fair employment, job creation, productivity improvement, and economic stabilization. We particularly see the need for macroeconomic policy to be conducted with a greater awareness of the labor market institutions whose decision-making such policies are designed to affect. Such an approach would require not only an understanding of these institutions—their rules, objectives, and constraints—but a sense of how to accomplish institutional change as well. Macroeconomic policy which is governed by an incorrect vision of the microeconomic institutions is not only likely to be ineffective, it may be counterproductive because it will fail to take into account the full set of factors, motivations, and goals of work groups which lie beyond the usual macroeconomic objectives of growth and stability.

Notes

1. See Piore, Michael J., "Notes for a Theory of Labor Market Stratification," in Richard C. Edwards et al. (Eds.), *Labor Market Segmentation* (Lexington, Mass.: D. C. Heath Co., 1975).

2. See, for example, Andrisani, Paul J., "An Empirical Analysis of the Dual Labor Market Theory," Unpublished Doctoral Dissertation, Ohio State University, 1973; Osterman, Paul, "An Empirical Study of Labor Market Segmentation," *Industrial and Labor Relations Review*, Vol. 28, No. 4 (July 1975), pp. 508–23; Dickens, William T., and Kevin Lang, "A Test of Dual Labor Market Theory," mimeo, National Bureau of Economic Research Workshop, November 1983.

3. See Hall, Robert E., "Employment Fluctuations and Wage Rigidity," *Brookings Papers on Economic Activity*, 1:1980, pp.91–123; Hall, Robert E., "The Importance of Lifetime Jobs in the U.S. Economy," *American Economic Review*, Vol. 72, No. 4 (September 1982), pp.716–24; Tobin, James, "Inflation and Unemployment," *American Economic Review*, Vol. 62, No. 1 (March 1972), pp. 1–18; Solow, Robert M., "On Theories of Unemployment," *American Economic Review*, Vol. 70, No. 1 (March 1980), pp. 1–11; Okun, Arthur M., *Prices and Quantities: A Macroeconomic Analysis* (Washington, D.C.: The Brookings Institution, 1981), chap. 3, pp. 81–133.

4. See Wachter, Michael L., "Primary and Secondary Labor Markets: A Critique of the Dual Approach," *Brookings Papers on Economic Activity*, 3:1974, pp. 637–80; Cain, Glen G., "The Challenge of Segmented Labor Market Theories to Orthodox Theory: A Survey," *Journal of Economic Literature*, Vol. 14, No. 4 (December 1976), pp. 1215–57; Ryan, Paul, "Segmentation, Duality, and the Internal Labour Market," in Frank Wilkinson (Ed.), *The Dynamics of Labour Market Segmentation* (London: Academic Press, Inc., Ltd., 1981).

5. See Bosanquet, Nicholas, and Peter B. Doeringer, "Is There a Dual Labour Market in Great Britain?" *Economic Journal*, Vol. 83 (June 1973), pp. 421–35; Piore, Michael J., "Dualism in the Labor Market: A Response to Uncertainty and Flux, The Case of France," *Revue Economique*, Vol. 19, No. 1 (January 1978); Piore, Michael J., and Suzanne Berger, *Dualism and Discontinuity in Industrial Society* (Cambridge: Cambridge University Press, 1980); Doeringer, Peter B., and Michael J. Piore, "Unemployment and the Dual Labor Market," *The Public interest*, No. 36 (Winter 1975), pp. 67–79.

6. See Maurice, Marc, et al., "The Search for a Societal Effect in the Production of Company Hierarchy," in Paul Osterman (Ed.), *Internal Labor Markets* (Cambridge, Mass.: MIT Press, 1984).

7. See Dore, Ronald P., *British Factory-Japanese Factory: The Origins of National Diversity in Industrial Relations* (Berkeley: University of California Press, 1973); Dore, Ronald P., "The Labour Market and Patterns of Employment in the Wage Sector of LDC's: Implications for the Volume of Employment Generated," *World Development*, Vol. 2, Nos. 4 and 6 (April-May 1974), pp. 1–7.

8. See Kaufman, Roger, "Why the U.S. Unemployment Rate Is So High," in Michael J. Piore (Ed.), *Unemployment and Inflation: Institutionalist and Structuralist Views* (Armonk, N.Y.: M. E. Sharpe Inc., 1979), pp. 155–69.

9. See Dunlop, John T., *Industrial Relations Systems* (New York: Henry Holt, 1958).

10. See Medoff, James L., and Katherine G. Abraham, "Experience, Performance, and Earnings," *Quarterly Journal of Economics*, Vol. 95 (December 1980), pp. 703–36, and Freeman, Richard B., and James L. Medoff, *What Do Unions Do?* (New York: Basic Books, 1984).

11. See Foulkes, F. K., *Personnel Policies in Large Nonunion Companies* (Englewood Cliffs, N.J.: Prentice Hall, 1980).

12. See Katz, Harry, *Shifting Gears: Changing Labor Relations in the U.S. Auto Industry* (Cambridge, Mass.: MIT Press, 1985).

13. See Osterman (1983), and especially Osterman, Paul, "White-Collar Internal Labor Markets."

14. See ibid.

15. Verma, Anil, and Thomas A. Kochan, "The Growth in Nature in the Non-Union Sector within a Firm," in Thomas A. Kochan (Ed.), *Challenges and Choices Facing American Labor* (Cambridge, Mass.: MIT Press, 1985).

16. For example, see Elbaum, Bernard, "Labor and Uneven Development: Unions, Industrial Organization, and Wage Structure in the British and U.S.Iron and Steel Industry," Unpublished Doctoral Dissertation, Harvard University, 1982; Edwards, Richard, *Contested Terrain: The Transformation of the Workplace in the Twentieth Century* (New York: Basic Books, 1979).

17. Brody, David, *Workers in Industrial America: Essays on the Twentieth Century Struggle* (New York: Oxford University Press, 1980); Piore, Michael J., and Charles Sabel, *The Second Industrial Divide, Possibilities for Prosperity* (New York: Basic Books, 1984), chap. 5, pp. 111–32.

18. See Becker, Gary S., *Human Capital* (New York: National Bureau of Economic Research, 1964).

19. See Oi, Walter Y., "Labor as a Quasi-Fixed Factor," *Journal of Political Economy*, Vol. 70, No. 6 (December 1962), pp. 538–55.

20. See Azariadis, Costas, "Implicit Contracts and Underemployment Equilibria," *Journal of Political Economy*, Vol. 83 (December 1975), pp. 1103–1202; Bailey, Martin Neil, "Wages and Employment under Uncertain Demand," *Review of Economic Studies*, Vol. 41 (January 1974), pp. 37–50.

21. See Lazear, Edward P., and Sherwin Rosen, "Rank-Order Tournaments as Optimum Labor Contracts," *Journal of Political Economy*, Vol. 89 (October 1981), pp. 841–64.

22. See Williamson, Oliver E., Michael L. Wachter, and Jeffrey E. Harris, "Understanding the Employment Relation: The Analysis of Idiosyncratic Exchange," *Bell Journal of Economics*, Vol. 6 (Spring 1975), pp. 250–78; Williamson, Oliver E., *Markets and Hierarchies: Analysis and Antitrust Implications* (New York: The Free Press, 1975).

23. For example, see Mueller, Dennis C., *Public Choice* (Cambridge: Cambridge University Press, 1979).

24. See Olson, Mancur, Jr., *The Logic of Collective Action* (Cambridge, Mass.: Harvard University Press, 1965); Williamson (1975).

25. See Sahlins, Marshall, *Cultural and Practical Reason* (Chicago: Chicago University Press, 1976). Also see Sahlins, Marshall, *Stone Age Economics* (Chicago: Aldine Publishing Co., 1972); Berger, Peter, and Thomas Luckman, *The Social Construction of Reality* (Garden City, N.Y.: Anchor Books, Doubleday and Company, 1967); and Berger, Peter L., *The Sacred Canopy: Elements of a Sociological Theory of Religion* (Garden City, N.Y.: Anchor-Doubleday, 1969), pp. 29–45.

26. Berger and Luckman.

27. For a layman's introduction to the concept of structure in this sense, see Gardner, Howard, *The Quest for Mind* (New York: Knopf, 1973). Also, perhaps, Furth, Hans G., *Piaget and Knowledge, Theoretical Foundations* (Englewood Cliffs, N.J.: Prentice-Hall, Inc., 1969).

28. Gardner.

29. And even then, one must ask what new probability distribution they put in

place of the old in that event. This problem could be formulated in terms of the incentives for choice between two probability distributions. But, in fact, the problem suggested here is that of how the economic actors get the distributions which enter into their "choice-theoretical" in the first place.

30. See Leibenstein, Harvey J., *Beyond Economic Man* (Cambridge, Mass.: Harvard University Press, 1976).

31. Freeman and Medoff, op. cit.; Clark, Kim B., "The Impact of Unionism on Productivity: A Case Study," *Industrial and Labor Relations Review*, Vol. 33, No. 4 (July 1980), pp. 451–69.

32. See Dore (1973, 1974, 1983); Doeringer, Peter B., "Non-Competing Groups: Employment Systems, Legitimacy, and Economic Performance," Boston University (mimeo), Department of Economics, May 1984; Doeringer, Peter B., Philip Moss, and David Terkla, "Employment Systems and Economic Change: Jobs, Income, and Ethnicity in New England's Fishing Ports," Boston University (mimeo), 1985; Elbaum, Bernard, and William Lazonick (Eds.), *The Decline of the British Economy* (Oxford: Oxford University Press, 1985); Piore and Sabel (1984).

33. Most recently, for example, Peters, Thomas J., and Robert H. Waterman, Jr., *In Search of Excellence: Lessons from America's Best Run Companies* (New York: Harper and Row, 1982); Kantor, Rosebeth Moss, *The Changemasters: Innovation for Productivity in the American Corporation* (New York: Simon and Schuster, 1983).

34. Hall, Robert E., "Employment Fluctuations and Wage Rigidity," *Brookings Papers on Economic Activity*, No. 1 (1980), pp. 91–120; Flanagan, Robert J., "Wage Concessions and Long-Term Union Wage Flexibility," *Brookings Papers on Economic Activity*, No. 1 (1984).

Chapter 1

Introduction

This volume is the outgrowth of a series of labor market studies conducted over the last six years. These studies reflect the variety of policy concerns of the 1960's—structural unemployment, technological change and automation, inflation, racial discrimination, and the employment and training of disadvantaged workers. These problems were initially approached with the traditional analytical tools of economic theory. But, in one way or another, each of the issues strained the conventional framework and required the introduction of a number of institutional or other *ad hoc* explanations. Reliance upon market imperfections or nonmarket institutions to explain deviations from the results predicted by conventional economic theory can be, at best, intellectually unappealing. At worst, it neglects, or even masks, variables significant for policy formation. In this volume, a number of these variables are identified and incorporated into a more comprehensive approach to labor market analysis than that provided by the competitive labor market model.

The Internal Labor Market

The central concept around which this volume is organized is that of the *internal labor market,* an administrative unit, such as a manufacturing plant, within which the pricing and allocation of labor is governed by a set of administrative rules and procedures.[1] The internal labor market, governed by administrative rules, is to be distinguished from the *external labor market* of conventional economic theory where pricing, allocating, and training decisions are controlled directly by economic variables. These two markets are interconnected, however, and movement between them occurs at certain job classifications which constitute *ports of entry and exit* to and from the internal labor market.[2] The remainder of the jobs within the internal market are filled by the promotion or transfer of workers who have already gained entry. Consequently, these jobs are shielded from the *direct* influences of competitive forces in the external market.

The rules governing internal labor allocation and pricing accord certain rights and privileges to the internal labor force which are not available to workers in the external labor market. The internal labor force, for example, has exclusive rights to jobs filled internally, and continuity of employment, even at entry ports, is protected from direct competition by workers in the external labor market. The phenomenon of internal labor markets is thus closely akin to the problems which other authors have identified as "industrial feudalism," "the balkanization of labor markets," and "property rights" in a job.[3]

The scope and structure of internal labor markets varies considerably among industries and occupations. The production and maintenance units of a steel plant with their limited entry ports and lengthy promotion lines, the garment factory with its many entry ports, the military services, and the exclusive hiring hall in the building trades—each constitutes a type of internal market. However, because the research upon which this volume is based focused primarily upon blue-collar employment in manufacturing, the concepts and applications presented have particular relevance for this sector.

Enterprise Markets

For blue-collar workers who are in manufacturing, the internal market is generally synonomous with the establishment. While several distinct types of internal labor market structures are found in manufacturing establishments, the predominant pattern appears to be one in which pro-

---

[1] John T. Dunlop, "Job Vacancy Measures and Economic Analysis," *The Measurement and Interpretation of Job Vacancies: A Conference Report,* National Bureau of Economic Research (New York: Columbia University Press, 1966).

[2] See Clark Kerr, "The Balkanization of Labor Markets," in E. Wight Bakke, *et al., Labor Mobility and Economic Opportunity* (Cambridge, Mass.: Technology-Press of MIT, 1954), pp. 92-110.

[3] Arthur M. Ross, "Do We Have a New Industrial Feudalism?" *American Economic Review,* vol. XLVIII, no. 5, December 1958, pp. 914-915, and Frederick Meyers, *Ownership of Jobs: A Comparative Study,* Institute of Industrial Relations, Monograph Series (Los Angeles: University of California Press, 1964), p. 11.

duction jobs are arranged in seniority districts or lines of progression. Entry job classifications tend to lie at the bottom of these lines and vacancies in other jobs are usually filled by the promotion of workers from the next lowest job classification in the line of progression.

The criteria governing entry to an establishment are fairly responsive to external market conditions. Thus the plant's "hiring standards" vary with the level of unemployment, the wage rates offered by competitors, the characteristics of the local labor supply, and the like. In contrast, layoffs and promotions to nonentry jobs are generally determined by relatively fixed standards of seniority and ability. The particular standards, especially the weight given to seniority relative to ability, vary from one plant to another. In any given plant the standards are subject to revision, but they do not change freely with external economic conditions or even in response to variations in the internal supply and demand for labor.

Both the field research and the industrial relations literature indicate that internal markets are by no means limited to blue-collar jobs or to manufacturing enterprises, but occur much more broadly in the economy. The parallel to blue-collar manufacturing markets is strongest for managerial employment, where jobs also tend to be organized in lines of progression. Managerial workers enter large corporations as trainees or lower-level supervisors. From these classifications their internal career ladders stretch to plant manager or to a series of positions in the corporate management hierarchy.

There are, however, significant contrasts between blue-collar manufacturing markets and those for managerial personnel. There is a tendency for managerial markets to span more than one establishment, frequently including all the plants of a corporation. Other contrasts include the stress placed upon ability in the rules determining promotions, often to the exclusion of seniority, and the provision of an implicit employment guarantee in many middle-level management jobs. The latter obviates the need for layoff procedures and reemployment rights which characterize blue-collar jobs in manufacturing.

Internal labor markets for other white-collar workers also tend to be structured in a vertical fashion with regard to entry jobs and internal promotion. They may follow either the blue-collar or the managerial variant. Markets for clerical workers and technicians tend to resemble the former, while markets for professionals tend to be more like the latter.

Craft Markets

In contrast to the predominant patterns of internal market structures found in manufacturing enterprises are those in the building trades, longshoring, and certain services. These tend to center around the local union, and the geographical and occupational jurisdiction of the local

union generally defines the boundaries of the market. The major problems of internal allocation are those of preparing apprentices or trainees
to be journeymen and of moving groups of workers of roughly equal skill
and rank among jobs of short duration.

The rules governing entry to the craft or occupational type of internal
market are more rigid than those found in manufacturing establishments.
Those governing internal allocation, however, may be more flexible. They
tend to emphasize equality of employment experience among the internal
work force somewhat more than the seniority and ability considerations
that are dominant in manufacturing. While occupational internal labor
markets predominate where the employment relationship is casual, elements of this pattern can even be found in some manufacturing industries,
such as printing, where craft traditions are strong.

Because craft markets contain skills that are utilized in many work
situations and because they do not generally contain jobs filled exclusively
through internal promotion, it could be argued that they are more directly
responsive to competitive forces than are enterprise markets. While the
evidence presented in this volume is far from complete, this argument does
not seem to be warranted. Within many occupational markets, the pricing
and allocating of labor are the subjects of administrative rules, just as they
are in enterprise markets. These rules create the distinction between the
internal and the external labor force which is so important to the definition of an internal labor market. The administrative rules are, of course,
different from those found in manufacturing and respond differently to
economic variables. But it is not at all clear from the research that they
respond any more readily to economic variables. This, as it will be suggested below, is the determining factor in establishing limits to the application of the construct.

Competitive Markets

Finally, it is useful, when discussing internal labor markets, to have
in mind some labor market in which the features of the internal market
are absent.[4] In the United States there are some jobs which are not contained within well-defined administrative units and for which the process
of allocating and pricing occurs in a more or less competitive fashion. The
market for migrant labor in California is the paradigm of such a competitive system, but there are numerous other work situations, some re-

---

[4] It is conceivable that no such market actually exists and that all jobs in the
economy lie within the jurisdiction of some set of administrative rules governing
the pricing, entry, and internal allocation of labor. It is also possible that industrial
economies evolve in the direction of gradually eliminating jobs outside of internal
labor markets. Forces tending to work in this direction are suggested in the next
chapter.

quiring considerable skill and others requiring little, in which administrative rules are either absent or so flexible as to argue against the applicability of the internal labor market concept.[5] It is with such competitive unstructured markets that the internal labor market should be contrasted.

The Internal Labor Market as an Analytical Construct

There is no doubt that internal labor markets, as evidenced by employment situations governed by administrative work rules, are present throughout the economy. Hiring, promotion, and layoff rules which create the distinction between the internal and external labor forces and which govern internal allocation are spelled out in collective bargaining contracts and in management manuals. Similarly, both contracts and manuals contain administrative rules and procedures for the determination of the internal wage structure.

But the utility of the internal labor market as an analytical construct does not depend upon the existence of administrative rules. It depends rather upon the *rigidity* of the rules which define the boundaries of internal markets and which govern pricing and allocation within them. If these rules are not rigid and respond freely to variations in economic conditions, their independent economic role will be minimal. Under such circumstances a preoccupation with these rules will only serve to obscure the operation of underlying economic forces. If, however, the rules are rigid, they will interrupt or transform economic influences causing the internal labor market to respond to dynamic economic events in a manner not readily predicted from conventional economic theory.

Rigorous proof of the rigidity of the internal labor market in the face of economic forces would require (1) the specification of a set of economic variables which should, in principle, govern the pricing and allocation of labor and (2) a demonstration that the rules which actually govern pricing and allocation are inconsistent with this set of variables. To the extent that there is a coherent labor market theory against which an internal market theory must be tested, it is that derived from neoclassical economics. Unfortunately, the requisite measures of neoclassical economic variables are unavailable at the microeconomic level, and the administrative rules which control internal labor markets in practice cannot be defined with sufficient precision to permit quantitative testing of their compatibility. As a result, the case for the internal labor market must rest on less satisfactory heuristic evidence.[6]

[5] In particular, see Chapters 3 and 8 of this book.
[6] For one recent attempt at quantitative testing of the internal labor market see Llad Phillips, "An Analysis of the Dynamics of Labor Turnover in United States Industry," unpub. dissertation (Harvard University, 1969).

There are several factors which indicate a rigidity in the rules of the internal labor market. First, many of the rules governing internal wage determination and allocation have survived over a considerable period of time. Longevity is not, of course, equivalent to rigidity, since a flexible structure may remain unchanged simply because the forces dictating its existence are constant. In many cases, however, the period over which internal markets have survived is long enough to create a strong presumption of variation in the underlying economic and technical contexts. Internal markets in steel, for example, can be traced to the late nineteenth century. For certain typographical, railroad, and construction crafts, the markets extend even further back in time.[7]

Second, a certain degree of rigidity in the rules governing the internal labor market can be inferred from the comments of both labor and management. Management is particularly vocal about the inefficiencies which the rules generate, and both unions and managements frequently speak of particular rules as if they were not only undesirable but sometimes even beyond the control of the parties to renegotiate them. Such comments suggest that the rules are not consistent with the pricing and distribution of labor which would prevail in a competitive market.

Third, the rigidity of the internal labor market appears to be connected with several phenomena at the workplace—investment in enterprise-specific human capital, on-the-job training, and the role of labor as a fixed or quasi-fixed factor of production—which have recently begun to receive attention from economic theorists.[8] These factors have been analyzed in a neoclassical framework, yet their effect is to weaken the assumptions of the competitive model and to interfere with the competitive determination of factor prices. Thus they appear to be highly consistent with the postulates of the internal labor market model.

Finally, there is a series of phenomena connected with the psychological behavior of work groups and the process by which customs are formed at the workplace which contribute to certain rigidities within the internal labor market. Through continuing interpersonal contacts with the internal labor market, workers appear to develop interdependent utility functions, similar to those postulated in the analysis of consumption and saving patterns.[9] These interdependencies contribute to the formation of rela-

---

[7] See for example, Lloyd Ulman, *The Rise of the National Trade Union* (Cambridge, Mass.: Harvard University Press, 1966).

[8] See Gary S. Becker, *Human Capital: A Theoretical and Empirical Analysis, with Special Reference to Education* (New York: Columbia University Press, 1964) and Walter Y. Oi, "Labor as a Quasi-fixed Factor," *The Journal of Political Economy*, vol.LXX, no. 6 (December 1962), pp. 538-555.

[9] James S. Duesenberry, *Income, Saving, and the Theory of Consumer Behavior* (Cambridge, Mass.: Harvard University Press, 1949).

tively fixed customs and traditions with respect to wage structures, promotion arrangements, and other work rules affecting groups of workers.

The Internal Labor Market as a Policy Instrument

The internal labor market appears to be a useful analytical device around which to group a series of related precepts which are not comfortably incorporated into conventional models of the labor market. The contrast between the internal labor market and competitive, neoclassical economic theory suggested by the previous discussion, however, should not be overemphasized. Many of the rigidities which impede market forces in the short run are eventually overcome, and there is probably a tendency for the economy to adjust, in time, in a direction consistent with the predictions of competitive theory. Moreover, many of the short-term phenomena associated with internal labor markets could perhaps be incorporated into a suitably modified neoclassical model. For example, even though monopolylike behavior is not necessarily characteristic of the internal labor market, the analysis of such markets is conceptually akin to monopolistic, or imperfect, competition and could be described in those terms. Nonetheless, such a presentation is not attempted here for two reasons. First, such an approach tends to be understood as a departure from some optimal set of arrangements and thereby connotes some inefficiency in the operation of the internal market. Many of the forces which encourage the formation of internal labor markets appear to be inescapable elements of the market behavior from which neoclassical theory abstracts, and it is not clear, in the context of these elements, whether the internal labor market is inefficient or suboptimal.

Second, adherence to neoclassical forms of analysis when possible can be advocated on the basis of its presumed generality. When, however, enterprise-specific phenomena are widespread, and the circumstances under which they arise easily identified, generality may be obtained only at the expense of relevance and applicability. It is in fact the generality of conventional theory which limits its utility for the analysis of the policy problems noted at the beginning of this chapter. In this sense, the policy problems under examination in this book provide further analytical justification for the concept. For example, the internal labor market plays a critical role in the recruitment and training of the labor force. Partly from necessity and partly from choice it has assumed many of the responsibilities for labor market information and labor force development assumed to be provided by separate systems in many traditional analyses. By internalizing such functions, the internal labor market can select from among a variety of wage and training options in acquiring an internal labor force.

Decisions regarding technological change are also made within the internal market. Many aspects of the relationship between technological change on the one hand and the training and wage costs of the internal labor force on the other can best be understood at the micro level. Technological change, training, and recruitment all affect labor costs and the composition of employment. These factors also play a large role in the process of labor force adjustment to structural change. These adjustment mechanisms in turn affect unemployment and earnings, especially among the less educated and less skilled.

Finally, custom, as a separate force in the internal labor market, has implications for manpower policy. Custom can provide beneficial stabilizing influences; it can be a process for easing labor force adjustments; or it can be a serious impediment to achieving efficiency or equal employment opportunity. The various effects of custom tend to be balanced in the aggregate, yet they are critical to many internal labor market operations.

These problems are largely microeconomic, in contrast with the aggregate issues of employment, wage levels, and national income which preoccupied economic policy in the three decades preceding the 1960's. The contrast suggests that the utility of the internal labor market as an analytical construct depends upon the level at which the analysis is conducted. For macroeconomic analysis, the administrative features of the internal labor market are treated, in effect, as random events which cancel out in the aggregate. But what is trivial on a macro level can turn out to be central on the micro level, where an understanding of the underlying market machinery is essential.

It is also possible that a recognition of the construct of the internal labor market will point to a new understanding of some of the unsolved macroeconomic problems of the postwar period. For example, it would seem to have particular relevance for understanding the role of the labor market in determining the trade-off between wage stability and full employment subsumed in the "Phillips Curve." Although the potential of the internal labor market for the understanding of aggregate economic problems is not fully explored in this volume, some applications are suggested by the analysis.

Research Methodology

The concepts developed in this volume are derived primarily from a series of interviews with management and union officials in more than 75 companies during the period 1964 to 1969. Most of the research was done with manufacturing companies, but interviews were also conducted in public and commercial enterprises and in construction and service industries. In most cases, managers from three areas — personnel, industrial engineering, and operations — were interviewed at both the corporate and plant levels. The interviews were open-ended; the majority were two to three hours in length with plant visits lasting one or two days.

Because of the extensive nature of the interviews and the sensitivity of the areas of inquiry, considerable cooperation on the part of managers and union officials was required. Personal contacts and cooperation took precedence over a scientific sampling procedure, but an attempt was made to select a heterogeneous group of plants. A variety of industries and labor markets was represented, but most of the establishments were of medium or large size.

These employer and union interviews have been supplemented by contacts with a variety of civil rights, poverty, and manpower agencies. These contacts provided frequent exposure to the disadvantaged labor force and were especially important for the sections of this book dealing with discrimination and low-income labor markets.

In addition to the interview materials, quantitative data on programs and personnel were occasionally collected. Some of this data are presented for illustrative purposes, but, on the whole, they are too fragmented to support any generally valid conclusions. The results, even when statistically significant, suffer from problems of sampling and statistical design which require caution in their interpretation.

The Plan of the Book

In Part One of this volume the theoretical concept of the internal labor market is developed. Some of the forces determining internal patterns of labor allocation, wage determination, and training are also examined. In Part Two, these analytical materials are applied to a series of topics of concern to manpower policy: adjustments to labor market imbalances, technological change, discrimination, and the disadvantaged labor force. Conclusions for manpower policy are offered in the final chapter.

Part One
The Theory of Internal Labor Markets

Chapter 2
The Origins of the Internal Labor Market

This chapter is devoted to an examination of the forces responsible for the existence of internal labor markets and for the determination of the rules which govern within them. Internal labor markets appear to be generated by a series of factors not envisioned in conventional economic theory: (1) skill specificity, (2) on-the-job training, and (3) customary law. These factors are defined and developed in the first section of the chapter. In the second section, they are combined with the economic forces recognized in conventional theory to develop an explanation of how internal markets arise and evolve over time. The analysis of this section abstracts from the behavior of managerial and trade union organizations and from actual historical events. These institutional and historical complexities are introduced in the third and fourth sections respectively. The final section of the chapter summarizes the discussion.

The Major Factors Generating Internal Labor Markets

Skill Specificity

The terms "specific training" and "general training" have been made current in the vocabulary of modern economics by Gary S. Becker. In Becker's terms, completely specific training is defined as "training that has no effect on the productivity of trainees that would be useful in other firms."[1] "Completely general training increases the marginal productivity of trainees by exactly the same amount in the firms providing the training as in other firms."[2]

In the present volume, *specific* and *general* are used in a somewhat different sense. Here they fundamentally relate to *skill* and to the frequency with which various skills can be utilized within different internal labor markets. A completely specific skill is unique to a single job classification in a single enterprise; a completely general skill is requisite for every job in every enterprise. The terms *specific* and *general* may also be applied to training, as in Becker's usage. Training is more or less specific according to the type of skill which it provides.

Skill specificity has two effects important in the generation of the internal labor market: (1) it increases the proportion of training costs borne by the employer, as opposed to the trainee, and (2) it increases the absolute level of such costs. As skills become more specific, it becomes increasingly difficult for the worker to utilize elsewhere the enterprise-specific training he receives. This reduces the incentive for him to invest in such training, while simultaneously increasing the incentive for the employer to make the investment.[3] Skill specificity tends to increase the absolute cost of training (regardless of who provides it) because the less prevalent a skill in the labor market, the less frequently training for that skill is provided, and economies of scale in training cannot be realized.[4] Both of these effects encourage the employer to seek to reduce labor turnover.

Training is not the only labor cost affected by skill specificity. Recruitment and screening costs are influenced in much the same way. The reduction in turnover which skill specificity encourages increases the

---

[1] Gary S. Becker, *Human Capital: A Theoretical and Empirical Analysis, with Special Reference to Education* (New York: Columbia University Press, 1964), p. 18.

[2] *Ibid.*

[3] These results can be stated formally as follows: employers and employees will invest in training so long as the expected return is greater than the expected cost. For the employee, the expected return is equal to the difference between the income on the job to which the investment permits him to aspire and his income in his current job *weighted by the probability that he will obtain the job to which he aspires.* This probability is a decreasing function of specificity. The employer's expected return is equal to the difference in the productivity of the trained worker, and the productivity of the untrained worker corrected for any differences in wage rates which result from the training and *weighted by the probability that the worker will remain on the job.* This probability is also an increasing function of specificity.

[4] The effect of training scale upon absolute training costs may, however, be diminished if the specific skills are widely utilized in the internal market of the employer providing the training.

employer's willingness to accept these costs. Similarly, the absolute costs of recruitment and screening are reduced by economies of scale and standardization. Broad scale advertising campaigns and standardized testing procedures, for example, can be used to find and certify workers with skills which are in frequent demand, but these techniques are unsuitable for recruiting and screening workers with less common skills. These scale effects are further encouraged by specificity because it increases the amount of such activities in which individual employers engage.

Although, in the generation and operation of the internal labor market, it is the specificity of skills and training that is the key, it is not always the focus of managerial decisions. Such decisions often center instead upon *the job* or *the technology,* and the requisite skills appear to be derived incidentally from these decisions. Because the job and technology are so often the focal point of the decisions determining skill, it is useful to define and apply the terms "specific" and "general" to these concepts as well.

Job specificity. The specificity of a job, as that term is used here, is defined by its skill content. Jobs utilize a set of skills, and each of the skills in the set may be more or less specific. A completely specific job is one which utilizes only specific skills; a completely general job is one all of whose skills are general.[5]

Almost every job involves some specific skills. Even the simplest custodial tasks are facilitated by familiarity with the physical environment specific to the workplace in which they are performed. The apparently routine operation of standard machines can be importantly aided by familiarity with a particular piece of operating equipment. Even mass-produced machines have individual operating characteristics which can markedly affect work performance. In some cases workers are able to anticipate trouble and diagnose its source by subtle changes in the sound or smell of the equipment. Moreover, performance in some production and most managerial jobs involves a team element, and a critical skill is

[5] The reference of the term "specificity" to skill even when applied to a job, is important. It implies that a job could be unique to an enterprise, in the sense that the set of the skills which it utilized was not required elsewhere, and yet each skill in the set might be quite general. Such a job would *not* be enterprise specific.

A second source of confusion surrounding the concept of job specificity is derived from the instability in the definition of jobs in most enterprises. As will be seen subsequently in the discussion of on-the-job training, the skills and duties associated with a given job vary systematically as part of the internal allocative process, and this, plus the wide variation among enterprises in jobs with similar titles, makes the concept of the job a difficult and elusive one to work with. The concept is, nonetheless, necessary for an understanding of some phenomena. An employer, for example, may be induced to finance the training of the general skills required by a job because he knows that the specific training which the job also requires will minimize turnover.

the ability to operate effectively with the given members of the team. This ability is dependent upon the interaction of the personalities of the members, and the individual's work "skills" are specific in the sense that skills necessary to work on one team are never quite the same as those required on another.[6] There are no true examples of a completely general skill. In an industrial economy, however, generally transferable skills are approximated by basic literacy, by the ability to communicate, and by a commitment to industrial work rules.[7]

Technology specificity. Closely related to job specificity is the specificity of a technology, where technology refers to the entire set of tasks which comprises a work process. A technology, like jobs, utilizes skills of varying degrees of specificity. Technology does not impart specificity to skills so much through the motions of the tasks which it requires as through the speed and accuracy with which they are executed. In most manufacturing enterprises, for example, speed and accuracy of work are considered the critical determinants of labor cost. Both are heavily dependent upon the peculiarities of particular pieces of equipment, the type of materials, the particular product, the length of production runs, and the environment in which that product is being produced.

For example, the production of a pair of shoes requires some skilled operators and some skilled equipment repairmen. Similar operating and repair skills are utilized in many labor markets, and it is generally possible to engage new employees as machine operators. But operators familiar with the idiosyncracies of the particular pieces of equipment can produce much faster and are also able to anticipate machine breakdown, thereby minimizing equipment downtime. Downtime is further reduced when the repair crew is also familiar with the equipment so that the trouble can be quickly diagnosed and repaired. These skills are highly specific in character.

In one way or another every piece of equipment is unique, and every technology involves *some* skills which are specific in the above sense. But specificity can rise above this irreducible minimum, and, while its level is influenced by a number of variables beyond managerial control, discussion with managers and engineers suggest that they can exercise some discretionary restraint.

A general principle appears to govern many technologies: the greater the variety of tasks a machine is built to perform, the less efficient it tends to be in the performance of any one of them. Since production depart-

---

[6] Edith T. Penrose, *The Theory of the Growth of the Firm* (New York: Wiley and Sons, 1959) and Robin Marris, *A Managerial Theory of Capitalism* (New York: Free Press of Glencoe, 1964).

[7] See Clark Kerr *et al., Industrialism and Industrial Man* (Cambridge, Mass.: Harvard University Press, 1960).

ments are under continued pressure to minimize costs, the operation of this principle results in the tendency for technology to become increasingly enterprise specific over time. Line supervision, and sometimes operatives and maintenance crews as well, are forever modifying equipment in order to improve its efficiency. Such changes accumulate quickly and can produce considerable movement toward specificity.

Countervailing pressure against specificity is generated by the savings in fixed capital costs and fixed labor costs associated with standardized equipment which can utilize widely available skills. Economies of scale in production generally make standardized equipment cheaper than custom-made machinery. The availability of standardized parts reduces repair and maintenance costs and the need for spare-parts inventories. Standardized equipment also tends to reduce the cost of adjusting to changes in the composition of demand.

Specific technologies are also less apt to be described formally in blueprints, operating instructions, or repair manuals for several reasons. First, technologies often become specific through a long series of minor changes in initially standard equipment, each of which is too trivial to warrant recording. Second, many of the factors which make machinery and jobs idiosyncratic, such as the sounds and smells of equipment, are extremely difficult to describe. Finally, there are fixed costs for developing and maintaining detailed written instructions and designs. If this investment cannot be spread over many pieces of equipment, it is less likely to be undertaken. When not formally recorded, the technology exists only in day-to-day operations, and the skills required tend to be the unique possession of the internal labor force. This in turn further enhances the importance of the internal labor force as a stable and self-perpetuating body and thus fosters rigidity in the rules governing internal training.

On-the-Job Training[8]

The second factor critical in the development of internal labor markets is the process of on-the-job training. In the past, economists have tended to ignore this phenomenon altogether. Economic theory, when it has considered training at all, has assumed that it occurs in a formal educational institution which is implicitly treated as a part of a separate educational industry. There has been a recent upsurge of interest in on-the-job training, but analysts have viewed such training primarily as a shift in the locus

---

[8] Much of the material in this subsection appeared initially in Michael J. Piore, "On-the-Job Training and Adjustment to Technological Change," *The Journal of Human Resources,* vol. III, no. 4 (Fall 1968), pp. 435-449; and Peter B. Doeringer and Michael J. Piore, "Labor Market Adjustment and Internal Training," *Proceedings of the Eighteenth Annual Meeting,* Industrial Relations Research Association, New York, December 1965, pp. 250-263.

of the educational process and in the distribution of training costs.[9] Very little attention has been paid to the training *process* and its effect upon the establishment in which it occurs. It is the process, however, which is important in understanding internal labor markets and which is examined in this section.

By far the largest proportion of blue-collar job skills is acquired on the job.[10] Such training appears relatively less important for white-collar professional and managerial jobs where formal education attainment requirements tend to dwarf skills previously acquired on the job.[11] But, even for these positions, formal education is often used more as a screening device for selecting people with certain aptitudes and social backgrounds. On-the-job training then provides either the larger proportion of skills actually utilized in the performance of work or is a prerequisite for the successful utilization of formal education.[12]

For blue-collar manufacturing jobs, the hallmark of on-the-job training is its informality. The process is variously described as "osmosis," "exposure," "experience," or "working one's way up through promotion." Very often on-the-job training is not recognized as a distinct process at all; it is simply assumed that a worker who has "been around" for a while will know how to do certain things. For relatively simple operating jobs, new

[9] See, for example, R. S. Eckaus, "Economic Criteria for Education and Training," *Review of Economics and Statistics*, May 1964, pp. 181-190; Kenneth J. Arrow, "The Economic Implications of Learning by Doing," *The Review of Economic Studies*, June 1962, pp. 155-173; Jacob Mincer, "On-the-Job Training: Costs, Returns, and Implications," *Journal of Political Economy Supplement*, vol. LXX, no. 5, part 2 (October 1962) pp. 50-79; and Walter Y. Oi, "Labor as a Quasi-Fixed Factor," *Journal of Political Economy*, vol. LXX, no. 6 (December 1962), pp. 538-555.

[10] See U.S. Department of Labor, "Formal Occupational Training of Adult Workers," *Manpower/Automation Research Monograph No. 2*, December 1964, Table 11, pp. 43-45. See also U.S. Department of Health, Education, and Welfare, Office of Juvenile Delinquency and Youth Development, *Getting Hired, Getting Trained* (Washington, D.C.: U.S. Government Printing Office, 1965); National Manpower Council, *A Policy for Skilled Manpower* (New York: Columbia University Press, 1954), pp. 208-233; and Department of Labour, Canada, *Acquisition of Skills*, Research Program on the Training of Skilled Manpower, Report 4 (Ottawa: Queen's Printer and Controller of Stationery, 1960). George Strauss's study indicates that the training of construction craftsmen is often equally informal; see "Apprenticeship: An Evaluation of the Need" in Arthur M. Ross (ed.), *Employment Policy and Labor Market* (Berkeley: University of California Press, 1965).

[11] *Ibid.*

[12] See Lester C. Thurow, "The Occupational Distribution of the Returns of Education and Experiences for Whites and Negroes," in *Federal Programs for the Development of the Human Resources,* papers submitted to the Subcommittee on Economic Progress of the Joint Economic Committee, U.S. Congress (Washington, D.C.: Government Printing Office, 1968), vol. I, pp. 267-284.

workers are typically given a brief job demonstration. They then begin to produce on their own, receiving occasional help from foremen or neighboring operators. On more complex jobs, particularly those involving maintenance or repair, the novice may serve as an assistant to an experienced employee. In other cases, training takes place along a promotion ladder in which work on the lower-level jobs develops the skills required for the higher level. Workers may also learn other jobs by observing their neighbors and by practicing on, or "playing around with," equipment during lunch hours and other production breaks. Learning often occurs by observing neighboring workers. Sometimes even the trainee is not conscious of the learning process. Thus, even when the jobs within a department are not skill-related, the ability to perform them is correlated with the length of time the worker has "been around."

The informality of on-the-job training makes it difficult to identify the precise nature of the process, but the following elements appear to be involved. First, training typically occurs in the process of production, partly through trial and error. It is the production process that disciplines the learning process and provides indications of success and failure. Both monetary and psychological rewards and penalties stimulate the mastering of the skills.

Second, when instruction of one kind or another is required, it is usually provided by a supervisor, by the incumbent worker, or by workers on neighboring jobs. The experienced workman deliberately demonstrates new tasks to novice workers; a superior may delegate a portion of his tasks to a subordinate; or the subordinate may, after brief instruction, fill in for his superior during temporary absences. In all cases, the "instructor" generally continues to discharge his productive responsibilities. The participants in the training process therefore assume dual roles: one in the production process, as supervisors or subordinates, the other in the learning process, as instructors or students.

Third, the very process of on-the-job training tends to blur the distinction between jobs. In many respects, on-the-job training might best be described as one of a rolling readjustment of tasks between experienced and inexperienced workmen. The experienced workman begins by assigning novices the simpler parts of the jobs which he originally performed. He then gradually assigns more complicated tasks connected with teaching and supervision. As the workman shifts more complex tasks to the trainee, he also reduces his supervisory and teaching efforts, and reabsorbs some of the simpler tasks to allow the trainee time to master the complex work. Somewhat the same thing occurs when on-the-job training occurs through temporary assignments of trainees to the job of the experienced workman. The novice performs the routine aspects of the work, and the more complex tasks are either performed by a superior or are postponed until the experienced man returns.

In all of these cases, the formal distinction between one job classification and another is maintained. Work assignments are referred to as temporary or permanent, and different wage rates are attached to the jobs. But the wage rates and the job definitions tend to be somewhat arbitrary. They are artificial distinctions, imposed upon a situation where one job merges into another and where the skills acquired and the tasks performed are continually changing in subtle ways. For example, screw machine operators may normally perform set up and minor maintenance tasks on four or five machines. When a "green hand" is hired, the skilled operator may assume setup and maintenance responsibilities for seven or eight machines. The trainee will observe the operation of these machines, and keep the tool bit clean and oiled. Gradually the trainee will absorb the more complex tasks and operate more machines until he is weaned from his reliance upon the experienced worker, except for an occasional problem.

Sometimes training in manufacturing plants is described as "formal." But, in many cases, this involves little more than a systemization of informal procedures which leave the underlying nature of the training process unchanged. For example, vestibule training, which is usually called formal, often involves the development of a separate production facility where the slower pace of new workers does not interfere with the operation of experienced personnel. Another example is maintenance apprenticeship programs occasionally offered in manufacturing plants. These programs are described as formal, but the classroom portion is secondary to training on the job. The formal dimension of on-the-job training often involves little more than a systematic rotation of the trainee through enough job classifications to ensure exposure to the full complement of tasks which craftsmen are expected to perform. Similar managerial arrangements are utilized for training college graduates entering large corporations and for medical interns.

The prevalence of on-the-job training appears to be associated with several different factors. These factors, because they determine when the training occurs and also because they may influence other aspects of the work environment, are worthy of note. First, for certain jobs there is no alternative to training on the job. These jobs exist only as work performed and cannot be duplicated in the classroom. Incumbent employees have difficulty describing or demonstrating the skills they possess, except in a production context. In some cases they also have a strong incentive to hide what they do from management who might use this knowledge to extract greater output from them or to correct a loose incentive rate. Hence, managers find it impossible to develop a formal curriculum which might be taught in classrooms and must rely, by default, upon a teaching technique in which skills are directly transmitted from the job incumbent to his replacement.

Because so much of the learning process is automatic and dependent upon the individual's curiosity about what goes on around him, as well as his desire to master a job for its extrinsic and intrinsic rewards, it tends to seem "natural" in the eyes of both management and workers. Such training also seems costless, and thus little attention is paid to the training process. Moreover, managers can often capitalize on the "natural" learning process by breaking technological processes into jobs and arranging the physical proximity of workers in order to increase the amount of automatic learning which occurs. One example of this is the promotion unit: each job in the progression line develops skills requisite for the succeeding job and draws upon the skills required in the job below it.

It should be emphasized, however, that not all on-the-job training is in fact free. The process frequently involves waste of material, machine damage, reduction in product quality, and sacrifices in the productivity of both the trainee (whose attention is diverted from his current job to that of a neighbor or superior) and the instructor who becomes preoccupied with training and supervising his subordinates. These costs are difficult in practice to separate from the costs of production, but virtually all managers are aware that they exist.[13]

Some of the resources absorbed by the training process, moreover, might otherwise be wasted. Such is the case when the novice learns by playing around with idle equipment during a production break, when scrap material is used to demonstrate a new technique, or when the instruction is provided during lulls in the production process when workers would otherwise be resting. Frequently the best learning situation coincides with the most efficient staffing arrangements. Subordinates, for instance, often learn by filling in during the temporary absence of their superiors. The subordinate might not perform the job as efficiently as the experienced workman, but the arrangement may still be less expensive than the alternative of having redundant experienced replacements available to substitute for skilled workers during unexpected absences.

On-the-job training may be more economical than formal instruction in several other respects as well. Because on-the-job training is derived from the content of the job itself, it is confined only to those skills required for the job and involves no excess training. Since much of the training takes place through demonstration rather than verbal communication,

---

[13] The presence of such costs does not necessarily deter on-the-job training. Given the automatic character of the learning process, it may be impossible to prevent these costs. Where training alternatives exist, they may be even more costly to operate.

persons incapable of teaching in the classroom can serve as instructors. When the number of trainees required at any given time is small, and the training period short, the economies of scale provided by classroom instruction cannot be obtained. The cost of on-the-job training is further reduced by the output produced by a trainee which is unavailable when training is conducted outside the plant.

Even when more costly, on-the-job training has certain advantages over classroom instruction. Instruction on the job is individual and can be tailored to the learning capabilities and idiosyncracies of each trainee. Moreover, the relevance of the instruction is immediately apparent, which tends to make the trainee more attentive. Vestibule training, which is occasionally used for blue-collar jobs in manufacturing, represents a compromise between on-the-job training and classroom training. Such programs only partly prepare a worker for job performance despite attempts to simulate work conditions.

As should be apparent from the preceding analysis, on-the-job training is closely related to skill specificity. Specificity tends to promote this type of training by reducing the number of people learning a particular skill at a given time. By precluding large-scale, standardized training, formal instruction is discouraged. Moreover, to the extent that skill specificity leads to unrecorded knowledge, it necessitates the process of direct skill transmission from incumbent to successor in the process of production— the essence of on-the-job training.

The relationship between skill specificity and on-the-job training, however, runs in both directions. The narrowness of this training, which makes for economies, makes the skills which it produces highly specific to the context in which they were acquired. Reliance upon on-the-job training also encourages the mutation of technology in the direction of increasing specificity. Skills change with time as they are transferred from one worker to the next. Since instruction does not depend upon formal records or the use of skill developed by formal classes, there is little incentive to maintain standard jobs. Operators and repair crews are allowed latitude to modify equipment on their own, and innovations are frequently introduced by engineers and supervisors without written record.

Custom

Custom is the third of the major factors important to an understanding of internal labor markets. Its role in economic activity has only occasionally been recognized by economists, most frequently in discussions of wage relationships. But it is generally used as a residual explanation: one which is used as a catchall to account for events which cannot otherwise be explained.[14] Economists have not attempted to define the concept of

---

[14] See, for example, J. R. Hicks, *The Theory of Wages* (London: Macmillan Co., 1963), especially pp. 316-319, and J. S. Mill, *Principles of Political Economy* (New

custom precisely or to explain when it is generated and how it might be changed.[15]

Custom at the workplace is an unwritten set of rules based largely upon past practice or precedent. These rules can govern any aspect of the work relationship from discipline to compensation. Work customs appear to be the outgrowth of employment stability within internal labor markets. Such stability, as will be seen from the following discussion, is of value to both the employer and the work force, and one of the factors producing internal labor markets is the desire to effectuate stability. When employment is stable, the same workers come into regular and repeated contact with each other. The result is the formation of social groups or communities within the internal labor market. Communities of this type—in a workplace or any other social setting—tend to generate a set of unwritten rules governing the actions of their members and the relationship between members and outsiders. Eventually, these rules assume an ethical or quasi-ethical aura. Adherence to these rules tends to be viewed as a matter of right and wrong, and the community acts to retaliate against behavior which is at variance with them. It is to such rules that the term "custom," as it is used in this volume, applies. The generation of custom in the internal labor market closely resembles the development of customary law in medieval Europe, and both appear to be the product of the psychological behavior of groups.[16] Indeed, the feudal manor, to which medieval custom has reference, can be viewed as a self-contained internal labor market.

The existence of customary law at the workplace is indicated by the "ethical" phrases which appear in the language of industrial relations: "just cause for discharge," "equal pay for equal work," "a fair day's pay for a fair day's work," and so forth. At each workplace, the vague terms "just," "fair," and "equal" are given meaning largely by past practice and precedent. Workers who violate the code are subject to discipline, either by supervision or by their co-workers. For example, fighting or

---

York: Longmans, Green, and Co., 1926), pp. 242-248. More recent examples can be found in Lloyd G. Reynolds, *Labor Markets and Labor Relations* (Englewood Cliffs, N.J.: Prentice-Hall, 1968), p. 509; and George W. Taylor and Frank C. Pierson (eds)., *New Concepts in Wage Determination* (New York: McGraw-Hill Co., 1957), pp. 117-172.

[15] Considerably more work has been done in this area by sociologists, legal historians, and psychologists. This section draws heavily upon articles by Edwin Sapir and Charles S. Lambinger in *The Encyclopedia of Social Sciences* (New York: Macmillan Co., 1931), vol. IV., pp. 658-667, and Marc Bloch, *Feudal Society*, L. A. Manyon (trans.) (Chicago: University of Chicago Press, 1964), vol. I, pp. 113-120. The connection between legal behavior and economic behavior is suggested by Justice Douglas in the Supreme Court's opinion in *United Steelworkers of America vs. Warrior and Gulf Navigation Co.*, 363 U.S. 574 (1960).

[16] See Bloch, *op. cit.*

drinking at work may result in discharge or suspension by management; exceeding output norms which the internal work force has determined as "fair" may result in verbal abuse by the work group, or, in the extreme, being "sent to coventry" or being subject to sabotage or physical harm.

Customary law is of special interest in the analysis of internal labor markets both because of the stabilizing influence which it imparts to the rules of the workplace and because the rules governing the pricing and allocation of labor within the market are particularly subject to the influence of custom. These rules become constrained and less responsive to market forces, thereby explaining much of the apparent rigidity of internal wage and allocative structures.

The central question posed by this phenomenon is: how can customary laws at the workplace continue to command allegiance in a context where institutional survival is dependent upon economic success?

The ultimate sanctions upon the operation of custom are indeed economic. For example, the willingness and ability of the internal labor force to punish management's violations of custom operate through economic pressure, the extreme form of which is the strike or sabotage. Short of such extreme action, however, a dissatisfied internal labor force can harass management in a variety of ways—reduced work pace, "misplaced" tools and materials, epidemics of minor equipment breakdowns, increase in defective outputs, and minor infractions of rules too small to punish individually.[17] Such minor, unorganized economic harassment, for which it is impossible to pinpoint responsibility, is the form of economic pressure which managers appear to fear most when customs are violated. Adherence to work customs may also have its costs. Where customs are in conflict with economic efficiency and fail to adjust in order to resolve this conflict, economic constraints begin to affect profits, wages, and employment. The ultimate sanction against custom is economic failure.

Managerial adherence to work customs cannot be understood, however, in purely economic terms.[18] To a certain extent, management, especially lower-level management, belongs to the work group and abides by custom for the same reasons that other group members do: because it cannot conceive of alternatives, because alternatives that are conceivable are discomforting and seem wrong, or because it fears the sullen hostility of the work force and the implied social ostracism. Thus custom has a direct influence upon management decisions as well as being a constraint.

The most important factor in understanding the relationship between custom and economic efficiency, however, is not the pressure, social or

---

[17] See, for example, Stanley B. Mathewson, *Restriction of Output Among Unorganized Workers* (New York: The Viking Press, 1931).

[18] John T. Dunlop, *Industrial Relations Systems* (New York: Henry Holt, 1958).

economic, that the group generates in its behalf, but the character of custom itself. Here, its operation can best be illustrated by reference to medieval European society. Marc Bloch, for example, emphasizes (1) the dependence of customary law upon past practice and (2) the fact that customary law is essentially unwritten.[19] Both characteristics, he suggests, give considerable flexibility to custom.

Dependence upon "past practice" means that any procedure, if repeated, becomes customary. Hence, a new practice, even if it initially countervenes the customary procedure, will eventually supersede it, if the new practice is repeated sufficiently. Dependence upon memory to recall practices which have not been recently applied also facilitates change. To quote Bloch, "The human memory is a marvelous instrument of elimination and transformation especially what we call the collective memory."[20] People remember past practice selectively, and individual recollections may conflict. Moreover, since even repetitive events differ slightly, the applicability of a given practice to a current event is usually ambiguous, or past practices having differing implications may seem equally relevant.[21]

This characterization of custom makes it an essentially passive phenomenon which tends to grow up around whatever exists. It implies that a workplace begins essentially as a *tabula rasa* without work rules. Management, at least in nonunion enterprises, is free to establish whatever set of work rules are most conducive to economic efficiency. Once these rules are established, custom begins to form around them through the process of application. If underlying economic conditions are stable, no conflict between efficiency and custom will emerge, and custom will not be recognized as a separate force. It is only if the initial economic conditions change and the customary procedures become inefficient that conflict arises.

In the face of such a conflict, management can attempt to shift the customary practice toward an efficient practice by relying upon the ambiguity of past practice. If the requisite ambiguity is not present, management might accept the cost of the inefficient practice as being less than the cost of change. Or it might introduce the new practice, relying on the ability of repetition to establish new custom and hoping that any reaction of the labor force will be of short duration.

The description of work customs as essentially a passive outgrowth of procedures initially determined purely by efficiency needs to be modified in one important respect. Certain customs are imported by the work

[19] Bloch, *op. cit.*, vol. I, pp. 2-12.
[20] *Ibid.*, vol. I, p. 114.
[21] See Richard P. McLaughlin, "Custom and Past Practice in Labor Arbitration," *Arbitration Journal*, vol. XVIII, no. 4 (1963), pp. 205-228.

group from the larger community in which it resides. They are sanctioned by outside social groupings, and workers who rise to their defense do so as members both of the narrow work group and of extended social groups outside the enterprise. Even in a new plant, management cannot violate widely held customs without encountering the pressure of worker dissatisfaction. Nor can it easily supplant them with new customs simply by repetition of an alternative. Indeed, some procedures, such as considering seniority in promotion and layoff, can become so embedded in custom outside the plant that they are exceedingly difficult to change.

The tendency of individuals to form the types of social groups which generate these customary laws is rooted in certain basic principles of group and individual psychology that can only be briefly sketched here. What we have described as group custom appears to be the aggregate of habits common to the individuals comprising the group. Habits are patterns of behavior which individuals develop through a conditioning or reinforcement process in which the pattern is repeatedly associated with a reward. The classic example of conditioning is the Pavlovian experiments. The strength of a habit is defined as its ability to survive in the face of a destructive process in which the habit is not reinforced for long periods, or is even punished. Experimentation with animals indicates that habit strength is a functon of the frequency and pattern of reinforcement and of the interval between reinforcements.[22]

Early experiments emphasized reinforcement derived from basic physical needs such as food and sex, and most psychologists believe that all habits are ultimately related to needs of this kind. But once a habit is established, it can, in turn, become a reinforcing experience because it is symbolically associated with basic rewards. Such habits are called secondary reinforcers. They are divorced from primary needs and may generate further habits. It is secondary reinforcement that appears to be central to the development of custom.

One of these secondary reinforcers is the habit of imitation. Individuals learn in early childhood that the imitation of those around them is rewarded. Since imitation constitutes a successful means of adaptation to the environment, it eventually becomes an independent mode of behavior. In a group situation imitation clearly facilitates the development of modes of behavior common to the members of the group. For many individuals, the habit of accommodation to a group situation is in itself a secondary reinforcer. This leads them more or less automatically to accept the norms of the groups to which they become attached and encourages them to impose group norms upon others. Group habits therefore become reinforced

---

[22] See Ernest R. Hilgard and Donald G. Marquis, *Conditioning and Learning,* 2nd ed., revised by Gerald Kimble (New York: Appleton-Century-Crofts, 1961), Century Psychology Series.

by both the frequency of repetition and by the sense of reward which members experience.

The relation between custom and habit implies that it is possible to apply learning theory in identifying a set of variables which determine the ability of a custom to persevere in the face of contrary economic pressures. Among these variables is the number of times which the practice has been repeated and the interval between repetitions. Also included would be a series of variables governing the effectiveness of secondary reinforcement mechanisms. Homogeneity in the work group tends to facilitate the development of custom, since a diverse group will offer many competing habits for its members to imitate. Similarly, the stability of the group will facilitate the development of custom, as new members would tend to dilute group behavior, at least until they have been assimilated into the group.

Finally, it is worthwhile to note that the behavioral phenomena from which custom derives are collectively called "learning theory," and that this theory is often used to analyze various kinds of "training." This implies that the process through which custom is generated at the workplace is closely related to the development of job skills. On-the-job training, for example, depends heavily upon individual habits formed by a set of reinforcements generated by the productive process on the one hand, and through the imitation by inexperienced workmen of neighboring employees on the other. The latter effect is essentially what is meant by the terms "osmosis" and "exposure"; terms by which the training process is frequently described. Some skills and habits required for successful job performance are in fact group customs, and the development of these skills is facilitated by the social cohesion and group pressure which enforce customary law.

This conclusion suggests that internal markets may be especially effective for training, precisely because they become social institutions. But it also suggests that social variables may be particularly important in the economic performance of individuals within such markets. This, as will be seen in later chapters, has important implications for remedying discrimination in employment and for developing policies to facilitate the employment of disadvantaged workers. Furthermore, learning theory and the role of groups in the formation of both individual preferences and customary law are critical to the process of internal wage determination.

The Process of Internalization

While skill specificity, on-the-job training, and custom appear to be critical factors in the generation of internal labor markets, they do not operate alone. Rather, they work in combination with those forces recognized in neoclassical economics. An understanding of the origins of internal labor markets can be approached through study of the canons of conventional theory. The procedure adopted in this section is to postulate an unstructured, competitive labor market in which there is no commitment to a continuing employment relationship, but in which skill specificity, on-the-job training, and custom can develop. The analysis is then directed at identifying and examining the circumstances which will lead the competitive market to internalize pricing and allocation functions.

To simplify this exercise, it is assumed that internal labor markets are initiated solely at the discretion of management and that managers seek to minimize their labor costs. It follows from the latter assumption that jobs will be awarded to workers on the basis of their costs and qualifications—the job going to the lowest bidder unless the high price of a competing worker is compensated for by high productivity. Naturally, workers will seek to sell their services to the highest bidder. This competitive market procedure will be replaced by internal labor market arrangements only if costs are thereby reduced. Three kinds of cost considerations appear to militate in favor of internal markets: (1) the value of such markets to the labor force, (2) the cost of labor turnover to the employer and the role of such markets in the reduction of turnover, (3) the technical efficiencies of an internal labor market in the recruitment, screening, and training of labor.

Value to the Labor Force

The comments of workers and union officials suggest that the members of the labor force place a positive value upon internal markets. To the extent that they do so, they should be willing to sacrifice earnings to acquire and retain employment in such markets. The savings implied by these wage sacrifices should act in turn as an inducement to management to internalize pricing and allocation. The size of the savings and the strength of the resulting inducement will depend upon the variables governing the value which workers place upon internal allocation.

The benefits which workers receive from internal labor markets appear to derive primarily from enhanced job security and chances of advancement available within them. Wage sacrifices necessary to attain access to an internal labor market thus represent a trade-off between present and future income. As such, they should be responsive to such variables as the time horizon of the labor force and the rate of discount between present and future income, increasing as the former expands and the latter declines. The acceptable sacrifice should also be affected by the prevalence of other arrangements which ensure against insecurity. Internal markets may thus be viewed as a substitute for public or private pension and unemployment insurance programs. The size of the acceptable wage sacrifice will also depend upon broader variations of income and employment. It will be greater in periods of recession than in periods of prosperity and in industries with strong seasonal and cyclical fluctuations than in those with stable labor demand.

A secondary factor augmenting the value of internal markets to the work force is the association of such markets with equity and due process. The rules which govern an internal market are thought to effectuate standards of equity that a competive market cannot or does not respect. The standards at stake include not only the criteria upon which pricing and allocative decisions are made, but also administrative procedures such as union grievance procedures and managerial "open door" policies through which these criteria are applied and reviewed. The value of equity does not appear to vary with any obvious set of economic variables such as those determining the value of security and advancement. It is, however, connected to the phenomena of customary law, to the political dynamics of trade unions, and to problems of managerial control.

In principle, internalization of market functions can also yield an indirect benefit to the labor force: the opportunity to share in savings in recruitment, screening, and training costs generated by internal markets. These benefits, however, do not receive much attention judging by the comments of workers in manufacturing. In construction, on the other hand, where the casual nature of employment requires frequent job changes, workers are much more conscious of these benefits.

Turnover and Turnover Reduction

One effect of internal markets upon labor turnover follows from the fact that such markets are valued by the labor force. Because they are, turnover requires some sacrifice on the part of the work force, and this should act as a deterrent to movement. Further reduction in turnover results when, as is common for blue-collar manufacturing workers, the amount of security and advancement which the market affords is made a function of length of service. The employer can then assign to his most senior workers those jobs for which the cost of turnover is greatest.

The impact of a given change in turnover patterns upon the incentive to institute an internal market depends upon the relationship between turnover and cost. In traditional economic theory turnover has no cost. Labor is treated as a variable factor of production, and employers are assumed to hire their work force by the hour or by the day at an hourly or daily rate. Turnover begins to carry a cost only when labor becomes, to borrow Walter Oi's term, a quasi-fixed factor of production.[23] Labor then takes

[23] Oi, *op. cit.*

on some of the properties traditionally attributed to capital, and management incurs costs if a worker leaves and must be replaced, irrespective of the time worked. Such costs are of two kinds: the cost of *replacement* and the cost of *termination*.

There are three major components of replacement cost: (1) *recruitment*, the cost of attracting job candidates; (2) *screening*, the cost of assessing the qualifications and attributes of candidates; and (3) *training*, the cost of raising the performance level of a newly hired or promoted worker to that of his predecessor. As was seen in the preceding section, the primary reason for the employer encountering these costs is *skill specificity*. As skill specificity increases it becomes less likely that workers possessing the required skills will be available from the external market. Consequently, for any given level of skill, specificity results in an increase in the absolute level and proportion of training, screening, and replacement costs incurred by the employer.

The second aspect of turnover costs, the price of termination, can also fall on both workers and employers. As indicated earlier, workers undergo costs of job search and job replacement and therefore seek to limit the employer's freedom to initiate terminations. By placing constraints upon the conditions under which discharges or layoffs can occur, hiring decisions cannot be easily reversed, and a premium is placed upon careful (and expensive) screening of applicants. Managers claim that union restrictions upon discharge and formal grievance procedures are a major deterrent to employer-initiated terminations.

The termination costs for employers are largely the product of employee insurance and benefit programs. Some of these—severance pay and unemployment insurance, for example—are deliberately designed to impose termination costs. Other costs appear to be an incidental result of the method by which the benefits are financed. The ceiling on the social security tax base, for example, makes it expensive to terminate an employee whose cumulated earnings exceed the ceiling if he is replaced by someone whose earnings have not.

Certain insurance programs—both public and private—increase replacement as well as termination costs by shifting the cost of some economic contingencies from the employee to the employer. The employer then has an incentive to avoid high-risk workers and screens job candidates even more carefully. It can also result in more extensive recruitment efforts to find acceptable candidates and, occasionally, in the development of specialized training programs, such as health and safety education, which attempt to reduce insurable risks.

Technical Efficiencies in Recruitment, Screening, and Training

In addition to the effects of recruitment, screening, and training upon turnover costs, the efficiency with which these functions are performed also encourages the development of internal markets. The efficiency of internal recruitment and screening derives from the fact that existing employees constitute a readily accessible and knowledgeable source of supply whose skill and behavioral characteristics are well known to management. Information about internal candidates is generated as a by-product of their work history in the enterprise. Supervision has an opportunity to observe the subtleties of the candidate's personality and the ease with which he adapts to new skills. Management also has a record of his attendance, punctuality, and willingness to operate within established work norms.

In contrast, potentially interested outsiders must first be located and then screened. Detailed information on work performance can be gathered for external candidates only through extensive testing and reference checks. The problem of identifying the variables which will completely predict a new hire's work performance, however, is generally viewed as either insoluble or soluble only at a prohibitive cost. Outsiders must also be provided with information about the workplace and must learn to assess this information. The internal work force will already have accomplished much of this process by drawing upon its own experience and that of a network of friends among the incumbent employees.

The advantages of internal screening and recruitment may be outweighed by factors operating in the other direction. The internal labor force may be less qualified than externally available workers, and the cost of training may more than absorb the savings generated by internal recruitment and screening. Internal promotion may simply transfer the vacancy to another job where the cost of external recruitment and screening is equal to or greater than the original vacancy. The extent to which these factors are controlling varies among industries and occupations, but the prevalence of both is reduced by the nature and efficiency of on-the-job training.

As was seen in the preceding section, training on the job is heavily dependent upon the natural curiosity of people about what is going on around them, the desire to show off to others what they are doing, and the reinforcement value of imitation.[24] Thus, in any workplace, learning and teaching occur automatically, and often at little cost.[25] Consequently, the

[24] As indicated earlier, the desire to demonstrate, or "show off," skills to others is operative only when such transmission of skills does not pose an economic threat to the "teacher." When training will jeopardize an incentive rate or increase competition for promotion, the incumbent employee may be exceedingly reluctant to disclose his skills. See below pp. 33, 83-84.

[25] However, under certain circumstances the costs of on-the-job training can rise for the very reason that it is automatic and therefore not organized systematically. This problem is most likely to arise under "payment by results" systems

internal labor force tends to be more qualified in the performance of plant jobs, even those which it does not hold, than do outsiders. This is true even when the production process is relatively standard and the required skills fairly general in the economy. When jobs are enterprise specific, the advantages of internal training are even greater.

Both the automatic character of the learning process and its efficiency can be increased by designing jobs, and sequences of job assignments, so that skills absorbed in one job can contribute to the training required to perform the next job in the progression. In manufacturing, these progressions become promotion units, with unskilled jobs at the bottom and the more highly skilled and highly paid jobs at the top. Such promotion sequences not only give rise to technical efficiencies in internal training but also reduce the recruiting and screening costs required to fill some jobs relative to others. Finally, the promise of internal promotion which the market affords increases the incentive to learn, thereby reducing training costs.

Constraints Upon Efficiency

These three factors—the value of the labor force, turnover costs, and technical efficiencies in recruitment, screening, and training—are responsible for the initial generation of internal labor markets. They are also important in shaping the rules which govern the internal allocation structure and the internal wage structure. For the most part, these rules may be understood as a response to the economic and technical contexts within which the internal market operates. But the rules are not freely responsive to changes in these variables and, at any moment in time, tend to be rigid. Over time they are generally capable of gradual revision. More rapid revisions usually can be obtained only at considerable cost.

The major constraint upon change is that imposed by customary law. As explained previously, wage relationships and sequences of promotion which are followed repeatedly tend to become customary. They are then viewed as equitable by employees, and efforts to change them suddenly will encounter resistance.

In addition to custom, changes in the rules are subject to several other types of constraints. One of these is inherent in the nature of skill specificity and of on-the-job training. Both place a tremendous amount of power in the hands of the experienced labor force. The training process requires

---

where the incumbent employee is not adequately compensated for earnings which he must forgo while providing instruction. Under these circumstances, on-the-job training will be haphazard and may encourage turnover among trainees who suffer earnings losses as a result of inadequate on-the-job training instruction. See Paul Pigors and Charles A. Myers, *Personnel Administration,* 6th ed. (New York: McGraw-Hill Co., 1969), pp. 747-751.

the acquiescence and often the active cooperation of experienced workmen. Where skills are specific, the knowledge of the experienced work force is indispensable to training. Training is also a process through which the supply of skilled labor is increased. Allocative and pricing rules which respond freely to variations in the supply of trained labor create a tremendous incentive for workers to frustrate the training process whenever possible. A certain degree of wage rigidity and job security is therefore necessary for on-the-job training to operate at all. Indeed, since much of the training is automatic, and the effort to stop it would involve each worker in hiding what he is doing from those around him, wage rigidity and job security may also prove essential to efficiency in plants where interaction among workers is an important part of the productive process.

One example from a men's garment plant may serve to illustrate these points. In a pressing department, where all workers were paid piece rates, an informal arrangement existed where experienced pressers would instruct new hires in shortcuts they had discovered in exchange for some of the trainee's production "tickets" over a two-to-three month period. Most new hires chose to invest in improved training because of the higher income which such training yielded. Experienced workers were compensated for time spent in instruction through higher take-home pay or greater leisure.

Another set of constraints leading to rigidity in the rules governing internal markets derives from their role in the provision of employment security and advancement. The rules, as we have seen, affect the relationship between present and future income within the market. The worker accepts employment with the expectation that the rules will operate in the future to improve his income. Such expectations assume a certain stability in the rules, and the employer who later changes them to the detriment of the existing labor force reneges on an implicit contract. A violation of expectations through a change in rules affects the incumbent work force and may induce sanctions against management. It also affects recruitment by calling into question the credibility of any offer of security which management might wish to make in the future. This acts as a deterrent to changes which *reduce* the security of the work force. Similarly, short-run changes which enhance security, unless they are costless, are deterred by the knowledge that they are irreversible.

The job security provided by the internal market, holding economic conditions constant, depends upon the rules insulating the labor force from external competition and the rules rationing scarce jobs internally. This dependence further constrains changes in the rules.

Insulation from external competition can be affected in one of two ways. One is through restrictions upon entry. Craft unions, particularly those in the building and printing trades, rely heavily upon this procedure.

The result is a highly rigid set of entry rules but a relatively flexible set of rules governing the internal allocation of labor.

A second method of insulating workers from external competition is seniority. In the case of strict seniority, jobs are allocated to workers in the order in which they entered the internal market. Because senior workers are guaranteed precedence in employment and promotion over those with less seniority, workers are indifferent to those entering the market after them. Enterprise internal labor markets tend to rely heavily upon seniority, particularly in the allocation of scarce jobs when layoffs are required. As a result, the set of rules governing internal allocation in enterprise is considerably more rigid than that found in the building trades, but the rules with respect to entry are considerably more flexible.

Rationing jobs within the internal labor market is also a constraint upon rule changes. Normally, job security and promotion opportunity cannot be increased for the internal labor force as a whole. When the internal demand for labor falls, every worker who retains his job under a set of internal allocative rules does so at the expense of some other member of the internal labor force who is laid off. Every worker who is promoted forecloses a promotion for someone else. This generates a final set of rigidities in the rules governing internal labor markets. Change, or even discussion of change, inevitably brings different groups of workers into conflict with each other. Such conflicts are particularly costly to trade union organization which relies for its strength upon solidarity, and to trade union leaders who see in them the potential support of rival candidates for office. Thus when internal allocative procedures are negotiated jointly by managers and trade unions, the union tends to act as a deterrent to change.

In general, management is also disposed to avoid such issues since any gains to be had from their divisive effects within the union tend to be counterbalanced by the effect of a volatile union leadership upon the stability of labor-management relations. Moreover, divisive conflicts among the work force on so important an issue as job security can be detrimental to productive efficiency quite outside the union-management framework. These factors tend to deter changes in internal allocative procedures even in unorganized shops where management is the sole custodian of the rules.

Trade Union Organizations and Managerial Controls

Most of the preceding analysis has omitted reference to the organizational behavior of trade unions or of managements. The omission has been deliberate. Much of the empirical information available on enterprise internal labor markets comes from studies of manufacturing plants that are organized by trade unions or that are sufficiently large to require formal managerial structures. This facilitates the understanding of internal labor markets because allocative, training, and wage decisions become the subject of written records and of explicit review by union and management officials. The same policies frequently prevail in less-structured organizations, but, because they evolve informally and exist only as plant custom, they are more difficult to recognize and discuss. Nonetheless, the impact of worker and managerial organization is not completely neutral, and this section attempts to identify its most important effects.

Trade Union Organizations

The existing analytical literature tends to view trade unions either as economic or as political institutions.[26] In the former view, union policy is seen as the outcome of an attempt to maximize the economic welfare of the membership. In the latter, it is understood in terms of the pressures playing upon a leadership which is attempting to maintain its position in office. Many of these views are most appropriate for the analysis of union policy on the national level, where there is a more distinct cleavage between the leadership and the rank and file and where policies are more often conceived in the light of recognized economic and political constraints.

The rules governing internal labor allocation, and to a large extent the internal wage structure as well, are, however, the province of local negotiations and the local union. At the local level, social relationships may equal economic or political relationships in importance. Local union officers do not clearly distinguish between themselves and their constituency: they tend to think and act as "one of the boys," and their policy as often represents their assessment of the collective view of the group as it does calculation and an attempt at leadership. In this sense, the local union becomes a vehicle for the expression and enforcement of customary law.

The existence of the local union clearly strengthens employee pressure at the workplace. Prior to the advent of a union, custom at the workplace is enforced only by unorganized and sometimes unconscious expressions of discontent. After union organization, the threat of organized, deliberate economic reprisal results in raising the cost to management of changing customary procedures.

A second result of trade union organization is the codification of un-

[26] See, for example, John T. Dunlop, *Wage Determination Under Trade Unions* (New York: Macmillan Co., 1944), Arthur M. Ross, *Trade Union Wage Policy* (Berkeley: University of California Press, 1948), and Richard E. Walton and Robert B. McKersie, *A Behavioral Theory of Labor Negotiations* (New York: McGraw-Hill Co., 1965).

written custom into collective bargaining agreements. The effect of this is to limit whatever flexibility custom derives from its dependence upon past practice and memory. This effect should not, however, be exaggerated, for much of customary law is simply brought under the umbrella of the contract's enforcement provisions without ever being committed to written form. This is accomplished through vague contract language, such as "just cause" in discharge, that has concrete meaning only within the context of a given work situation and which depends for its interpretation upon unwritten traditions. Many contracts include a clause explicitly sanctioning past practice. These interpretations are subject to much the same process of mutation over time as is customary law.

The third effect of trade unions is to provide an organized channel for deliberate change in customary practices through collective bargaining. In this respect, trade union organization may actually enhance the flexibility of custom and reduce the conflict which it poses for economic efficiency. For example, collective bargaining provides a framework for identifying trade-offs between customs which have become repugnant to management and new work rules which are equally valued by the work force but are less costly to the enterprise.

The scope for flexibility through collective bargaining increases to the degree that the local officers act as leaders and innovators rather than simply as spokesmen for the existing rank-and-file. This, in turn, depends upon a variety of factors. As a rule, large locals are more likely to have full-time elected officials than small locals, and these officials will more often have larger political ambitions that encourage leadership.[27] But, on some issues, even large locals can be dominated by cadres operating as a social group, and all locals will be dominated by group social pressures on some issues. Finally, the interest of the national union in the affairs of the local union or in the particular issue with which the local is concerned can introduce an element of leadership into a local otherwise disposed to act as a social group.

Managerial Organization and Control

Large hierarchical management organizations produce many of the same effects as does trade union organization. The attempt of higher-level managers to control the actions of work-level managers leads to the formalization of rules and regulations. This tends to freeze the rules and limit the flexibility which unwritten work rules provide.

As in union contracts, however, the terminology in "management rules"

[27] See Derek C. Bok and John T. Dunlop, *Labor and the American Community* (New York: Simon and Schuster Co., 1970). Also Leonard R. Sayles and George Strauss, *The Local Union: Its Place in the Industrial Plant* (New York: Harper & Bros., 1953).

is often vague enough to leave considerable latitude for custom to govern. Moreover, formal regulations may be accompanied by a set of administrative procedures for review and amendment. When the work force accepts these procedures as equitable, it often restores some of the flexibility lost in committing the rules to writing.

The need for formal regulations, it should be noted, is not independent of the existence of internal markets. Where allocative and pricing decisions are strictly determined by a competitive market, as they are assumed to be in economic theory, managers have little discretion. It is the weakness of market discipline, and the consequent increase in managerial discretion that creates the need for administrative controls to ensure allegiance to the goals of the enterprise.

The dynamics of social groups and of customary law enhance the need for such controls. The tendency for custom to grow up around repeated practices makes it particularly important to prevent inadvertent deviation from efficient procedures. Line supervisors, who are particularly susceptible to social pressure from the work group, have a tendency to give greater weight to custom than is consistent with economic efficiency. The opposite danger, which formal regulations are also designed to avoid, is that the line foreman will organize the labor force for personal advantage, and use his position in a corrupt or inequitable manner.

The Historical Origins of Internal Markets

The analysis or "origins" of the internal labor market has largely been metaphorical. Nonetheless, there are indications that internal markets, at least in the United States, have evolved in the course of economic development from a far more open, fluid, and competitive economy in the nineteenth century. That this is the case was certainly the dominant view among labor economists in the 1950's when the question was last subject to widespread discussion.[28] There has been no attempt to undertake the historical research required to subject this hypothesis to careful review. But many of the forces identified in the preceding sections as generating and governing internal markets lend plausibility to the hypothesis, and it appears appropriate to summarize that argument here.

First, a general presumption that internal markets have become more prevalent over time is created by their irreversibility. The tendency of custom to grow up around the practice of filling certain jobs from within, of workers to accept employment in the expectation that the practice will continue, and of job skills to become increasingly specific once dependence upon the outside market is reduced all make it easier to move toward

[28] See, for example, Arthur M. Ross, "Do We Have a New Industrial Feudalism?" *American Economic Review,* vol. XLVIII, no. 5 (December 1958).

internalization of market functions than away from it. These particular forces, moreover, may come into play without a conscious decision on the part of the employer to institute an internal labor market.

Second, the factors responsible for internal markets imply mechanisms which create a tendency for internalization, once begun by a single employer, to spread from one establishment to another within an initially competitive labor market. One such mechanism derives from the role of internal labor markets in the provision of job security. A certain amount of security is also provided by open, competitive labor markets. But the relative security of an open market is a function of its size and of the diversity of industries within it. If any employer withdraws jobs from a competitive market and allocates them internally, the job security of workers in other establishments is thereby reduced, and the value of an internal market to them is correspondingly enhanced.

Skill specificity creates a similar effect by increasing the value of internal markets to the employer. The concept of specificity refers essentially to the inability of workers to transfer their skill to alternative employment. Since the internal labor market reduces the accessibility of workers within it to competing employment offers, internalization by one employer increases the effective specificity of jobs within competing establishments and, hence, the incentive for those establishments to resort to internal job allocation.

Third, it appears likely, on balance, that the value of internal markets to the labor force, the cost of turnover to the employer, and the effectiveness of such markets in reducing turnover have all increased in the course of American economic development. Of these effects, the increase in the value of such markets to the labor force is the most debatable. That value is influenced, in part, by the prevalence of alternative arrangements of ensuring future income. These arrangements clearly have expanded with the introduction of unemployment insurance and social security in the 1930's and the development of collectively bargained insurance protection in the war and postwar periods. While the expansion of such programs may have operated to promote internal markets in other ways, it has probably worked to reduce their economic value to the labor force.

Working in the opposite direction has been the effect of economic fluctuations. It is here that the irreversibility of internalization comes most prominently into play. The great depression of the 1930's and the automation scare of the late 1950's have encouraged private arrangements for protecting the employment security of the internal labor force. These protections have not been reversed by the ensuing periods of prosperity or by the generally enhanced stability of the economy in the postwar period taken as a whole.

Finally, it is likely that the cost of turnover to the employer has risen in the course of economic development. One factor clearly working toward this end has been the growth of insurance programs and other forms of nonwage compensation, which indirectly raise turnover costs. A second factor which can be argued to be working in the same direction is the trend in manuacturing technology, in some sectors, to replace the all-round craftsmen with various forms of unskilled and semiskilled workers who work with the aid of specialized machinery. While these developments have reduced the overall skill requirements of jobs, they may also have increased the specific skill component, and to this extent they will have raised fixed employment costs and the penalties for turn-over that they impose.

Summary

It has been argued in this chapter that internal labor markets are a logical development in a competitive market in which three factors (usually neglected in conventional economic theory) may be present: (1) enter-prise-specific skills, (2) on-the-job training, and (3) custom. Enterprise-specific skills are those which can only be utilized in a single enterprise in contrast to *general* skills which can be transferred among many enter-prises. The effect of skill specificity is twofold: it encourages employers, rather than workers, to invest in training; once the investment has occurred, it leads employers to stabilize employment and reduce turn-over so that they can capture the benefits of the training.

On-the-job training is characterized by its informality. In many ways it appears to occur almost automatically by "osmosis" as the worker observes others or repeatedly performs his job. Because on-the-job train-ing is informal, is a joint output of the production process, and is limited to the skills required by work actually being performed, it appears to be an economical training process. Skill specificity tends to promote on-the-job training by reducing the number of persons learning a particular skill, thereby deterring more formal training programs with their concomitant fixed costs. Moreover, because skill specificity is often the result of ele-ments of work which are difficult to codify in a formal training curric-ulum, on-the-job training may be the only way to transmit skills from one worker to another. The informality and adaptability of on-the-job training, in turn, permits skill specificity to increase inasmuch as the need to codify or standardize the training process is not a constraint upon the evolution of job content.

Custom, or customary law, is the natural outgrowth of the psychological behavior of stable groups. Where stability of employment is encouraged, a work group will begin to develop customs based upon precedent and repeated practice. As work rules become customary through repetition at the workplace, they come to acquire an ethical, or quasi-ethical, status within the work group (and violations of these customs tend to be punished by the group). Even where work rules may have initially reflected economic forces, custom imparts a rigidity to the rules and makes it difficult to change them in response to dynamic economic forces. Custom seems to form most strongly around wage relationships and internal allocation procedures. This accounts for much of the long-term stability in the wage and allocative structures of internal labor markets and is an important influence in the maintenance of internal labor markets over time.

When one internal labor market emerges in a previously competitive labor market, some workers and some jobs are withdrawn from general market competition, thereby encouraging other workers and managers to institute internal labor markets within their enterprises. Managers will do so in order to retain their "competitive" position in both product and labor markets. Incumbent workers will do so in order to protect or enhance their employment security and promotion opportunity. Once these markets are prevalent, workers and managers will seek to stabilize the work relationship and to reinforce further the internal labor market. Much of the interest of trade unions in seniority, internal promotion, job control, and equitable treatment at the workplace can thus be interpreted in the light of these effects. Similarly, management's interest in stabilizing its work force and in maintaining flexible work assignment procedures reflects its desire to retain an efficient work force while protecting its prerogatives from the encroachment of customs which will interfere with the profit of the enterprise.

Stability of employment is the most salient feature of the internal labor market. With stability comes rigidity and irreversibility in the administrative rules governing such markets. Not only are they irreversible, but, as argued above, they tend to spread and to grow stronger over time among all enterprises. Internal labor markets are favored by employers because they reduce the costs of turnover among workers who have been provided with enterprise-specific skills. Because skills are not transferable among enterprises, because employers seek to induce stability through economic incentives, and because mobility is frustrated by actions taken in other internal labor markets, workers become increasingly protective of such markets and the privileges which they confer. Finally, the gradual removal of the industrial work force from its agricultural antecedents, the decline in economic fluctuations, the increased specialization of machinery, and the rise in nonwage compensation and social welfare payments have all worked to gradually increase the stability, and the incentives for stability, within the internal labor market.

Chapter 3
The Allocative Structure of Internal Labor Markets

Introduction

The allocation of labor is one of the major functions of the internal labor market. As indicated earlier, there are two basic types of internal labor markets, *enterprise* and *craft,* both of which are governed by similar principles. The analysis in this chapter, as in other parts of the book, centers upon enterprise markets, although some reference will be made to craft markets as well.

While no national surveys are available, estimates of the proportion of the labor force within these two types of internal labor markets are available from data on employment by size and type of enterprise, and by craft union membership. Table 1 suggests that about 80 per cent of the employed labor force works in internal labor markets, while the remainder works in agricultural and service occupations.[1]

[1] General practitioners, street "hustlers," free-lance writers, some nonunion craftsmen, and the like operate primarily as unorganized independent entrepreneurs. The best illustration of an unstructured occupational labor market is that of harvest labor. Harvesting is primarily unskilled and casual. Because of its transient nature and the piece-rate method of wage payment which standardizes labor costs per unit of output, employers make few attempts to identify differences in worker productivities. Moreover, the labor force follows the geographic and climatic pattern of crop maturation so that work is always temporary, and the formation of "social"

TABLE 1.   Employment Distribution by Type of Internal Labor Market, 1965

TYPE OF LABOR MARKET	PERCENTAGE OF EMPLOYMENT	
Structured		81.4%
Enterprise type		54.4
Military services	3.2	
Workers in public enterprises	11.8	
Workers in institutions (includes hospitals, universities, museums, etc.)	2.9	
Union workers in large enterprises	11.8	
Nonunion workers under industrial agreements	1.3	
Workers outside the bargaining unit in large enterprises	7.0	
Workers in large nonunion enterprises	7.0	
Workers in small enterprises	27.0	
Craft type		
(Workers in craft unions)		9.4
Unstructured		18.4
Proprietors and self-employed family workers	12.0	
Farm laborers	1.5	
Domestic workers	2.4	
Self-employed professionals in offices and laboratories	1.6	
Workers performing odd jobs, service and repair work	.9	
Total		100.0

SOURCE: Derived from Orme W. Phelps, *Introduction to Labor Economics* (New York: McGraw-Hill Co., 1967), p. 48. (Total does not equal 100.0% because of rounding.)

Types of Allocative Structures

The allocative structures of both enterprise and craft internal labor markets may be analyzed according to three characteristics: (1) the degree of *openness* to the external labor market as measured by (a) the proportion of ports of entry or exit,[2] the job classifications connecting the internal and external labor markets, and (b) the restrictiveness of the criteria for entry; (2) the *scope* — size, geographical, and occupational

---

attachments between employers and workers is precluded. Lloyd Fisher has described this labor market as "particularly well suited to accommodate and usefully employ labor of almost any description. The market is without any structure of job rights or preference." Lloyd Fisher, *The Harvest Labor Market in California* (Cambridge, Mass.: Harvard University Press, 1953), p. 7.

[2] See Clark Kerr, "The Balkanization of Labor Markets," in E. Wight Bakke, *et al., Labor Mobility and Economic Opportunity* (Cambridge, Mass.: Technology Press of MIT, 1954), pp. 92-110.

— of the internal labor market; and (3) the rules which determine the *priorities* for distributing workers among the jobs within the internal market.[3]

The Degree of Openness

Ports of entry. Two polar types of internal labor markets can be postulated: *closed* and *open*. All jobs within closed internal markets are filled internally through transfer or upgrading from a single entry job classification. Such closed structures are to be found in production and maintenance units in industries such as steel, petroleum and chemicals, as shown in Figure 1. Workers in these plants are hired almost exclusively into low-skilled job classifications, and most blue-collar skills, including maintenance and repair, are developed internally.[4]

At the opposite extreme is the *open* market in which vacancies in all job classifications are filled directly from the external labor market. Craft markets generally follow this model. The number of job classifications is extremely limited, and each constitutes a port of entry. This extreme case is also characteristic of certain enterprise markets. In the garment and shoe industries, for example, a high proportion of all production job classifications are entry ports, as shown in Figure 2, and internal mobility is infrequent. In the men's tailored clothing industry, promotion sequences are rarely found and usually occur only in response to serious employment dislocations or critical skill scarcities.

Because such open markets are exposed to the external labor market at a large number of points, hiring often appears to respond to external market conditions in the manner hypothesized in economic theory. This appearance, however, is deceptive. The allocation of work assignments, the determination of wages, and the procedures followed in periods when work is scarce are all governed by administrative rules that are not wholly responsive to market forces and that distinguish sharply between the internal and the external labor force.

Most enterprise internal labor markets lie between being completely

---

[3] Mobility within enterprise labor markets is of three types: (1) upgrading or downgrading, corresponding to secular trends in employment; (2) vertical and lateral movements as a result of seasonal or cyclical fluctuations in output; and (3) temporary reassignments to fill vacancies created by unplanned variations in production and in the attendance of the internal labor force. There are also three types of mobility in craft internal labor markets: (1) from low skill to higher skill; (2) among employers in the same geographical area; and (3) from one regional mobility cluster to another.

[4] For a study of an internal labor market which develops all of its operating and maintenance skills through internal training and upgrading, see Edgar Weinberg and Herman J. Rothberg, *A Case Study of a Modernized Petroleum Refinery* (Report No. 120) U.S. Department of Labor, Bureau of Labor Statistics, Studies of Automatic Technology, No. 4 (Washington: Government Printing Office, 1957).

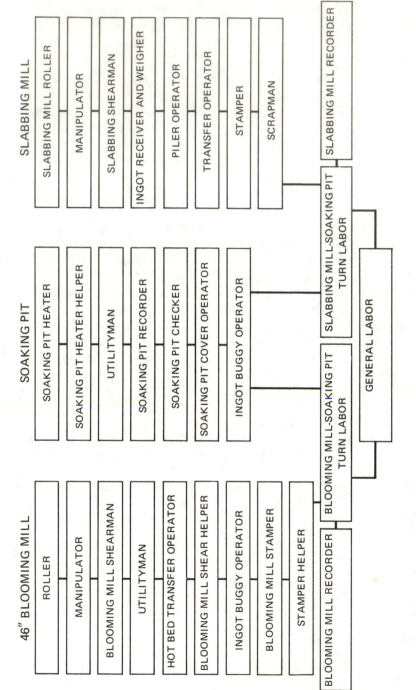

Figure 1. Line of progression: 46" blooming mill—soaking pit—slabbing mill.

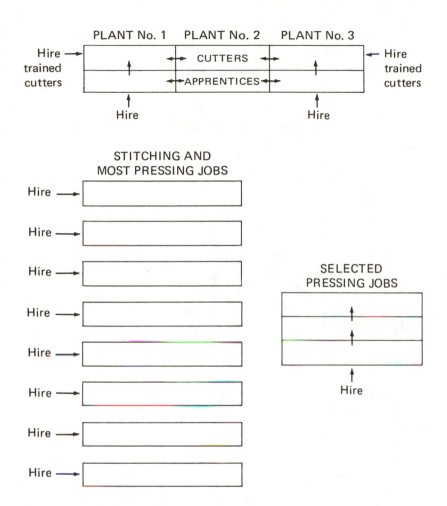

Figure 2. Internal labor market—men's garment industry.

open and completely closed. In manufacturing for example, hiring classifications for production work are typically low skilled: laborer, sweeper, machine cleaner, packer, assembler, shipping clerk, and the like. Most semiskilled and high-skilled production jobs are filled internally. Job classifications such as maintenance electricians, painters, pipefitters, masons, and machinists which exist in many enterprises, and in which a general skill is a major component of job content, may be filled either from external sources or by upgrading less-skilled members of the internal labor force. Such a market is depicted in Figure 3.

Internal markets for clerical workers are generally more open than those for blue-collar labor. Each skill or occupational grade may be an

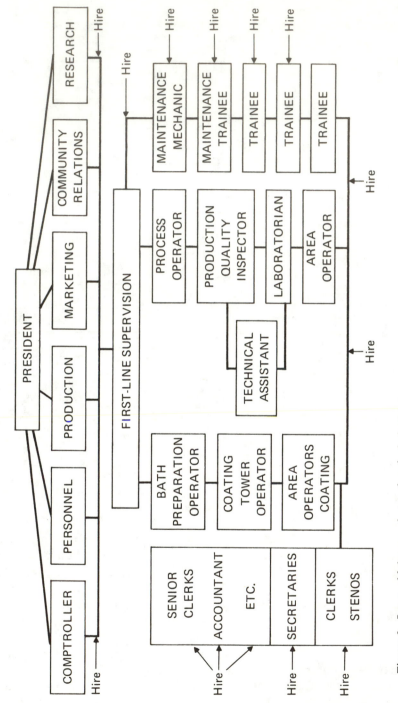

Figure 3. Internal labor market—chemical plant.

entry port so that mail clerks, clerk typists, stenographers, and various grades of secretaries can all be hired from the external labor market under certain circumstances. The permissible circumstances are sometimes limited, however, and a *mixed* system using both hiring and internal promotion as sources of labor are not uncommon.

For managerial and technical work, internal training and promotion policies are followed whenever possible although, as for clerical workers, mixed systems may also arise.[5] Experienced executives, scientists, and engineers, for example, may be hired from the external market, especially when suitably qualified employees are not available for upgrading. Professional personnel, such as lawyers, physicians, and nurses are usually hired into jobs at a skill and pay grade commensurate with their education and experience, with little or no prospect of internal mobility.[6]

Some enterprises utilize formal training programs as entry ports when they wish to prepare workers for particular jobs or progression patterns that require high levels of skill and background qualifications. This approach may be more efficient than training through other patterns of hiring and upgrading. It may also enable the enterprise to utilize more selective hiring standards for trainees than are ordinarily required. Management training programs for specially selected college graduates, apprenticeship programs designed to provide persons destined for supervisory jobs with shop experience, and vestibule training programs for equipment maintenance are examples of such entry ports.

Criteria for entry. A second determinant of the degree of openness of internal labor markets is the selection criteria governing entry. These criteria, expressed most often in terms of educational attainment, aptitude test scores, personal interviews, work experience, physical fitness, and so forth, are used to define gradations of "quality" among workers in the external labor market.[7]

Entry into enterprise internal labor markets is customarily controlled by hiring standards determined by management. These standards ostensibly reflect the skill or worker-trait requirements of entry jobs, and of

[5] See Edith T. Penrose, *The Theory of the Growth of the Firm* (New York: Wiley and Sons, 1959) and Robin Marris, *A Managerial Theory of Capitalism* (New York: Free Press of Glencoe, 1964).

[6] See also Theodore Alfred, "Checkers or Choice in Manpower Management," *Harvard Business Review*, vol. XLV, no. 1 (Jan.-Feb. 1967) pp. 157-169.

[7] In the past, union membership, race, sex and age have also been used as screening criteria, but these are now subject to various legal constraints. Federal legislation requires that entry into internal labor markets not be limited or discriminatory with respect to such factors as union membership, sex, race, and national origin. See Secs. 7, 9(a) (3) and 8(b) (2) of the Labor Management Relations Act, 1947, and Secs. 703(a) (1), 703(c) and 703(d) of the Civil Rights Act of 1964. These statutes, however, do not preclude the establishment of certain nondiscriminatory criteria for entry. See Sec. 8(f) of the Labor Management Relations Act, 1947, and Sec. 703(e) of the Civil Rights Act of 1964.

related jobs which are filled internally. However, they are usually free to vary with the tightness of the labor market. In this sense, the openness of enterprise markets may be said to vary with labor market conditions.

Applicants for apprenticeship programs in craft internal markets must usually meet similar qualifications. The journeyman's category in such markets can be reached through a "mixed system," either through "promotion" from an apprenticeship program or by "picking up" the requisite skills. In the latter case, skill proficiency must be demonstrated by passing a journeyman's qualification test or by working regularly in the trade. Temporary clerical help services, another example of a craft market, usually test applicants for minimum typing, shorthand, or office machine skills before accepting them into their referral systems. Placement systems for professional occupations, such as nursing, typically have specific education or training criteria for their services, formally incorporated in licensing requirements.[8] For example, the placement services of state nurses' associations may be available only to nurses who have completed approved or accredited programs of nursing education.

Qualifications for entry into craft internal labor markets are usually based on the level of vocational skill required by the occupation, although monopsonistic control over a work jurisdiction is very often also a factor.[9] As the level of occupational skill decreases, entry into the occupationally oriented internal labor market becomes less restricted. In longshoring, for example, much of the work is unskilled, and entry criteria are often minimal or nonexistent, so that anyone may be allowed to "shape" at the hiring location.[10]

Entry criteria in occupational markets are not as a rule free to vary with labor market conditions. They are more often the subject of labor-management agreements than are standards in enterprise markets and are frequently the subject of legal restrictions and governmental licensing requirements as well.[11]

[8] See *Report of the National Advisory Commission on Health Manpower* (Washington: U.S. Government Printing Office, 1967), vol. I.

[9] Waivers of entry requirements for occupational internal markets can occur when labor demand is high. Such waivers operate through devices such as work permits, which allow less skilled workers to enter the trade only temporarily.

[10] See Vernon Jensen, *Hiring of Dock Workers and Employment Practices in the Ports of New York, Liverpool, London, Rotterdam, and Marseilles* (Cambridge, Mass.: Harvard University Press, 1964); U.S. Department of Labor, *Manpower Utilization: Job Securitiy in the Longshore Industry* (Washington: Government Printing Office, 1964); and Francis M. McLaughlin, "The Development of Labor Peace in the Port of Boston" *Industrial and Labor Relations Review,* vol. XX (January 1967), pp. 221-233, for the complete details of hiring practices in longshoring. In the port of New York, for example, a medical examination must be passed. Moreover, from time to time the medical card rolls may be closed to control the number of workers in the referral system.

[11] See Richard A. Lester, *Hiring Practices and Labor Competition,* Princeton University Research Report No. 88 (Princeton: Princeton University Press, 1954).

Ports of exit. Internal markets typically have definite rules relating to exit, as well as to entry. Exit rules do not generally change an internal market's classification with respect to openness, but because they are of interest in the analysis of other problems, they are considered here.

Exit rules are generally defined for the purpose of controlling *involuntary* mobility. With the exception of markets controlled by the military or penal authorities, the worker is always free to quit his job, to relinquish his union affiliation, or to remove his name from a labor referral system.[12] In enterprise internal labor markets, exit rules deal with a variety of forms of involuntary movement: temporary and permanent layoffs, sabbatical leaves, termination for lack of work, disability, or discipline, and compulsory or early retirement. They determine the location in the job structure of the involuntary exit ports and the conditions under which termination will occur.

The rules for leaving craft markets differ from those in enterprise markets. Neither the number of workers nor membership in the craft markets are directly related to the volume of employment in the market at any point in time. Consequently, involuntary separation from the market does not normally occur as a result of a lack of work.[13] A worker, however, who fails to pay his union dues or referral fees when required, who violates rules governing performance or behavior within the market, or who fails to conform to stipulated minimum annual employment requirements may lose his eligibility for referral or employment.[14]

The Scope and Structure of Internal Labor Markets and Internal Mobility Clusters

The scope of craft and enterprise markets is defined in terms of their occupational and geographical boundaries. Within these boundaries there are often subdivisions which define the *internal structure* of each market.

[12] On the historical development of the asymmetry between the employees' and the employers' rights in the employment contract see Frederick Meyers, *Ownership of Jobs: A Comparative Study,* Institute of Industrial Relations, Monograph Series (Los Angeles: University of California Press, 1954), Ch. I.

[13] The correspondence between the size of the internal work force and the number of jobs is much less perfect in occupational internal labor markets than in enterprise-oriented internal labor markets. In the building trades, for example, the number of journeymen within the referral system may be less sensitive to the particular phase of the business cycle than employment in industrial plants. See Daniel Quinn Mills, "Factors Determining Patterns of Employment and Unemployment in the Construction Industry," unpub. diss., Harvard University, 1967.

[14] For example, a minimum of 700 hours a year are required for a worker to remain eligible for referral and are part of the administrative rules governing the allocation of work in longshoring on the New York waterfront. See *Manpower Utilization — Job Security in the Longshore Industry — Port of New York* (Washington, D.C.: U.S. Department of Labor, 1964).

For example, entry ports are typically connected to internal *mobility clusters,* the groupings of jobs within which an employee is customarily upgraded, downgraded, transferred and laid off.[15] Both the scope and structure of internal markets are determined by factors such as job content, predictable changes in the supply and demand for labor, and custom.

The structure of enterprise internal labor markets. Jobs within mobility clusters share one or more of the following elements: (1) related skills or work experience (lines of progression in steel mills); (2) similar levels of job content (as when janitors, sweepers, and machine cleaners constitute a single unit cutting across several departments in a manufacturing plant); (3) a common functional or departmental organization (such as "maintenance," in which many occupations—electricians, pipefitters, millwrights, machine mechanics, and so forth—are grouped); (4) a single focus of work (such as a computer and its related software).[16]

In the enterprise, the dimensions of the mobility clusters may vary with the type of movement (that is, promotion, layoff, lateral transfer, and so forth) and they tend to be narrower for upward mobility than for downward mobility.[17] In the steel industry, for example, workers are promoted along progression lines within departments. For layoffs, on the other hand, workers can apply seniority rights to employment in an employment "pan" consisting of the lower job grades in two or more departments. The patterns of internal movement may also differ for temporary and permanent moves, with more flexibility usually permitted for the former than the latter.

Mobility clusters have both a *vertical* and a *horizontal* dimension. The

---

[15] These mobility clusters are closely related to the concept of the "job cluster" developed by Dunlop to identify groups of jobs within the enterprise which are seen by workers and managers as linked together in the process of determining the internal wage structure. See John T. Dunlop, "The Task of Contemporary Wage Theory," George W. Taylor and Frank C. Pierson, eds., *New Concepts in Wage Determination* (New York: McGraw-Hill Co., 1957), pp. 117-139. Job clusters may be empirically defined by identifying those jobs which are compared to one another for purposes of job evaluation and internal wage setting. In most cases these clusters will be found to follow upgrading progressions.

[16] Other factors can also determine the shape of internal mobility clusters. Prior to the passage of Title VII of the Civil Rights Act of 1964, for example, formal or informal designations of race or sex were sometimes applied to jobs, and separate mobility clusters were established. Similarly, NLRB election unit determinations may also separate skilled production or maintenance units from the blue-collar industrial units in manufacturing plants or other enterprises.

[17] See Sumner H. Slichter, James J. Healy, and E. Robert Livernash, *The Impact of Collective Bargaining on Management* (Washington: The Brookings Institution, 1960), pp. 154-210, for a discussion of the various types of internal markets for promotions and layoffs in manufacturing.

former is defined by the range of "skill" content of the jobs within the cluster. The horizontal dimension measures the number, degree of specialization, and diversity of the jobs at any level of skill.

In enterprise internal markets, broad mobility clusters are typically associated with jobs having low variation in the levels of job content and a low proportion of specialized jobs. For example, plantwide mobility clusters are found in many food product companies, in supermarkets, and in small, mass-production electronics companies. Narrow mobility clusters are found in establishments where the job structure is divided into departments. In some manufacturing plants—steel, chemicals, autos, and petroleum, for example—there are further internal subdivisions, or *lines of progression* within production departments. These progression lines may be only one job classification wide, or they may consist of multiclassification steps or branching lines of progression. The narrowest type of mobility cluster in enterprise internal labor markets consists of a single job classification, and each classification constitutes an entry port. Such clusters reflect the high specialization, training time, and unrelated skills among the jobs in the internal labor market.

For managerial and technical jobs, mobility clusters may embrace a number of establishments within a single enterprise since managerial skills are not establishment specific to the same degree that blue-collar skills are, and since exposure to different work experiences is an important component of a manager's training. Multi-establishment mobility clusters are less common for blue-collar workers, appearing most often in times of serious employment dislocation, or when new plants are being established.[18]

The structure of craft internal labor markets. The geographical scope of craft markets ranges from narrow, locally oriented markets to those which are multistate or even nationwide. The geographical scope of these markets is determined by (1) the relationship between the demand and supply for the occupation and its distribution over the work year in a geographical area; (2) the potential mobility of the internal labor force; and (3) the geographical area of the product market within which the employers participating in the internal labor market compete.[19] In the case of union-operated referral systems, negotiating strategies and bargaining

---

[18] See Slichter *et al., op. cit.,* pp. 154-158, for further descriptions of layoff systems and bumping rights. David B. Lipsky provides an interesting example of transfer rights during plant relocation. See David B. Lipsky, "Interplant Transfer and Terminated Workers: A Case Study," *Industrial and Labor Relations Review,* vol. XXIII, no. 2, January 1970, pp. 191-206.

[19] See John T. Dunlop, "The Industrial Relations System in Construction," in Arnold R. Weber, *The Structure of Collective Bargaining* (New York: The Free Press of Glencoe, 1961), pp. 271-272.

strength may also be important in determining the geographical area to be served.[20]

Internal labor markets for longshoremen, carpenters, and plasterers tend to be narrow in scope because the employers typically operate within a limited geographical area, and employment opportunities are relatively stable within the area. For boilermakers and operating engineers, on the other hand, the employment opportunities are relatively more scarce within any particular locality, so that their internal labor market must encompass a larger region to provide equivalent employment opportunity. Moreover, such an internal market facilitates labor recruitment in heavy construction, where contractors may have to bid on work over a large region in order to ensure adequate utilization of their capital equipment.[21] Where labor demand is occasionally subject to wide fluctuations among geographical areas, special linkages such as union "traveling cards," temporary work permits, "shipping letters," or other transfer arrangements are likely to be developed to augment customary allocative procedures.[22]

The geographic scope of the market is also influenced by the potential for administrative economies. Labor negotiations, economic agreements, apprenticeship programs, dispute-settling procedures, pension plans, and the efficient utilization of business agents all engender fixed administrative costs. These costs encourage internal labor markets which are large enough to achieve economies of scale and an adequate dues-paying base.[23]

The control of employment opportunities in craft markets. As indicated

[20] See Gordon W. Bertram and Sherman J. Maisel, *Industrial Relations in the Construction Industry: The Northern California Experience* (Berkeley: Institute of Industrial Relations, West Coast Collective Bargaining Systems Monograph no. 2, 1955), p. viii, and Gordon W. Bertram, *Consolidated Bargaining in California Construction* (Los Angeles: University of California Institute of Industrial Relations Monograph, no. 12, 1966), p. 7.

[21] This relationship has been detailed by Bertram. (See Bertram, *ibid*, pp. 7-67.) The rising capital-labor ratio for heavy contractors, for example, provides a motivation for wider bidding on contracts and more uniform labor cost arrangements over large geographical areas, especially for the operating engineers' craft. Uniformity of collective agreements in turn encouraged more interlocal labor mobility, especially when work was plentiful and created incentives, both for the contractors and the unions, to reduce geographic jurisdictional barriers and to encourage movement of labor over a broader area.

[22] For a discussion of the historical development of such transfer arrangements in craft type internal labor markets see Lloyd Ulman. *The Rise of the National Union*, rev. ed. (Cambridge, Mass.: Harvard University Press, 1966), pp. 49-152. Bertram indicates that such arrangements for interlocal movement are common, but not numerically substantial. Although figures were not available, Bertram states that most interlocal movement occurs among iron workers and operating engineers, primarily in response to the shifting location of larger construction projects. See Bertram, *op. cit.*

[23] See Dunlop, "The Industrial Relations System in Construction," *op. cit.*, p. 271, and Bertram, *op. cit.*, p. 64.

earlier, craft markets encompass a number of employers. Such markets may have total responsibility for allocating workers among the jobs in the market, or may serve as an adjunct to other methods. In the building and maritime trades, these two systems are often referred to as *exclusive* and *nonexclusive* referral arrangements.

Under *exclusive* referral arrangements, the internal labor market is the sole source of workers for the employers within it, subject to certain qualifications. If the referral system fails to provide competent workers within a limited time period, the employer is usually free to obtain labor elsewhere.[24] Employers may also be allowed to hire certain "key employees" (such as foremen) and a percentage of "regular" employees, without recourse to the referral system.[25] This is often the case where contractors operate in a number of different regions.

Under the *nonexclusive* referral arrangement the employer may utilize both the referral system and the external labor market in general. Such nonexclusive internal labor markets are found in the building trades, temporary help services, and among professional associations which operate placement services.[26]

Priorities for internal mobility. The rules which determine the priority or ranking by which workers move within a mobility cluster depend upon such factors as ability, seniority, and frequency of work. These criteria, however, may be limited in various ways, and employees may or may not elect to accept assignments for which they are eligible under a given set of criteria.

---

[24] In the maritime and construction trades this time limit is usually 24-48 hours. However, when emergency situations require labor immediately, the limit may be waived. For example, in the referral systm for hotel service employees in New York City run by the New York State Employment Service, a 48-hour time limit for referrals is automatically reduced to one hour in emergencies.

[25] Key people typically possess critical supervisory or craft skills. These people are familiar with an employer's work practices and equipment, and their presence in a job may be crucial to productive efficiency, especially among small general contractors or builders who may have developed employer-specific production techniques. (See Bertram and Maisel, *op. cit.,* p. 47).

[26] A study of building trades workers in the Boston labor market indicated that one third of the construction craftsmen utilized union referral systems in the process of obtaining employment, one third had a regular attachment to an employer or foreman, and the remainder found their jobs through casual search. (Abraham Belitsky, "Hiring Problems in the Building Trades," unpub. diss., Harvard University, 1960, p. 25). Bertram and Maisel suggest that, in the building trades, the size of jobs as well as the type of work may be a factor in the mix between regular workers and reliance upon union referrals in a nonexclusive referral system. They postulate that turnover, and contractor-specificity of experience and skills, affect efficiency and that efficiency is more important on small jobs than large. (Bertram and Maisel, *op. cit.,* p. 47). The stability of contract volume is also important as the proportion of keymen who can be economically retained will depend on how much a contractor's labor needs fluctuate.

Enterprise Internal Labor Markets

Seniority and ability. Although some enterprise internal labor markets rely exclusively upon either seniority or ability in deciding priorities for internal movement, most employ some combination of the two.[27] In any particular enterprise, a different combination may be used for promotions than for layoffs. In large and medium-sized manufacturing plants, for example, straight seniority predominates in determining layoffs within production and maintenance units. Those plants which do not use seniority for layoffs generally provide some other form of employment security, such as employment guarantees or work-sharing procedures.[28]

Most promotions and lateral transfers, however, are determined by ability factors as well as seniority. The emphasis upon ability varies from complete reliance upon merit and ability to automatic promotion of the most senior employee, subject only to his ability to perform the job after a trial period. Some enterprises apply both criteria to all types of internal movement; others use a "float line" system where seniority exclusively determines internal movement among job classifications below a certain job grade, and ability governs movement above that grade. This arrangement is common in parts of the flat-glass industry and applies informally in many others.

Reliance upon seniority as a criterion for internal mobility is often

[27] Because on-the-job training, seniority and ability are generally correlated, a study by James J. Healy found that arbitrators were continuing to follow the "head and shoulders" principle, which emphasizes the seniority factor in promotions unless an obvious case of ability distinction exists, and that there is a substantial amount of management satisfaction with the subsequent work performance of the senior employee. He concluded that "in an industry in which semi-skilled jobs predominate, clearly discernible differences in ability among a large group of employees is so slight that they do not govern the selection of persons for promotion." James J. Healy, "The Factor of Ability in Labor Relations," in *Arbitration Today, Proceedings of the Eighth Annual Meeting of the National Academy of Arbitrators* (1955), p. 53.

[28] Internal labor markets containing jobs which are insulated, to some degree, from the external labor market antedate the widespread appearance of formalized rules structures. In a study by Roy W. Kelly, *Hiring the Worker* (New York: The Engineering Magazine Co., 1918), 20 per cent of the firms surveyed had some formal promotion plan. Only one firm in thirty had a plan which involved seniority; the rest relied upon personal judgment (usually a foreman's) in selecting candidates for promotion. One firm did not replace older workers with younger, more able people, in order to sustain morale (pp. 27-30). A later study by Paul Gemmil, "Methods of Promoting Industrial Employees," *Industrial Management,* vol. LXVI (April 1924), of a sample of 150 large companies (100 or more employees), found that 141 had a policy of promotion from within. Two of these firms promoted the most senior worker, and 97 used seniority when "merit" was equal among alternative employees. See also Sumner H. Slichter, *Union Policies and Industrial Management* (Washington: The Brookings Institution, 1941), pp. 276-279, pp. 542-543.

identified with trade union objectives, but some unorganized firms also adhere to promotion by straight seniority. Most enterprises which rely solely on merit criteria, however, are unorganized.

Bumping rights. Bumping rights are closely related to the issue of ability and seniority. They define the sequence in which workers displace one another when being downgraded and laid off. This sequence, in turn, affects the relative job security of individual workers and the retraining costs incurred by the employer. For example, *chain bumping,* in which a bump by one employee initiates a series of consecutive bumps down a progression line before a layoff results, produces the greatest average number of reassignments per redundant employee. This introduces costs and frictions into the redundancy procedure since each move requires some retraining and reorientation to work. When these costs are significant, management will prefer narrow downgrading districts. Alternatively, it will seek to limit the number of bumps by requiring that surplus employees in higher-skilled classifications bump directly into the lowest-skilled jobs or by permitting workers with, for example, ten years of seniority to bump only those workers with five or less years of seniority.

Posting and bidding. The priorities for internal movement are sometimes affected by "posting and bidding" arrangements. These are rules for notifying workers of internal vacancies and for allowing them to select opportunities for internal movement. Internal job vacancies are made available to the internal labor force in a variety of ways. Notifications of vacancies may be formally "posted" on bulletin boards or communicated by supervisors and co-workers. Workers may then "bid" for jobs or otherwise signify their interest in reassignment. Such procedures determine the group of applicants to which management will apply the selection criteria described above when filling a particular internal vacancy.

Craft Labor Markets

The priorities for movement in craft labor markets often depend upon a system of categories of workers. These categories may be based upon a combination of factors such as length of previous work experience with employers under a particular collective agreement, length of work experience in a craft, or the period of residency in a particular geographic area.[29]

---

[29] For example, a referral priority clause in an International Union of Operating Engineers agreement might read as follows:

Group A. All applicants who have worked as operating engineers for the past four years; who have been employed for an aggregate time of at least one year during the last four years by employers who are parties to collective bargaining agreements with the union . . . and who have maintained residence for the past year within the geographical area constituting the normal construction labor market . . .

Group B. All applicants for employment who have worked as operating engineers for the past four years and have been employed for an aggregate time of at least

All workers in the most preferred category are referred to employment before workers from the next category are eligible. Assignment or referral within each category is then made according to a principle of rotation. Often the principle of "first in, first out" is used so that the first job opportunity goes to the worker with the longest period of continuous unemployment. This system may be modified to equalize earnings by considering total days worked as well as frequency of employment. Sometimes, personal factors, such as health and family problems, may be taken into consideration as well.

Craft labor markets do not ordinarily recognize *enterprise* seniority as a basis for referral priorities. Consideration of internal market seniority, however, is not entirely absent. For longshoring in New York, for example, length of service governs assignment priorities within "pier," "section," "borough," and "port" referral categories. In Chicago, Local 134 of the International Brotherhood of Electrical Workers uses seniority in developing priorities for both referral and layoff. A journeyman acquires seniority, for purposes of referral, either by having worked one year with a single employer or two years with more than one employer under contract with the Chicago local. Once a worker has been employed for six months by a single employer, layoffs, with the exception of those lasting three days or less, are governed by seniority within that employer's work force.

Skill and ability may also be criteria for referral in craft markets. For example, the Operating Engineers would not refer a worker who could handle only scrapers and bulldozers to a job vacancy which required a crane or derrick operator.[30] Among temporary help services, ability is usually the exclusive criterion for referral.

The Determinants of the Allocative Structure

There is a unity and coherence to the rules governing the internal allocation of labor which implies that a change in any one dimension will nor-

---

six months during the last four years by employers who are parties to collective bargaining agreements with the union . . .

Group C. All applicants for employment who have worked as operating engineers for the past two years and who have maintained residence for the past year within the geographical area constituting the normal construction labor market . . .

Group D. All applicants for employment who have worked as operating engineers for one year.

Group E. All other applicants for employment.

(Suggested Hiring Hall Clauses; Internal Union of Operating Engineers.)

[30]See Garth L. Mangum, *The Operating Engineers: The Economic History of a Trade Union* (Cambridge, Mass.: Harvard University Press, 1964) pp. 270-275.

mally require adjustment along other dimensions as well. For example, limitations upon the employer's freedom to assign and utilize his work force will be reflected in highly selective hiring criteria; employment guarantees are associated with considerable managerial freedom to modify jobs and to redeploy the internal labor force. As a result, internal labor market structures exist in an almost bewildering array of combinations.

Nonetheless, the classification scheme outlined in the preceding sections suggests a set of features which they share in common. These features reflect the forces identified in Chapter 2 as responsible for generating internal markets and for governing their behavior. The structure of the enterprise internal market is influenced by management's interest in internal allocation as a means of promoting efficiency by reducing training and turnover costs. The structure most efficient in these terms, however, is compromised by the work force's interest in the internal market as a means of enhancing job security and advancement. Further distortions are introduced by the rigidities of custom which inhibit the response of the allocative structure to changes in the interests of labor and management.

Allocative Efficiency

The employer's interest in the allocative structure is to minimize the cost of turnover. If all vacancies could be filled without cost, the *employer* would be indifferent toward various market structures.[31] When turnover costs are present, the employer seeks to design jobs and arrange them in mobility clusters which reduce such costs. The openness of a market and its internal structure will therefore be subject to the influence of the various factors determining turnover costs. Ultimately, these are the technology embodied in existing capital equipment, the volume of production, the product mix, and the characteristics of the external labor supply. These fundamental variables are reflected in the levels of job skill, the mix of specific and general skills which the jobs require, and the skill relationships among the various jobs, all of which exercise a direct influence upon turnover cost.

Where the skill content of jobs is low, recruitment, screening, and training requirements are small, and turnover costs are trivial. Under these circumstances, the job structure exercises relatively little influence upon the internal allocative structure, and broad internal mobility clusters often emerge. Similar structures also develop when the content of jobs is closely related so that workers can be interchanged with few retraining costs.

---

[31] Workers, however, would still perfer a system which relied upon internal upgrading unless the opportunity costs of inter-enterprise mobility costs were also zero.

When each job requires skills which are essentially independent of other jobs and which are developed through an extended period of on-the-job training, there are no efficiency gains from internal movement. Each time a worker changes jobs internally, the full expense of training must be incurred. In this case, workers are not ordinarily transferred among jobs in the internal market. Moreover, in periods of work force redundancy management has little incentive to develop layoff procedures or to utilize seniority. Since both recent hires and experienced workers are equally trained, costs cannot be minimized by laying off junior workers. Instead, there is a tendency to emphasize work-sharing arrangements as a means of retaining the entire complement of trained workers. The open markets of the garment and the shoe industries are good examples of this phenomenon.

A different type of internal labor market structure is the *line of progression*. This structure occurs in enterprises where jobs are differentiated by levels of skill and fall, or can be designed to fall, into natural skill progressions. Work on one job develops the skills required for the more complex tasks on the job above it, and those at one point in the line constitute the natural source of supply for the next job along the line. Ideally, the training required to learn any given job in the progression occurs on the job below it, and workers are fully qualified by the time they are promoted. Layoffs are made in reverse order of progression. Such an allocative procedure captures the training opportunities inherent in natural skill progressions, and layoff in reverse order of progression ensures that workers with the most training will be retained in employment longest.

Efficiency under these circumstances favors narrow allocative districts synonomous with these natural lines of progression. It also favors the restriction of entry to jobs at the bottom of the progression line. Consequently, strict screening of candidates for entry is utilized to ensure promotability to the more skilled jobs in the line. Lines of progression are found in steel mills, paper mills, petroleum refineries, and in other process industries.

Jobs may also differ widely in terms of turnover costs, regardless of skill relationships. Some jobs involve heavy employer investments in training, screening, and recruitment; for others, these investments are minimal. Because the allocative structure of the internal market is designed to reduce turnover costs, it is important to control the incidence of turnover within the job structure. Some promotion sequences therefore arise where jobs are ranked by turnover cost, with minimal-cost jobs serving as ports of entry and exit. In most cases, jobs are designed and placed into mobility clusters that are consistent to some extent with both reducing costs and utilizing skill relationships. This pattern resembles that of a line of progression, except that the internal labor force is not completely trained for promotion by work on lower-level jobs. Consequently, a period of training and adjustment after promotion is generally necessary before peak efficiency is reached. Very often a readjustment period is also required in demotion during a layoff to regain peak efficiency in a job previously performed. Such training and readjustment periods create costs to internal movement and generate an employer interest in reducing the amount of movement when layoffs or promotions occur.[32]

Employee Interests

While the underlying structure of an internal market tends to reflect the requirements of allocative efficiency, the actual structure is generally modified to a greater or lesser extent to accommodate employee interests. These interests center upon the role of the internal market in enhancing job security and advancement. They therefore favor broad mobility clusters with wide geographic and occupational coverage, entry confined to a few low-skilled jobs, and reliance upon uniform criteria such as seniority in the internal allocation of jobs.[33]

These characteristics are favored because, in the absence of employment guarantees, income and employment are insured only so long as the displacement of a worker on one job coincides with a vacancy on another job to which he has access. The chances of this occurring are greater the larger the size of the internal market. They are further enhanced by technical and economic diversity which reduces the possibility that a technical change or an economic contingency which eliminates one job will affect other jobs in the internal market as well. Rules which limit entry and which allocate jobs on the basis of seniority-related criteria protect the worker from the competition of those outside the market or those entering the market after him.

Worker interests produce classic industrial relation conflicts over the design of internal market structures. Among these is the conflict between seniority and ability in job allocation. Another is the clash between the wide mobility districts favored by workers and the narrow districts which employers tend to prefer. The resolution of these conflicts varies depending upon the pressure which the work force can muster in its behalf and the sacrifices in wages and other aspects of the employment offer which it is willing to make to obtain allocative concessions. But in virtually all cases these are sufficient to induce some departures from the allocative structure that the employer would otherwise design.

The Interaction of Allocative Efficiency and Employee Interests

The relationship between allocative efficiency and employee interests can perhaps be best illustrated by the allocative rules designed to deal with

---

[32] See, for example, the discussion of "chain bumping," p. 55.
[33] See Phillip Selznick and Howard Vollmer, "The Rule of Law in Industry: Seniority Rights," *Industrial Relations*, vol. I, no. 3 (May 1962).

anticipated fluctuations in the supply or demand for labor within the internal labor market.

Most internal markets are designed to accommodate certain more or less anticipated fluctuations in the supply of workers on the external labor market and in the demand for labor internally. Procedures for handling such fluctuations are often embodied in the rules governing internal labor allocation, and the content of jobs is sometimes designed to facilitate the accommodation to these fluctuations.

The outstanding example of anticipated variations are seasonal and cyclical fluctuations in the demand for production workers. Such variations often generate an elaborate set of rules and customs governing transfer, layoff and recall. Because these rules constitute an acceptable compromise between the narrow allocative efficiency desired by management and the workers' interest in employment security, such fluctuations place no strains upon the internal market structure.

The structure of markets for production workers contrasts with that of markets for managerial and professional employees. The latter are not in general subject to, or prepared to accommodate, wide variations in demand for labor. Workers in this market have acquired, by precedent, an implicit employment guarantee which makes layoffs a jolting experience. The nature of this phenomenon is most clearly illustrated by the aerospace industry, with its large technical labor force and employment fluctuations determined by unpredictable vagaries in government contracts. At present the industry appears to be seeking a new market structure which will facilitate the transfer of workers among enterprises to take advantage of the greater stability of industry, as opposed to enterprise, employment.

Employment declines are only one type of fluctuation which internal market structures can be designed to accommodate. Another fairly common type is the internal scarcity of various skills. For example, some markets have several internal sources of supply. The preferred candidates for promotion might be the incumbents of neighboring jobs, but if these workers do not have sufficient experience or refuse the job, internal recruitment might be extended to a worker in another department who possessed related skills. There are similar choices between internal promotion and external hiring. The auto industry, for example, normally hires skilled craftsmen from the external market. A secondary route of entry is through an apprenticeship program to which incumbent employees have access on a competitive basis with outside candidates. A third route, the "temporary skilled craftsman," is opened only in a very tight market when external craftsmen are not available and apprentices are not yet ready for advancement. The "temporary skilled craftsman" is a kind of "paraprofessional" position for which production workers are trained on the job.

Variations in product demand also have their effects upon the internal market structure. Diversified establishments accustomed to frequent changes in the composition of product demand generally train workers more broadly than firms producing one or a few standardized products. Mobility sequences typically involve rotating employees through a variety of different jobs of similar difficulty before they are permitted to progress to a higher-skill level, much like the pattern for managerial trainees in many large corporations. Similar broad training is usually provided in plants which undergo frequent technological change, and the implications of a change in technology are totally different from those in firms whose market structures are predicated on a relatively stable technology.[34]

Custom

Custom is the third force playing upon the design of allocative structures. Because one effect of custom is to inhibit change, it causes the allocative structure to reflect the efficiency considerations, employee interests, and balance of negotiating power prevailing at some time in the past. A general outline of the nature of custom has been developed in the preceding chapter and need not be repeated here. However, several facets of the way in which custom affects the allocative structure should be emphasized.

For example, in discussing the way in which internal markets are structured to accommodate anticipated fluctuations in labor supply and demand, the customary nature of these arrangements should be borne in mind. Even when they are negotiated and spelled out in contracts, their true sanction is precedent and past practice, and they become "rusty" or difficult to evoke if they are not frequently reaffirmed. For instance, a set of procedures for reassigning workers in cases of product change will lose its legitimacy in the eyes of the labor force unless it is regularly utilized. Also the work force forgets many of the skills which facilitate work on other products if it continually exercises only the skills specific to one product.

A second aspect of custom that requires emphasis in the present context is the role of vested interests and expectations which grow up around existing allocative structures. These tend to reflect pressures for change in odd ways, producing structures totally different from those which would emerge if the interested parties were free to establish internal labor market

---

[34] It is to be noted that some of these accommodations to fluctuations in demand and supply involve not only the allocative structure but the job structure as well. For example, in autos, when temporary skilled craftsmen are used in the place of journeymen, work assignments must be revised to ensure that the really complex jobs are separated from other work and assigned to the available journeymen. Jobs may also be designed to require a broad range of skills as a means of accommodating the work force to frequent changes in products. See Chapters 5 and 6.

structures *de novo*. This often gives such structures a random, or haphazard, appearance in which it is difficult to recognize the core forces of efficiency and work force security which were originally influential.

Typical of this process are the changes introduced by attempts to maintain economic parity among lines of progression in different departments. Technological change often operates over time to shorten some lines and reduce the number of high-paying jobs at the top. This creates resentment among workers already in those lines whose expectations of future income are frustrated and who see junior workers in other districts moving above them in pay and status. It also leads workers to refuse assignment to jobs in these lines in anticipation of vacancies at the bottom of longer lines with greater opportunities for advancement. The efficient solution to this problem is to merge the shortened progression lines with other lines in the plant. However, this is generally resisted by workers in preferred lines who fear the competition of senior workers from whom they would otherwise be insulated. The alternative is typically an effort to improve the attractiveness of short lines by adding new jobs at the top. The added jobs often have little relationship in skill, geographic proximity, or turnover cost and the result is sometimes a promotion sequence consisting of a hodgepodge of unrelated jobs.

A final aspect of the internal market structure where change is constrained by custom is in the relative weight given to seniority and ability. Managements are perpetually concerned that technological changes will make employees with promotion expectations unqualified. This results, in many plants, in the imposition of entry criteria far in excess of the requirements necessary to master even the top job in a line of progression developed for the current technology. It also biases management in favor of ability as a selection criterion, even when seniority and ability are almost perfectly correlated.

Whenever custom results in the loss of allocative flexibility to the point that efficiency is seriously impaired, it can often be regained only by instituting some form of employment or income guarantee, or by relocating the plant. When employment guarantees are developed, they are accompanied by the introduction of a distinction between incumbent employees to whom the guarantee applies, and new workers who have lesser employment rights. In the extreme, the employees hired after the guarantee is installed are treated as temporary workers, with few employment rights. This procedure has been used in sugar refineries, and it is also a component of many longshoring markets.

Summary

In this chapter, the allocative structures of enterprise and craft internal labor markets have been described. These structures can be analyzed according to (1) the degree of openness to the external labor market; (2) the scope of the market and the patterns of mobility within it; and (3) the rules determining priorities for internal movement.

Each internal labor market structure reflects a compromise between managements' concern with efficiency and workers' interests in enhancing job security and advancement opportunity. Patterns of entry and internal mobility are typically designed to capture natural on-the-job training sequences and to reduce turnover costs. Priorities for internal movement combine ability and seniority in varying ways, also according to training and retraining costs.

These structures are designed to accommodate predictable changes in product demand, in technology, and in the availability of skills on the external labor market. Where such change threatens the security of the internal work force, allocative procedures involving seniority, wide mobility clusters, and other arrangements favoring the protection of employment rights tend to take precedence over efficiency considerations in determining the internal allocative structure.

The allocative structure of the internal labor market is a focal point around which strong customs are formed. Consequently, present market structures will often reflect the influences of earlier economic and techno-logical conditions. Custom makes the allocative structure stable and en-courages internal training, informal job redesign, and other activities helpful to efficiency. However, when economic or technological factors change radically and in unanticipated ways, custom may be a deterrent to adaptation within the internal labor market.

Chapter 4
Wage Determination Within the Internal Labor Market

In conventional economic theory, wage determination and labor allocation occur simultaneously as part of the operation of the competitive labor market. In the internal labor market these two activities should also be connected, although administrative rules and custom, as well as economic forces, should presumably govern this relationship. For example, wage rates should, at least in principle, influence the movement of labor among the ports of entry in different enterprises, even when most jobs are removed from external competition by internal promotion arrangements. One would also expect the *internal* allocative process to carry implications for the wage structure within the enterprise. Although wages were not the central focus of the studies from which this volume derives, these expectations were, in fact, borne out by the comments concerning wage determination made by numerous respondents during interviews. Thus, although not under direct investigation, a picture did emerge of the wage determination process in manufacturing.

In this chapter the process of internal wage determination is examined in four sections. The first section is devoted to a description of the process. The problem of interpreting it and of identifying the forces which it expresses, or is designed to express, is discussed in the second section. It is argued there that, while it is possible to interpret many of the phenomena which occur in wage determination in manufacturing within the confines of competitive neoclassical theory, there are important aspects of the process which strain the neoclassical constructs. These appear to be related to the internal market and the forces which dictate its existence. This theme is developed in the two concluding sections of the chapter.

The Internal Wage Setting Process [1]

In the manufacturing plant, three dimensions of internal wage structure are recognized: (1) *the plant wage level,* (2) *the vertical differentiation of the wage structure,* and (3) *the horizontal or intralevel differentiation of wages.* The first term is actually used by managers and union officials in discussing wages. It is clear from the contexts in which it is used that the "wage level" is a summary statistic for describing the wage structure as a whole. The term is applied in different contexts, however, so that the precise statistic to which it refers is not always apparent. The term is frequently used to describe the plant wage level relative to other plants in the community: for example, "our level is the third highest in the community," or "our wage level is about average." A second use of the term is a weighted average of plant wage rates. This may be an average for all hourly workers, for production and maintenance workers, or for a category known as "direct" personnel. Occasionally the term makes reference to the plant wage bill or to the entry wage, the latter being the base upon which the internal wage structure is often built.[2]

Participants in the wage setting process do not have a clear terminology for the second and third dimensions of the wage structure, the vertical and horizontal differentiation of wages, but they are recognized. Vertical differentiation refers to differences in wage rates among individuals holding different jobs. This commonly takes the form of skill grades or wage

[1] Formal wage setting procedures have received little attention among economists. The presumed congruence between administered and market wages is largely responsible for economists' indifference toward administrative instruments. The following discussion is addressed primarily to that audience and it is designed to emphasize the relationship between formal procedures and the market forces identified in economic theory. The material covered will be more familiar to students of personnel administration; it is an abbreviated version of a topic extensively treated in every personnel text in comparison to which the present treatment will seem oversimplified, and for certain purposes, ill-conceived. Readers primarily interested in the practice of wage administration should certainly refer to other sources. See, for example, Paul Pigors and Charles A. Myers, *Personnel Administration,* 6th ed. (New York: McGraw-Hill Co., 1969), Chs. 20-22.

[2] Since the wage structure which the term seeks to summarize is a distribution and, as such, is not readily summarized by a single statistic, the several concepts to which the term is applied are understandable. It is to be noted, however, that none of the summary statistics describes the dispersion of the wage structure or the differentials between jobs.

steps and is generally referred to as the "internal wage structure."[3] The horizontal differentiation refers to differences in rates among individuals holding the same jobs.

The process through which these dimensions of the wage structure are established is most readily understood in terms of the formal instruments of wage administration: *job evaluation, community wage surveys,* and *engineered production standards.* Not all manufacturing plants, by any means, utilize these instruments, and only the larger and more sophisticated plants employ all three. The instruments do appear, however, to represent a formalization of the process through which wages are set in their absence and thus are the codification of a more general wage setting process.

Job Evaluation and the Vertical Differentiation of the Wage Structure

Job evaluation is a procedure for ranking jobs according to a consistent set of weighted job characteristics and worker traits. The specific factors evaluated and the weights attached to them vary among job evaluation plans. Such plans are typically constructed in three stages.

First, a set of categories is selected upon which differences in wage rates will be based. These generally include categories of characteristics relating to the job itself (skill, working conditions, responsibility for equipment, responsibility for directing other workers, for instance) and categories of characteristics pertaining to the individual holding the job (education, experience, and the like). Second, a maximum number of points or weights is assigned to each of the broad categories. Thus, for example, for the group of categories selected above, the point totals might be those displayed in Table 2. Finally, a set of criteria are established for awarding portions of the maximum number of points in each category to a job.

Certain of the evaluation factors can be unambiguously defined. Educational requirements, for example, can be measured in terms of years of school. The weighting system might assign two points for each school year and five additional points for the completion of high school. A job requiring a high school diploma would then receive 29 points for educational requirements.

Points for job characteristics with no such inherent scale of measurement are defined by reference to "benchmark" jobs. Benchmark jobs are carefully analyzed, defined in detail, and have had point totals assigned in each evaluation category. When the evaluation plan is applied, the evaluator looks for the benchmark which most closely resembles the job in question for the relevant attribute. Thus, for example, working conditions on a given job being analyzed are characterized as being better or

[3] Jacob L. Meij (ed.), *Internal Wage Structure* (Amsterdam: North-Holland Publishing Company, 1963).

worse than those on various benchmark jobs. In certain cases there may even be separate benchmarks for different aspects of working conditions, such as heat, noise, weight lifting, and dirt.

TABLE 2.   Model Job Evaluation System

FACTOR		MAXIMUM POINTS
Working Conditions		15
Noise	5	
Dirt	5	
Smell	5	
Responsibility for equipment		25
Responsibility for other workers		20
Skill		20
Manual dexterity	10	
Experience	10	
Education		35
Physical effort		10
Total points		125

JOB EVALUATION POINTS FOR LABOR GRADES			
Grades	Points	Grades	Points
I	10-20	VI	61-75
II	21-30	VII	76-90
III	31-40	VIII	91-105
IV	41-50	IX	106-120
V	51-60	X	121 and over

The process of job evaluation consists in rating a job in each of the factor categories and adding the points across categories to determine point totals. This is typically done once for all jobs in a plant when a job evaluation plan is first introduced. Jobs are then reevaluated only when they are thought for one reason or another to have changed. New jobs are, of course, evaluated when they are introduced.

The job-evaluation point totals serve as a device for arranging jobs in a pay hierarchy. Jobs are generally grouped in *labor grades,* which span a range of job evaluation points. Thus, for example, jobs with point totals of ten to twenty might be assigned to labor grade I; twenty-one to thirty, labor grade II, and so forth, as shown in Table 2.

In principle, it is possible to base actual wage rates upon job evaluation points. Thus, for example, each job evaluation point might be valued at ten cents an hour; a twenty-point job would then receive a $2.00 rate. In practice, this procedure is almost never followed. Wage rates are assigned to labor grades rather than directly to the job or to the evaluation point total. This procedure reduces the effect upon the basic rate for a job of differences in individual evaluations or of the minor changes in jobs which inevitably occur over time. The ordinal structure which job evaluation establishes is converted into the actual cardinal wage structure through the *community wage survey.*

Community Wage Surveys and the Plant Wage Level

A community wage survey is not necesarily representative of wage rates within a defined geographic area. Rather, it is a systematic procedure by which an enterprise appraises the appropriateness of its wage structure with respect to its major competitors for labor. The enterprise conducting the survey identifies wage rates paid for roughly comparable job classifications in a series of other enterprises, derives from these rates a target wage structure, and then seeks to adjust its own structure to the target. A given "survey" can thus be characterized by two parameters: (1) the enterprises whose wages are surveyed, and (2) the job classifications selected for survey.

The enterprises surveyed, and the particular job classifications within these enterprises, tend to be constant over time. The criteria governing their selection are central to an understanding of the role of the survey. The group of enterprises selected tends to include both product market competitors and firms utilizing workers from backgrounds similar to those employed by the surveying plant. These businesses are not necessarily direct competitors for labor, but they are usually highly visible in the labor market, and their wages are thought to affect workers' wage expectations.

Job classifications appear to be selected to insure, if possible, coverage of all labor grades. In practice, this means that all jobs which have close analogies in the surveyed enterprises are included. If cooperation can be obtained, the job evaluation plans of the enterprises surveyed may be used to identify substitute job classifications in labor grades for which there are no analogous jobs. In some cases, catchall classifications such as "semiskilled machine operator" are used to obtain comparability.

Generally, as much information as possible on compensation is sought. Data on straight time and overtime earnings, fringe benefits, and measures of the divergence between rates and earnings which might indicate the effect of incentive systems are often collected.

The earnings data collected from the surveyed enterprises are often displayed on a graph like that shown in Figure 4. The wage scale is measured along the vertical axis. The labor grades of the plant conducting the survey are laid out along the horizontal axis. In each plant the jobs whose wages are collected are assigned to one of the labor grades of the

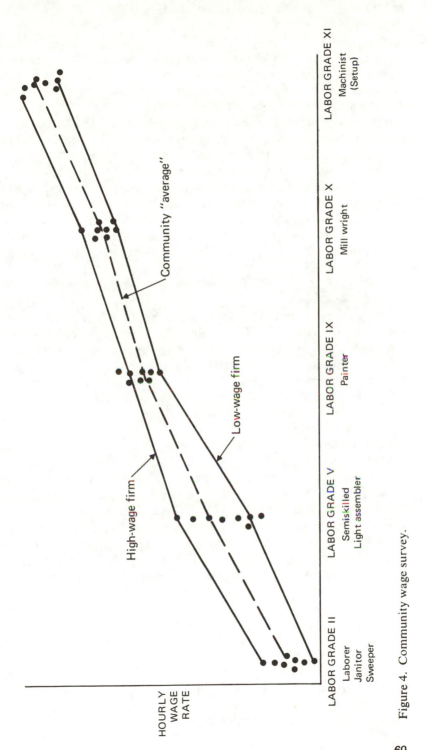

Figure 4. Community wage survey.

plant conducting the survey. This makes it possible to derive curves show-ing the wage structures of the various plants included. The target wage scale is then defined in terms of these curves, either in relation to the average wage scale over all the enterprises surveyed (for instance, "We pay at least 10 per cent above the average for every job.") or as a range within the community (for example, third highest-paying plant; or among the top three). Supplementary information about fringe benefits is some-times also displayed in this way, and separate fringe benefit targets are developed. In effect, the enterprise is attempting to meet the "community," not only in wage rates, but also in vacations, holidays, retirement benefits, and so on. In other cases, fringe benefit information is used to make rough adjustments in the target. For example, an enterprise may allow its wage rates to fall from third to fourth in the "community," arguing that its fringe benefits are far superior to that of the third highest-paying plant.

Engineered Production Standards and the Horizontal Differentiation of Wages

The wage rates attached to labor grades are based, in principle, upon the characteristics of jobs. The attributes of individuals holding the jobs are weighted only to the extent that the job requires these qualities, and all incumbents in a given job classification share the same basic rate. A number of enterprises, however, do make adjustments in wages for indi-vidual characteristics. These adjustments can be termed *horizontal differ-entiation*. Two techniques of horizontal differentiation predominate: merit rating and incentive systems.

Merit rating systems substitute a rate range for the single rate generally attached to each labor grade or job classification. Enterprises employing this system typically attempt to establish a set of uniform criteria for determining individual rates within the range, and require supervision to review each employee periodically in the light of these criteria. The formal criteria almost always emphasize the use of merit rate progression as a reward for performance but, in practice, merit ratings tend to be highly correlated with length of service. This sometimes reflects on-the-job learning but is more often indicative of a tendency for merit increases to become automatic.

On certain jobs it is difficult to distinguish between merit rating as a means of horizontal differentiation among individuals holding essentially the same job, and vertical differentiation among different jobs in a skill progression. This is especially true in craft jobs where it is common to have a hierarchy of subclassifications for the same craft. In such cases the work performed by the different classifications tends to overlap, but move-ment between classifications, and hence pay rates, is based upon some formal review or test of individual skills.

The second common form of horizontal differentiation is "payment by results." The central feature of all such payment systems is that they reward output. Such systems vary widely from straight piecework, becoming increasingly rare, to complicated group incentives. Most common are individual incentives based upon engineered standards.

Time and motion engineering studies are used to determine the output of the average employee working at a regular pace. From this measure, a standard or baseline output is defined. The job incumbent is guaranteed the basic wage, as set through job evaluation and community surveys, for standard output and receives a bonus for output in excess of this standard. Incentive systems vary in their yield, but most standards are set deliberately low so that even the average worker gains a bonus.

Interpretation of Formal Wage Determination

It is frequently argued that the wage determination process outlined in the preceding sections can be interpreted, within a competitive economic framework, as a passive institutional procedure for expressing market forces. The instruments of wage determination may give the illusion of influencing wages independently of the market, but this is only because the market forces governing wage determination are relatively stable. Were these forces to change, the instruments would rapidly be adjusted.

Under this interpretation, the community wage survey becomes the principal transmitter of market forces. It provides wage data about market competitors to which the internal wage structure can then conform. Job evaluation is a secondary instrument, designed to simplify the setting of wages by relating job classifications for which competitive data are obtained to job classifications not included in the survey. Similarly, horizontal wage differentiation permits the enterprise to reward differential productivity within job classifications, much as the competitive market is expected to function.

A more sophisticated version of the competitive interpretation takes cognizance of other functions of the instruments of wage determination. In this version, wage administration is concerned not only with expressing *short-run* market forces, but is part of a larger system of management control directed at ensuring the *long-run* responsiveness of the enterprise to market forces. Without these instruments, supervisors might neglect market forces under pressure of other responsibilities, or they might respond to immediate labor market conditions in a manner which would jeopardize the longer-term profitability of the enterprise. Internally, an absence of some unifying control over wage decisions might lead to favoritism and wage inequities which would impair work force morale and productivity.

Community wage surveys encourage a regular reassessment of an enterprise's wage position with respect to other enterprises. Because the survey process is a continuing one, it also provides managers with a longer-range perspective on the labor market which moderates the risk of short-run wage adjustments which are incompatible with the enterprise's long-run interests. Within the enterprise, job evaluation and engineered production standards ensure the establishment of uniform rates of compensation for similarly situated and similarly productive workers.

By encouraging response to *long-run* labor market forces, by continually examining the parity of internal and external wage relationships, and by encouraging standard wage rates within the enterprise, it can be argued that the control function of the administrative instruments of wage determination will closely approximate the predictions of competitive economic theory. A competitive interpretation of wage determination is, of course, congenial to economists because it permits administrative instruments to be neglected in favor of a direct analysis of market forces. The operation of these instruments of wage determination is also broadly consistent with this interpretation. The enterprises included in a wage survey do more or less correspond to those which would be in competition in an open labor market. Some firms are unwilling to cooperate with surveys because they may foster pirating of workers or of production techniques. The supremacy of the market forces reflected in the wage survey is further indicated by the practice of "fudging" job evaluation points to reconcile the internal wage structure with the structure of wages in the external market. Common techniques for circumventing an internal wage structure which is inconsistent with the external labor market involve reevaluating jobs to produce the desired structure or adjusting rates within "merit" ranges.[4]

The difficulty with competitive market interpretations of wage determination, however, is that they imply an inversion of the relative importance accorded to job evaluation and community wage surveys within the enterprise. Contrary to the expectations of competitive theory, wage administrators customarily give job evaluation far greater attention than community wage surveys. Internal consistency of wages receives much more consideration than is the case with external wage consistency. As a general rule, conflicts between ranking jobs in the community wage structure and the order dictated by job evaluation are resolved in favor of the latter.[5] Fudging the job evaluation plans to produce wage adjust-

---

[4] Fudging is most readily accomplished when a plan is first introduced. When a conflict develops after a system is in operation, it is necessary to assert that a job has changed in order to have it reevaluated. If the natural evolution which jobs undergo over time is not sufficient to justify such an assertion, a sufficient change can generally be engineered.

[5] See Jack Stieber, *The Steel Industry Wage Structure* (Cambridge, Mass.: Harvard University Press, 1959).

ment in conformity with market forces occurs largely in response to market pressures so gross that no survey was required to uncover them, and large divergencies from target wage structures are tolerated for longer periods of time than are seemingly minor internal wage disparities. Moreover, examples are not uncommon where wage rates dictated by job evaluation are maintained in the face of conflicting market pressures. The conflicts are often resolved ultimately by automating the job or subcontracting the work rather than compromising the evaluated wage structure.

The relative priority accorded job evaluation and wage survey results is paralleled by differences in the manner in which they are developed and applied. Job evaluation plans invariably represent considerable investment of time and energy in development and negotiation. The initial introduction of a job evaluation plan is viewed as a major business decision, comparable to the purchase of an expensive piece of capital equipment, and it is not unusual for the evaluation of a single job to consume the full day of an industrial engineer. Although the procedure of job evaluation is acknowledged by most to lack scientific precision, it is nonetheless conducted with a seriousness and attention of detail characteristic of scientific work.

By contrast, the construction and conduct of community wage surveys is cavalier. Uncooperative enterprises are avoided, and large occupational gaps are often condoned. There is the concern that the surveys might be inadvertently biased by the limited selection of enterprises and job classifications. In short, survey procedures, the lack of concern with maintaining external wage parity, and the sanctity of internal wage relationships do not support a competitive interpretation of wage determination, except within wide limits. It is, therefore, difficult to avoid forces distinct from the competitive market. Wage surveys permit the enterprise to monitor the external market constraint and to make deliberate responses to it when appropriate, but the emphasis upon internal forces points toward an independent role of the internal labor market in the process of wage determination.

Technical and Market Constraints

A theory of wage determination consistent with the wage setting process outlined above recognizes two sets of technical and market pressures upon the wage rate of a particular job: (1) External pressures generated by the factors emphasized in neoclassical theory but, given the existence of an internal labor market, not in themselves definitive, and (2) pressures deriving from the exigencies of internal allocation. Generally, these two sets of pressures constrain the wage structure and do not interact to determine a unique structure but rather *a range* or family of feasible wage structures. In some cases, the constraints may conflict so that wage rates consistent with one set of constraints are inconsistent with the other. For example, most large enterprise internal markets have one or a few jobs (and sometimes a whole department) for which wage rates consistent with the internal labor allocation are seriously out of line with the external labor market constraint. The result is generally a series of trying, but not insurmountable, operating and industrial relations problems. In the extreme case, however, the problems generated by conflicting constraints can drive a firm out of business. For most jobs, the constraints are more or less consistent, leaving the particular structure to be determined by social and institutional forces operating within the constraint.

The Neoclassical Constraints

The central results of neoclassical wage theory are twofold. First, an enterprise will pay each employee a wage commensurate with what he could obtain elsewhere. Second, the wage will be equal to the worker's marginal product. These results are dependent upon two assumptions seldom made explicit in the development of the theory: the absence of fixed employment costs and the temporary nature of the employment relationship. As was seen in Chapter 2, both assumptions are generally abrogated by the internal labor market. Internal markets tend to be accompanied by significant fixed costs of recruitment, screening, and training, and are designed to create a permanent relationship between the worker and the enterprise.

The formal implications of these changes have been worked out by Walter Oi and Gary Becker within the framework of competitive theory.[6] In that analysis, the presence of fixed employment costs creates an incentive for employers to stabilize the employment relationship. While the two phenomena are treated together, fixed employment costs are the central focus, and the permanency of employment is derivative or incidental. In the present context, however, it is useful to examine the two separately.

Fixed labor costs. Because fixed costs of recruitment, screening, and training occur in internal labor markets, wages (a *variable* cost) are no longer the sole component of labor costs, nor are they the single variable controlling labor allocation. These fixed labor costs operate in several ways to introduce an element of indeterminacy into wages. They do so first because nonwage employment costs reflect the existence of instruments other than wages through which the enterprise can adjust to external labor market conditions. This implies that, where nonwage

---

[6] See Gary S. Becker, *Human Capital: A Theoretical and Empirical Analysis, with Special Reference to Education* (New York: Columbia University Press, 1964) and Walter Y. Oi, "Labor as a Quasi-Fixed Factor" *Journal of Political Economy*, December 1962.

adjustment costs exist, the equality between wages and productivity predicated in neoclassical theory will no longer occur under competitive conditions. The marginal product of labor in the internal market must be sufficient not only to compensate the employer for wage costs, but also for nonwage expenditures on hiring and training.

The second, and most important, implication of fixed labor costs is that they represent an investment by the employer in the incumbent work force. The payoff period on this investment is a function of the length of tenure of each worker, and the replacement costs are incurred only when the employment relationship is broken. As a result, a variety of institutional arrangements are developed to encourage a permanent employment relationship with workers in whom the employer has invested heavily. The most significant of these arrangements is the internal labor market itself.[7]

For example, in an economy where many jobs are internally allocated, entry ports are often limited to the lower-level jobs at the bottom of promotion ladders. Therefore, employees who have reached higher-level jobs are generally earning well above the wages on entry jobs elsewhere. Turnover and interfirm mobility among such employees are therefore discouraged by the immediate earning loss which would result. This in turn implies that the wage rates on jobs filled through internal promotion are insulated from the direct influence of external labor market competition and that competitive market pressures upon the wage structure are felt almost entirely at entry-level jobs.[8]

A third consequence of fixed employment costs is that they endow the incumbent employee with bargaining power at the workplace. As noted above, many nonwage labor costs are investments which the employer must make at the time of hire and which he incurs again only if the worker must be replaced. Once the investments are made, the threat of quitting provides employees with a bargaining weapon which may enable them to extract wages above their immediate marginal productivity. Where such bargaining occurs, its effect is to contribute further to the elimination of the equality between wage rates and productivity, even for entry-level jobs. The administrative machinery surrounding the wage setting process and the consequent regularities in the wage structures may be understood partly as an attempt to forestall this bargaining.

In summary, when a permanent employment relationship is established as a result of fixed labor costs, profit maximization no longer compels the firm to equate the wage and marginal product of labor in every

---

[7] Other arrangements include work sharing and nonvested pensions.

[8] This is not to say that labor market competition will have no repercussions elsewhere in the wage structure. But the forces which produce these repercussions are not generally of the kind envisioned in neoclassical theory.

pay period. Following Becker, employers should be willing to pay a wage greater than the marginal product in early periods provided they are compensated by marginal product in excess of wages in some subsequent period. Correspondingly, workers should be willing to accept wages below those available to them elsewhere if they expect to receive higher wage payments later on. Factors such as the bargaining power of workers and the desire of employers to pay a wage increment to ensure against turnover, both the product of employer investments in fixed labor costs, further interrupt the nexus between wages and marginal productivity.

Permanency of employment. Neither Becker nor Oi emphasized the startling implications for neoclassical wage theory of the permanent employment relationship. As noted, when the relationship is permanent, neither employers nor workers necessarily concern themselves with the connection between wages and marginal productivity at any point in time. There is instead a much more liberal, but nonetheless competitive, constraint that relates labor costs, earnings, and productivity streams over the employee's entire work career within the enterprise. As a result, there is a set of internal wage structures consistent with this constraint.

Where the worker typically holds a number of different jobs over the course of his employment life within the enterprise, this constraint implies little or nothing about the wage on any particular job. The disruption of the neoclassical equivalencies between the wage and the marginal product in each pay period, in other words, involves the disruption of these equivalencies for a given job as well. The worker, therefore, may *never* produce enough in a particular job classification to cover his wages during the period in which he is employed in that classification. Both worker and management decisions will, as a result, center upon a structure of wages over the series of jobs which the individual is likely to hold over his career in the enterprise, not upon particular wage rates. The wage structure, which in neoclassical theory results from a series of separate decisions upon individual job rates, becomes itself the focus of decision making.

This is no doubt part of the explanation for the use of summary measures such as the "plant wage level" when wage decisions are being made. It may also explain the tendency of engineers, when designing or selecting capital equipment, to estimate labor costs by using an average wage rather than the rate for the particular workers by the equipment.[9] Since the jobs required by a given technology must be fitted into a promotion sequence within the plant, an average wage may be a closer approximation of the cost of the job than would the wage actually paid for it. If the actual wage on the new job is lower than the jobs it replaces, wages elsewhere in the sequence may have to be raised, and vice versa.

[9] A discussion of this process is presented in Chapter 6.

These results, which follow essentially from the permanency of the employment relationship, are indicative of a major divergence between neoclassical theory and the complications of the world which it seeks to describe. In theory, wages are paid to workers, as a factor of production. In many jobs in the economy, wages are not attached to workers, but to jobs, and much of the discussion of wage rates in this chapter actually refers to *job* rates. This distinction is not in conflict with traditional theory so long as one can argue that the rate paid for a job is really a reflection of the marginal product of the workers who hold that job. Such an argument is valid in a competitive market where a temporary employment relationship is assumed. It is not valid in the internal labor market. In that market neoclassical analysis does not provide a theory of wages. It provides, at best, a theory of income. And, in fact, it is toward an analysis of income that Becker's examination is directed.

Finally, it should be noted that, even at entry ports where it would seem most likely that wage rates and worker productivity should be closely related, employment and wage decisions generally apply to *groups* of workers rather than to *individuals*. The group may be defined by characteristics such as age, race, or education as is common at entry ports, or by seniority and job classification as in the case of jobs filled internally. When wage determinations are made for groups of workers, the influence of economic constraints—labor costs, productivity, and so forth—is estimated in terms of the *expected value* for the group as a whole and not for individuals. As a result, the productivity of some workers drawn from any particular group is likely to differ from the expected value of the group. Some will therefore receive wages below their individual productivity, and some will receive wages above it. Thus, a worker who produces more quickly than average seldom reaps the full gain, but rather he subsidizes the worker who produces less than average. Similarly, the worker who stays with an employer longer than average tends to subsidize the fixed employment costs of workers who stay for less time.

The linkage of wages either to the output or to the seniority of the individual worker reduces these effects but probably does not eliminate them. Their existence implies that changes in the groups from which employers customarily hire, or changes in precision with which individuals can be classified into groups, will effect the expected value of variables such as productivity and training costs, and may require basic changes in the wage structure.

In sum, the forces which in neoclassical theory yield a determinate wage establish, in the internal market, only a series of constraints. The equality between the marginal product of labor and the wage of a job postulated by competitive economic theory is reduced to an equality between the discounted present value of expected cost and productivity streams calculated over the distribution of *expected* employment tenure for various *groups* within the enterprise. Wage payment is not tied to individual productivity, and wage rates are applied to jobs more often than to workers. Such constraints are consistent with a variety of different wages for any particular job and a variety of internal wage structures as well. The other important neoclassical wage determinant, the wage on alternative employment opportunities, is also not a binding constraint. The employer can meet competitive pressure upon his wages through compensating adjustments in recruitment, screening, and training. Moreover, where internal markets are widespread and many of the higher-paying jobs in the economy are allocated internally, employees in nonentry jobs in one enterprise often have access only to entry-level jobs in other enterprises. The latter will often pay substantially less than those which the employees currently hold and, as a result, turnover will be discouraged.

Internal Allocative Constraints

The firm's commitment to internal allocation of labor according to a set of administrative rules places a second set of constraints upon the internal wage structure. The wage on every job must be high enough relative to the job or jobs from which it is supposed to draw its labor and low enough relative to the jobs to which it is supposed to supply labor to induce the desired pattern of internal mobility. The actual limitations which these constraints place upon wage rates depend upon several factors.

They depend first upon whether internal movement is voluntary or mandatory. In most blue-collar employments, permanent job vacancies are filled voluntarily. The employer posts the vacant job, interested employees bid for the vacancy, and the job is filled from among those bidding according to criteria such as seniority and ability. Wage rates, however, need not necessarily rise with rank in the line of progression in order to induce bidding. Superior working conditions, overtime opportunities, or the like may render a job more attractive than those below it and compensate for lower wages. The attraction of higher-level jobs which are accessible only through service in the job in question can also compensate for lower wage rates. But there is clearly some wage rate for each job below which the desired bids will not be forthcoming.

When movement is mandatory, employees can always be compelled to change jobs, and the wage structure is not so tightly bound by internal allocative requirements. But mandatory moves which are, from the employee's point of view, inadequately compensated are generally bad for employee morale. Where poor morale is thought to have an adverse effect upon productivity, it tends to push the wage structure in a direction conducive to voluntary acceptance of forced moves.[10]

Mandatory upgrading is uncommon for blue-collar jobs, although not for management jobs.[11] Mandatory movement is the rule, however, for reductions in force. The senior worker typically bumps down to a lower-level job in displacing the incumbent who either then bumps a junior worker, or is laid off. One of the effects of such mandatory movement is that enterprises experiencing long-term declines in employment often face pressure from employees to push the bottom of the wage structure upward.

The preceding discussion has been carefully phrased to leave open the options, in cases of conflict between the internal wage structure and the internal allocative structure, of revising the allocative structure or abandoning internal allocation in favor of direct hiring from the external market. The forces determining the viability of these options constitute another set of factors governing the relationship between the wage and the allocative structures.

Because wage structures and allocative structures must be consistent, changes in the wage structure can be used as a *strategic* instrument to induce changes in the allocative structure. For example, changes in technology may impair the effectiveness of traditional on-the-job training sequences. Reevaluation of the affected jobs may then be used as a device for altering the internal wage structure to make it consistent with *desired* promotion sequences instead of *actual* promotion sequences. Thus, apparent conflicts between the two structures at a particular point in time may only indicate a deliberate policy of adjustment in patterns of internal labor allocation.

The reasons for adopting such an indirect strategy are to be found in the employee expectations and customs which form around internal allocative structures. For example, changes in rules governing internal allocation often involve a redistribution of employment rights within the internal labor force which, in turn, may generate internal dissension within it. Union leaders may therefore prefer to permit changes in the allo-

---

[10] Views about the relationship between productivity and morale vary, but in blue-collar jobs they are generally related through the effect of morale upon the propensity to strike; in white-collar, especially managerial, jobs, the effects are probably more direct. See, for example, Douglas McGregor, *The Human Side of Enterprise* (New York: McGraw-Hill Co., 1960); see also Robert L. Kahn and Nancy C. Morse, "The Relationship of Productivity to Morale," *Journal of Social Issues*, vol. III, no. 3 (1951); and William J. Goode and Irving Fowler, "Incentive in a Low Morale Plant," *American Sociological Review*, 1949, pp. 618-624.

[11] See Theodore Alfred, "Checkers or Choice in Manpower Management," *Harvard Business Review*, vol. 45, no. 1 (January-February 1967), pp. 157-169.

cative structure to be made implicitly through changes in the wage structure rather than through explicit bargaining concessions. While the labor force is not easily deluded into accepting major structural revisions, minor revisions can sometimes be made acceptable in this way. The nature of customary law also favors this strategy: a change in the wage structure which induces even minimal movement between jobs which were not previously related may create precedents that at some later date can be used to justify formal changes in the allocative structure. Without these precedents, it might be impossible to gain worker acceptance of formal change.

While changes in the wage structure may be used as strategic devices to facilitate minor changes in the allocative structure, the allocative structure is, in general, more appropriately viewed as a constraint upon the internal wage structure. In particular, it is one factor which inhibits the responsiveness of the internal wage structure to external competitive forces. The effectiveness of this constraint will vary with the strength of the forces that promote internal allocation in the first place. For these purposes, the several forces identified in Chapter 2 may be divided into two groups: those which have to do with efficiencies in the recruitment, screening, and training, and those which promote the internal labor market because of its value to the internal labor force.

To a certain extent, allocative structures generated by the latter group of forces are determined by the wage structure. The internal market is designed to assign the "better" jobs to certain specific (generally senior) groups of employees, and the quality of the job in the eyes of the labor force is in part a function of the wage. Hence, if a change in the wage structure means that senior workers find a different set of jobs more attractive than those which they were previously encouraged to choose, their interests may continue to be as well served by having the newly preferred jobs placed at the top of the previous promotion sequence. Where this can be accomplished, the allocative structure cannot, in any meaningful sense, be termed a constraint. There are, however, few cases in which worker preferences are as simple as the preceding example suggests. In general, workers are not only concerned with wages but with working conditions as well. When workers are reluctant to substitute higher wages for these other characteristics—when, for example, the allocative system is designed to give senior workers not only the highest-paying jobs in the plant, but also the jobs having the least adverse impact upon their health —the allocative structure may again become a meaningful constraint.

For allocative structures dictated by economies in recruitment, screening, and training, the wage is constrained not only by the jobs above and below it in the standard promotion sequence, but also by the wages of workers in other promotion sequences or workers in the external market who constitute alternative sources of supply. If alternative sources of labor are used, the wage on the job to be filled must be at least sufficient to induce movement, but low enough to compensate for the costs of recruitment, screening, and training in excess of those imposed by the normal promotion pattern. Because allocative structures are so complexly interrelated, however, these incremental costs usually extend somewhat beyond those incurred in filling the specific vacancy. They may also include additional training to fill positions to which the vacant job normally leads; or there may be additional costs in filling vacancies created in the promotion sequence from which the alternative supply is drawn.

A third allocative factor affecting the internal wage structure is the shape of the internal mobility clusters. Their shape affects the number of candidates for a job: when this number is small relative to the number of vacancies to be filled, the wage rate required to induce the requisite movement will depend heavily upon the preferences of the particular individuals, or group of individuals, holding the jobs from which labor is drawn. For example, in the case of the line of progression consisting of a single job at each rung, the wage necessary to fill a job vacancy will depend upon the preferences of the incumbent in the job below it. Were management always able to set the minimum wage consistent with movement along this line, the wage would fluctuate with each vacancy. As will be seen shortly, the continual adjustment in the wage structure which this implies poses difficulties, and management generally sets a wage differential high enough to be consistent with the preferences of most of the workers occupying such jobs over the long run. As the job structure deviates from this extreme case toward a pyramidal structure in which the number of candidates is large relative to the vacancies to be filled, vertical wage differentials depend less upon preferences of particular individuals than upon those of individuals most anxious to accept promotion. Consequently, vertical wage differentials tend to be narrower.

Social and Institutional Constraints

The preceding section has identified a series of factors which, in one way or another, influence or constrain the internal wage structure. Under certain circumstances these constraints severely limit the wage structure, but only rarely do they establish a unique rate structure. In general, the factors identified above yield a set or family of wage structures. Consequently, an alternative to the competitive market mechanism must be developed to determine a single internal wage structure and to resolve conflicting pressures when they arise. One mechanism is implicit in the assumption that firms attempt to minimize costs (or maximize profits). This implies that the firm will weigh each of the variables impinging upon costs and select the wage structure for which total unit costs are at a minimum. This mechanism is, however, deficient in two respects. First, many of the relevant variables are dependent upon the preferences of one or a few individuals. To minimize costs, therefore, management must devise either a system for discovering these preferences or, at least, a rule for action in the face of uncertainty.

Second, given the constraints upon wage determination, the cost minimization assumption implies that the wage structure will be adjusted every time one of the variables impinging upon it changes. In a world of continual flux this would make the wage structure considerably more volatile than it in fact appears to be. Typically, wage changes occur at discrete intervals—annually in many enterprises and in longer periods in some organized plants. Therefore, if the assumption that cost minimization governs the wage determination process is correct, there must also be costs to making wage adjustments, and these too must be identified before the process can be completely specified.

The identification of both worker preferences and wage adjustment costs raises problems extending considerably beyond the internal market and cannot be fully explored here. But the internal market, and the factors associated with it, do influence both preference determination and adjustment costs in significant ways. The result is to make the internal wage structure rigid and to inhibit its response to changes in economic or institutional constraints.

Determining Worker Preferences

The problem of determining preference is inherent in any economic transaction, and, in this sense, every system of exchange is predicated upon some resolution of it. One resolution of the problem is market competition. When the number of buyers and sellers in a market is large, or when the transaction is consummated through an auction mechanism, each individual is forced to reveal his true terms of settlement. As competition recedes, exchange deteriorates into a bargaining game: the individual attempts to hide his true preferences from his adversaries on the other side of the market in an attempt to induce them to settle on more favorable terms.

Bargaining. Bargaining carries with it certain costs. There are the costs of the bargaining process itself and those of failing to reach an agreement. The latter will depend upon the particular bargaining situation. In union-management negotiations, for example, it is the cost of a strike; in international relations it is often the cost of war. The former involves the time and energy required to settle the bargain. When the costs loom large, an alternative means of settling upon a price will be to the advantage of the parties.

The internal market operates to raise the costs of bargaining. First, it restricts the number of candidates for a given job and hence reduces the pressure which competition places upon the parties to reveal their terms of settlement. In the extreme case where strict seniority determines promotion along a line of progression one job wide, the internal market dictates a pure bilateral monopoly. But in the more typical allocative structures, the internal market simply increases the probability that management will be forced into individual bargaining either because the pool of potential candidates begins to form bargaining alliances or because both parties no longer fear competition. Thus, to the extent that there are costs to bargaining, the internal market increases the likelihood that management will incur these costs.

Fixed labor costs. The second effect of the internal market derives from the fixed labor costs which tend to accompany it. They are a major component of the costs of failing to develop a wage structure which induces efficient promotion patterns. These costs are most obvious when the failure leads the preferred candidate to quit the enterprise, and a replacement must be hired. But certain fixed costs are also incurred when the preferred candidate simply refuses to accept promotion. In a line of progression, for example, training costs, and occasionally screening and recruitment costs as well, are reduced because the preferred candidate generally has the most experience working around the next job in the line and in filling it temporarily. The higher the additional fixed labor costs associated with filling a vacancy from a less-preferred source, the more likely is the employer to set a wage differential high enough to ensure against a preferred worker rejecting a promotion.

Fixed labor costs may also increase the time and energy required by the bargaining process even when satisfactory wage agreements are concluded with preferred candidates. The higher the level of fixed labor costs, the greater range between the maximum which the employer should be willing to pay before the alternative candidate looks preferable and the minimum the worker will accept before an alternative job will be accepted. Since both the number of possible settlements and the gains to the parties increase as this range expands, the difficulty of reaching an agreement would seem to increase as well. On the other hand, this effect may be counterbalanced by the costs to both parties of failing to reach an agreement, which should also rise with the level of fixed labor costs and should hasten the parties toward settlement.

On-the-job training and job specificity. The third effect of the internal labor market upon the cost of bargaining arises from on-the-job training and from job specificity. These, of course, tend to raise fixed labor costs and thereby affect the cost of bargaining. But they also have an independent effect upon bargaining costs generated by the strong bargaining weapons that they place in the hands of the experienced labor force. The effectiveness of on-the-job training depends heavily upon the willingness of experienced workmen to teach new workers. Incumbent employees are thus in a position to frustrate this training process simply by hiding what they are doing from the workers around them. In some cases, the employer can substitute alternative, if more expensive, training processes, but, in many cases, there are simply no alternatives. The cost of efforts to frustrate on-the-job training is frequently compounded by the fact that such training tends to occur automatically in the process of production, and any effort to stop it has an adverse impact upon efficient plant operation.

Job specificity operates in a similar manner. When the job is specific, the workman, as has been seen, tends to have a monopoly over a portion of the knowledge required to maintain and operate the technology. The importance of experienced workmen in the process of on-the-job training stems in part from this. But the monopoly also gives independent power to disrupt the production process. Given the fact that the technology is unwritten, and that part of the specificity derives from improvements which the work force itself introduces, workers are in a position to perfect their monopoly over the knowledge of the technology should there be an incentive to do so.

These characteristics of on-the-job training and of job specificity place a premium upon the development of wage setting procedures in which the labor force does not have an incentive to exercise its bargaining power. It may be noted that both also tend to promote procedures which avoid competitive processes for internal wage determination because, in a competitive wage determination system, the incumbent workers have an incentive to exercise their monopoly of training and skill to the detriment of both the firm and other employees.

Alternatives to bargaining and competition. Thus, in summary, the internal labor market operates to eliminate competition for internal vacancies — or, perhaps more accurately, arises under circumstances of reduced competition. As competition recedes, the choice is between the determination of wage rates through individual bargaining (the "haggle system" as it is called in some plants) which is inherently costly, and some alternative procedure which would establish rates acceptable to the parties without the time and energy demanded by bargaining or the threatened exercise of economic weapons inherent in it.

To a certain extent, the formal instruments and procedures of wage administration may be understood as such an alternative. Their quasi-ethical character and the laborious process through which they are applied lends a certain aura of legitimacy to them and makes them appear as "natural" a manner of wage determination as competition and bargaining.

To this extent, adherence to the formal procedures comes to be valued quite independently of whatever economic forces it expresses. This permits these procedures to continue to dictate the wage rate even when they come into conflict with economic forces, although at some point the cost of complete adherence to them will outweigh the costs of the bargaining process which they are designed to circumvent, and the procedures will be modified or abandoned. Though limited by economic forces, the formal procedures of wage determination can and do exert an independent influence upon wages. However, the set of rules upon which the parties rely to avoid the bargaining process is not limited to those formalized in the wage setting procedures outlined in the beginning of the chapter. Rules based upon workplace customs are also operative and probably exercise a more important influence than formal procedures of wage determination. For some purposes, the latter may even be viewed as merely a formal expression of customs.

Social Determinants of the Wage

While the cost of bargaining imposed by the internal labor market dictates an institutional solution to the wage setting problem, the particular form which that solution takes cannot be understood without reference to the series of social constraints within which the wage setting process operates. They are the product of custom, or customary law, strengthened by the role of wages and earnings as an indication of social status, and by the operation, on the individual level, of the psychological phenomena which work to generate custom and the group cohesion which supports it.

Custom and wage determination. Within an internal labor market, wage determination, like other industrial relations rules, becomes the focus of customs. The nature and effects of custom have been described generally in Chapter 2, and its effects upon wage setting follow from that description. Any wage rate, set of wage relationships, or wage setting procedure which prevails over a period of time tends to become customary; changes are then viewed as unjust or inequitable, and the work group will exert economic pressure in opposition to them. In a static world, custom would undoubtedly come to center upon the actual wage rate paid for each job, and any wage would thus become costly to change. The modern industrial economy does not experience this kind of stability, and custom tends to grow up around wage *relationships* rather than around specific wage *rates*.

The tendency for the rate and frequency of wage changes to become customary is often cited by management as one of the reasons why community wage surveys are not universally used. Managers apparently fear that regular patterns of wage change once established would become obligatory.

The role of custom in governing the wage structure also appears responsible for the nature of job evaluation procedures and the priority accorded to job evaluation by most managements. Basically, job evaluation is designed to reduce the conflict between custom and allocative constraints by directing the attention of the work force, and thereby the focus of custom as well, to the characteristics of the job rather than to its place in the job structure of the enterprise. It thus becomes possible to change the position of individual jobs in the wage structure in response to changes in job content.

The strictness with which internal *rank* order is maintained and the relative flexibility permitted management in changing the *amount* of wage differentials reflects the ambiguity of past practice. The historical ranking of jobs in the wage structure is not open to dispute. In a fluctuating economy, however, it is generally unclear whether wage relationships are fixed in *percentage* terms or in *absolute* terms, and this ambiguity permits occasional adjustments in wage structures to be dictated by wage surveys. A practice of continually varying wage differentials would, of course, enhance this ambiguity. But managers who do not exercise the latitude for wage variability and who fall into the practice of granting wage increases on the same percentage or cents-per-hour basis across the board find the practice difficult to break when economic forces dictate a change.

The ambiguity of precedent is also a factor in the resolution of conflicts between the internal ordering dictated by the job evaluation and the external ordering of community wage surveys. The multiplicity of external reference points and the variety of different economic pressures to which they are subject generally makes for less stability in external than in internal wage relationships. It is generally possible to point toward some employers with whose wage rates the historic relationship is maintained even when the relationship with other external rates is being broken.

Social status. A second factor operating to strengthen the influence of custom upon wage determination is the role of income as an indicator of social status. Income probably plays this role to a greater or lesser degree in every industrial society, but it is widely held to be more important in the United States where a strong class tradition is lacking than in countries with a feudal heritage.[12] The linkage between income and social status has a variety of implications for the wage structure which may be briefly summarized here. First, social status is required for effective performance of certain jobs, and the income level required to yield the requisite status is an important wage determinate. Thus, for example, workers whose jobs involve the direction and management of others must typically be paid

[12] Barbara Wooton, *The Social Foundations of Wage Policy* (New York: W. W. Norton and Co., 1955), pp. 25-32. Also James S. Duesenberry, *Income, Saving, and the Theory of Consumer Behavior* (Cambridge, Mass.: Harvard University Press, 1949).

more than their subordinates in order to perform this function effectively. This is recognized in many job evaluation plans by according weight to "the degree of responsibility for other employees." Another example of the same effect arises where the workers responsible for training feel their status threatened by the trainees.[13] As a result the training process operates effectively only if the wage determination process protects the status of incumbents by according considerable weight to seniority. These internal status effects constitute an important factor militating in favor of maintaining the existing internal wage structure when it is inconsistent with wages in the external market.

Second, there are occasionally wage relationships that are dictated by the status of a job which management is forced to recognize even though the job characteristics originally associated with the status are no longer present. This is most likely to occur in internal markets with promotion lines leading to jobs that are *considerably* more attractive than the entry-level jobs. Workers in such promotion lines develop expectations about promotion opportunities. Should technological change dilute the content of these better jobs, management cannot reduce their rank in the wage and allocation structure without frustrating workers' expectations and adversely affecting morale. The effect of changing the status of jobs and upsetting expectations is very much like that of violating a custom, but is stronger because of the economic value placed upon status. The steel industry is a case in point. It is an old industry in which job classifications such as "roller" carry a long history of high skill and prestige. The nature of many steel jobs has recently been changed in major ways by automation, but the ranking of job classifications in the internal wage structure has not undergone a comparable change. Technically, what appears to have happened is that a decline in skill content was counterbalanced in job evaluation by an increase in job responsibility, but the coincidence is suspect.[14]

Third, the role of income as a determinant of status is important in the interpretation of community wage surveys. It implies that these surveys, in addition to reflecting the wages of labor market competitors, also are used to maintain the status of the enterprise in the community. Comments by managers in some plants suggest that the status which employment with the company confers upon its employees was considered the major factor in its ability to recruit labor and that community surveys were primarily designed to maintain employer status. The sample of plants in the survey was thus literally a sample of the employer community rather than of the labor market as narrowly conceived, thereby explaining, in part, the

[13] One such illustration is the threat posed to older, unmarried clerical and secretarial help by pretty young girls.
[14] See Stieber, *op. cit.*

inclusion of employers whose economic relationship to the surveying firm was obscure. The role of the survey as an indication of company status also explains why wage adjustments indicated by surveys are readily ignored when they conflict with internal pressures. Departures from the target wage position in the community on one or a few jobs, or temporarily even for the plant as a whole, were considered unlikely to affect the company's general reputation.

Interdependent utility functions. The constraints imposed by group pressures to accede to customary law are augmented by responses to workers, as individuals, which operate in the same direction. Individual responses are derived from the same behavioral principles which control habit formation and imitation within groups. The most important implications of these responses for an understanding of wage behavior in an internal labor market may be summarized in two propositions. First, the utility of income to an individual depends upon the income of those with whom he comes into frequent contact, and the impact of the income of any particular individual upon the utility of another is a function of the frequency of contact between them.[15]

Second, workers become accustomed to certain levels of income relative to the income levels of those around them, and it becomes considerably more important to maintain these income levels than to exceed them. This proposition follows from the principle of habit formation, and the variety of habits of behavior and thought associated with relative income levels. Because of its dependence upon habit, the importance of maintaining a given relative income level is a function of the length of time it has been maintained.[16]

Thus, for very much the same reasons that the individual attempts to ward off threats to his relative consumption pattern by reducing his savings, he will also attempt to ward off such threats by exerting pressures at the workplace for wage increases. Such pressures may range from complaints to his foreman or shop steward to participation in group action, but all create a tendency for wage relationships to be stable and pressures to restore relationships whenever they are disturbed.

In the context of wage determination, the amount of individual pressure for maintaining customary parity of wage relationships is a function of the frequency of contact among the individuals holding those jobs. For

[15] This effect derives from the tendency of individuals to imitate the behavioral pattern of those around them, and the fact that insofar as those behavioral patterns are dependent upon consumption expenditures, imitation is constrained by income. See Duesenberry, *op. cit.*

[16] It may be noted, postulating a drive toward higher social status, that both propositions can be derived from the role of income as a determinant of social status. This, rather than imitation, is the foundation of these effects in Duesenberry's theory of consumption and saving.

the internal wage structure, this means that there will be an especially tight relationship among the wages of jobs whose incumbents have regular and frequent contact at the workplace. It also suggests that jobs which involve wide contacts with other workers acquire a strategic position in the internal wage structure which make it impossible to change their wages without adjustments throughout the system.[17]

Comparable phenomena govern the relationship between the enterprise wage structure and that of the community. An enterprise is under particular pressure to maintain wage rate parity between itself and those enterprises employing the relatives and neighbors of its work force. Large enterprises will therefore tend to dominate community wage movements through demonstration effects, even if they are not competitors in either the product market or the labor market.

Summary

The argument of this chapter may be summarized as follows: in the internal labor market, wages are administratively determined either by the formal procedures of job evaluation, community surveys, merit rating, and industrial engineering studies, or through less highly structured procedures which, nonetheless, appear to be similar in character and in effect. These procedures could be interpreted as merely the institutional form through which competitive market forces determine wages. But several features of the wage setting process, particularly the priority accorded internal relationships determined by job evaluation relative to the external relationships which community surveys define, are not easily reconciled with this interpretation.

An alternative interpretation has been developed in this chapter. When internal labor markets are present, the competitive forces emphasized in neoclassical theory place certain constraints upon the wage structure, but, in general, do not establish a unique wage rate for each job. Enterprises with internal markets are able to meet labor market competition through recruitment, screening, and training expenditures as well as through wage and employment adjustments so that a number of different wage structures are consistent with the same labor market conditions. More important, the job specificity and the stability of employment which the internal mar-

---

[17] Dunlop calls these internal patterns "wage clusters" and "key jobs" respectively. See John T. Dunlop, "The Task of Contemporary Wage Theory," in George W. Taylor and Frank C. Pierson (eds.), *New Concepts in Wage Determination* (New York: McGraw-Hill Co., 1957). It is to be noted that the individual psychology from which they are here derived makes it likely that they will exist in any employment situation: the stability of employment in the internal market, however, increases the frequency of contact and strengthens the habits upon which the effects depend and thus enhances these effects relative to other wage determinants.

ket is designed to achieve abrogate the necessity for the profit-maximizing firm to equate wages and marginal productivity in all job classifications, or even over the job tenure of all workers. These need not be equated in any pay period or on any particular job classification.

The rules governing internal allocation place certain additional constraints upon the wage structure. These sometimes narrow the range of feasible wages left by the traditional neoclassical constraints, but, except in unusual cases, individual wage rates remain indeterminate. The internal allocative rules, moreover, generally complicate the problem of selecting a wage within the permissible range. The restrictions which they impose upon the number of job candidates encourage individual bargaining or competitive bidding, either of which is expensive.

The institutional wage setting procedures are to be understood as a less expensive means of arriving at a determinate set of wage rates. The particular form which these procedures take, however, is greatly influenced by the social forces of custom, by the role of income as an indication of social status, and by related individual behavioral phenomena.

Part Two
Manpower Analysis

Chapter 5
Manpower Adjustment and Labor Market Imbalances

In this chapter the process of adjustment to labor market imbalance is examined. Both technological change and tightening labor markets pose essentially the same adjustment problem for internal labor markets. To an enterprise attempting to maintain a balance between its staffing requirements and the skills available on the external labor market, technological change is largely an exogenous factor affecting internal labor requirements; tightening labor markets are an exogenous change in the external availability of labor. In either case, manpower adjustment policies must be implemented to maintain a reasonably efficient balance between the internal and the external labor markets. Manpower adjustment policies are discussed in this chapter in terms of the problems posed by a tightening market, but the analysis can be generalized to include problems of adjustment to technological change.[1] Most of the materials relate to enterprise internal markets for blue-collar personnel. Except where indicated, the discussion is not necessarily applicable to other types of internal markets.

---

[1] The choice is made largely for expositional reasons. The discussion of adjustment of technological change is complicated by the fact that not all changes are exogenous. Some features of the adjustment process unique to technological change are discussed in Chapter 6.

Instruments of Adjustment Within the Enterprise

Changes in the external labor market are signaled to an enterprise in two ways: through the rate of turnover among incumbent workers and through the flow of applicants for its jobs. As external conditions change, the amount and the composition of turnover will systematically vary. Job applicants will exhibit similar variations. An enterprise can adjust to such variations through a number of instruments. Two of these instruments, the level of wage rates and the number of workers employed in various jobs, are conventionally recognized in economic theory. For an analysis of labor market adjustments when internal markets are present, however, explicit recognition must be given, at a minimum, to eleven instruments of adjustment: [2]

1. Wage and nonwage compensation.
2. Internal allocative rules.
3. The job structure.
4. Managerial procedure.
5. Job vacancies.
6. Subcontracting.
7. Overtime.
8. Hiring standards.
9. Recruitment procedures.
10. Screening procedures.
11. Training.

These instruments constitute alternative modes of adjustment to external market conditions. For example, an enterprise might raise wages when faced with increasing turnover and a declining quality and quantity of job applicants in a tightening labor market. Alternatively, it might attempt to attract more candidates at existing wages by changes in its recruitment procedures, or it might screen candidates more carefully to identify those actually qualified but rejected by cruder methods of assessing qualifications; or it could reduce hiring standards and accept candidates who are actually less qualified than those whom it is accustomed to hiring in a looser external labor market. The last policy could be combined with training, changes in the job structure, or new managerial

[2] See also Peter B. Doeringer and Michael J. Piore, "Labor Market Adjustment and Internal Training," *Proceedings of the Eighteenth Annual Meeting,* Industrial Relations Research Association, New York, December 1965, pp. 250-263. Peter B. Doeringer, "Enterprise Adjustments to Labor Scarcities," in *Proceedings of the International Conference on Employment Stabilization in a Growth Economy,* Organization for Economic Cooperation and Development, Manpower and Social Affairs Directorate, 1968, pp. 261-277; Michael J. Piore, "Technological Change and Structural Adjustment in the Labor Market," unpub. diss., Harvard University, 1966.

procedures to ensure previous levels of output and quality. Or a sacrifice in output and quality might be accepted as part of the policy.

The instruments through which enterprises react to the external labor market have various implications for the nation's social and economic goals. Reacting to labor scarcities by increasing wages, without accompanying adjustments in other instruments such as training, may produce an inflationary wage spiral without relieving much of the underlying scarcity of labor in the short run. Reductions in hiring standards may increase employment and change the distribution of employment opportunities among various social groups, but only at some sacrifice in labor productivity. Improved screening procedures can produce similar employment effects, but without impairing productivity. The combination of changed hiring standards and increased training could achieve these employment effects and, at the same time, increase labor productivity, at least over the long run. Skill-saving adjustments in job design through technological change may require an increase in the level of investment which might, through its impact upon aggregate demand, create further labor market stringencies.

It originally seemed that it would be possible to identify some relatively simple, recurrent patterns of labor force adjustment within the enterprise. One hypothesis was that the instruments of adjustment would fall into a clearly defined cost hierarchy. As the external market tightened, the enterprise would be forced to adopt progressively more expensive adjustment instruments within this hierarchy. For example, an enterprise might expand recruitment procedures as the unemployment rate falls from 5.5 per cent to 5 per cent and then utilize adjustments in screening procedures as well when unemployment falls from 5 per cent to 4.5 per cent. A second hypothesis was that the sequence of adjustment patterns would prove similar across enterprises.

Neither hypothesis could be substantiated. The mix and sequence of instruments vary considerably among enterprises. As a general rule, combinations of instruments will be used at any one time. Some will remain relatively stable over long periods, others will vary systematically with external labor market conditions. Selection among these instruments reflects estimates, often of an intuitive sort, of their relative costs and benefits.[3] There were, nonetheless, certain features of the adjustment process common to all, or most, of the enterprises studied. Broadly speaking, these common elements fell into two groups: (1) shared characteristics of the decision making process through which adjustments were made and (2) similarities in the nature of the variables affecting the choice among the adjustment instruments.

---

[3] A discussion of these estimates is presented in the Appendix to this chapter.

The Decision Making Process

Perhaps the most notable feature of the decision making process is that management makes little effort to anticipate staffing bottlenecks, either for entry jobs or along internal lines of promotion. Many large and otherwise sophisticated companies do not engage in manpower forecasting or planning for any segment of their labor force. The few which do are primarily concerned with managerial personnel.[4] The lack of even rudimentary manpower planning can be partly ascribed to the long period of relatively high unemployment during the late 1950's and early 1960's. The companies which began to develop elementary manpower forecasts during the 1960's did so under the pressure of tightening labor markets.

As a result, variations in labor supply are frequently met with unplanned and often *ad hoc* policies designed to overcome immediate labor shortages or to absorb unanticipated labor surpluses that the enterprise chooses to retain. The procedures for developing adjustments to the tight labor markets of the late 1960's are apparently similar to those utilized in World War II and during the Korean conflict.

Innovations in Adjustment Techniques

A second aspect of adjustment decisions is that each enterprise appears to have a series of customary adjustment strategies which it follows automatically in response to various internal and external signals of labor scarcity. For example, as the external market tightens, an enterprise will follow a fairly standard sequence of changes in recruitment procedures, moving from reliance upon unsolicited gate applicants to advertising in metropolitan newspapers and on the radio. It will strengthen contacts with public employment services, school systems, and social or religious organizations. Some companies will also pay bonuses to employees for referrals. Similarly, enterprises frequently have training or apprenticeship programs which they can activate in response to market conditions. One such example is the "temporary skilled trades" classification in the automobile industry mentioned in Chapter 3.

These customary strategies of adjustment may fail, or become too costly, forcing management to search for new techniques. The search is not very different from that for new methods of production. It proceeds to a great extent by trial and error, and it takes time. In the case of recruitment, for example, search may involve contributing instructors, equipment, and financial assistance to local schools in the hope that recruitment of their graduates would be facilitated. Other companies may initiate recruiting arrangements with ethnic churches and civil rights organizations for the recruitment of recent arrivals to the community.

---

[4] Peter B. Doeringer, Michael J. Piore, and James G. Scoville, "Corporate Manpower Forecasting and Planning," *The Conference Board Record,* vol. V, no. 8 (August 1968), pp. 37-45.

Because the development of these new techniques takes time, enterprises are often forced to utilize temporary, short-run adjustments which are more costly than those adopted in the long run. This point is of some importance in judging the inflationary response of the economy to tight labor markets. It is likely that the long-run adjustment response to a given level of unemployment will be less costly than the response when that level is first approached. Such is especially likely to be the case when a tight labor market occurs after a long period of looser markets during which the efficacy of standard adjustment techniques has not been tested.

Constraints Upon Adjustment

Finally, not all instruments of adjustment are equally flexible. Management views one group of instruments—the compensation structure, the job structure, the internal allocative structure, and many written managerial procedures—as being the subject of separate decision processes. Consequently, they are available for adjustments only under extreme circumstances. However, a second group of instruments consisting of hiring standards, screening procedures, training, recruitment procedures, subcontracting, job vacancies, and overtime are more amenable to management discretion. The latter bear the major burden of adjustment. The two groups may be termed the *more constrained* and the *less constrained* adjustment instruments.

The More Constrained Instruments

Each of the highly constrained instruments is the subject of its own decision making process. These decisions are seen as separate and distinct from decisions concerning the adjustment to external labor market conditions. The elements of that process for the internal allocative structure and for the internal wage structure have been outlined in Chapters 3 and 4. The external supply of labor is one of the variables impinging upon these decisions, but only rarely does it determine the outcome of the decision making process.

Compensation

The separation of wage decisions from those involving adjustment to external conditions reflects the constraints surrounding the internal wage structure. Because the structure is relatively rigid and tightly bound by the exigencies of internal allocation and by customary law, adjustments in the entry wage tend to exert a leverage upon all wages in the enterprise. This makes such adjustments a relatively expensive means of accommodation to market pressure since the marginal costs of adjustment rise more rapidly than the "supply price" of labor.

In addition, most managers, at least in medium and large enterprises,

seem to consider wage changes a relatively ineffective means of accommodating to labor scarcities. They fear that any changes in their own rates
will be matched by competitors, possibly generating a community wage
spiral without appreciably increasing the labor supply. The upward pressure upon wages in tight labor markets thus appears to come as much
from factors such as the changes in the relative cost of strikes to labor and
management, increases in prices and profits, and internal pressure to
maintain wage parity with other enterprises, as it does from attempts to
attract labor per se.[5]

With these *caveats* it should be noted that some discretion is permitted
within the internal wage structure. While widespread adjustments in
compensation are shunned, marginal adjustments are attempted, especially when they can be concealed within the existing compensation structure. Reclassifying entry-level jobs by a single job grade, upgrading new
hires more rapidly within rate ranges and between job grades, reevaluating
job classifications to move them into high labor grades, and raising guaranteed wage rates for new hires working under incentive programs were
examples of such adjustments found in many of the enterprises studied.
Occasionally new job classifications, such as machinist "B" and "C", were
created to provide greater wage upgrading opportunities.[6] To stave off a
raid by another employer, one company promoted its skilled machinists
to "group leaders" at a 20 cents per hour higher wage rate, and sustained
this rate until it was ruled improper in arbitration proceedings resulting
from grievances to reclassify other jobs.

While wage rates within the enterprise are customarily attached to job
classifications rather than to individuals, some adjustments in individual
rates can also be made in order to recruit or retain particularly valuable
employees. "Payment-by-results" plans and merit-rate ranges permit some
differentiation among workers holding the same job. Individual earnings
may also be increased by varying promotion rates slightly.

The Job Structure

The process through which the job structure is determined is also distinct from that of adjustment to external conditions. It is dominated by
engineers who seldom have direct contact with external market conditions
and are only rarely attracted by the problems which such conditions
cause. Most engineers appear to favor job simplification and the substitu-

---

[5] See Albert Rees, "Industrial Conflict and Business Fluctuations," *Journal of
Political Economy,* October 1952, pp. 371-382 and Orley Ashenfelter and George E.
Johnson, "Bargaining Theory, Trade Unions, and Industrial Strike Activity,"
American Economic Review, vol. LIX, no. 1 (March 1969), pp. 35-49.

[6] See E. Robert Livernash, "An Active Employer Manpower Policy," in the
Proceedings of the 19th Annual Meeting, Industrial Relations Research Association,
1966, pp. 208-218.

tion of capital for labor wherever decision making processes permit them to exercise discretion in these matters. While this implies a general bias toward "labor-saving" or "skill-saving" technologies, a bias conducive to overcoming labor scarcities, the strength of these biases and their influence upon the selection of technology does *not* seem to vary with external market conditions.

The separation of the job structure decision from the labor adjustment process reflects, like that of wage decisions, the constraints within which the enterprise operates. Given the enterprise's location, its product, and investment in existing plant and equipment, major changes in jobs to accommodate changing labor market conditions are, under most circumstances, prohibitively expensive.

A certain amount of minor job revision, however, takes place automatically as the character of the enterprise labor force changes. To this extent the job structure *is* responsive to market conditions. But the changes are for the most part unplanned and often unnoticed and do not form part of the enterprise's conscious strategy of adjustment.

The capacity for such change is inherent in the nature of the on-the-job training process. The process, as noted earlier, involves a kind of rolling readjustment and reassignment of tasks and duties. A skilled operator or supervisor initially assigns the unskilled tasks to the trainee, performing the skilled tasks himself, taking on the added responsibility of instruction and supervision, and possibly dropping, or at least postponing other duties during the training period. The trainee gradually takes on the more highly skilled tasks, the experienced workman reassumes the simpler job duties, and his supervisory responsibilities decline. When training is completed, the previous job structure is reconstituted.

When the external market tightens, and less qualified labor is admitted, the "training" may never be completed, and the job structure may stabilize with a distribution of tasks appropriate to some phase of training. The fact that on-the-job instruction is individualized also leads to a certain amount of accommodation of jobs to workers. The experienced workman may change the way he demonstrated the job to help the trainee master it. Sometimes this changes equipment and plant layout in small ways as well.[7] The process of adjustment in the job structure of the enterprise is explored more fully in Chapter 6.

The Allocative Structure

The process by which the allocative structure of the internal labor market is established does initially take into account external labor market forces, as indicated in Chapter 2. The location of entry ports is based upon

[7] See Michael J. Piore, "On-the-Job Training and Adjustment to Technological Change," *The Journal of Human Resources,* vol. III, no. 4 (Fall 1968), pp. 435-449.

the expectation that workers, with the traits required to fill the entry jobs and related job classifications, will be available on a continuing basis. By filling jobs with high turnover costs from within, the internal labor market also protects itself against costly turnover when external labor markets tighten. While such factors suggest that the internal allocative structure, and the on-the-job training sequences which it represents, might constitute a flexible instrument of adjustment, the value of the internal labor market structure to the labor force and considerations of custom severely constrain management's freedom to modify the allocative structure at will.

New entry ports cannot be opened in other than the lowest-skilled jobs without threatening the job security and opportunities for advancement expected by the incumbent labor force. Closing entry ports enhances the value of the internal labor market to the incumbent work force, but such actions tend to be irreversible, and are therefore discouraged. Industrial conflicts arise when managements have attempted to fill job vacancies from the external labor market when they had previously been filled internally.

Changes in the shape of mobility clusters also tend to be irreversible. When mobility clusters are made wider or narrower, there is apt to be a redistribution of promotion opportunities within the internal labor force. Giving benefits to some workers while taking them away from others within the internal labor market affects employee morale adversely and can also pose political and legal problems for union leadership. Many legal suits with respect to the union's obligation of "fair representation" have involved this issue.[8] Even more important, because movement along mobility clusters takes place in both directions, changes in the allocative structure which are designed to facilitate upgrading during a tight external labor market will later affect the job security of some workers during the contraction phase of the business cycle. Consequently, workers will seek to prevent changes in the internal allocative structure by raising the price which management will have to pay for change. The resistance among some employees to the negotiated merger of layoff districts in the steel plants in 1962 illustrates this point.

Movement within the allocative structure of the internal labor market is also a focus of custom. Patterns of internal labor mobility which are repeated become accepted by the internal labor force as natural and just. For the reasons discussed in Chapter 2, this too inhibits flexibility.

This is not to argue, however, that the internal allocative structure is immutable. As in wage and job structures, change can and does occur.

[8] See, for example, *Whitfield v. United Steelworkers Local 2708,* 263 F. 2d 546 (5th Cir.), *cert. denied,* 360 U.S. 902 (1959), and *Ford Motor Co. v. Huffman,* 345 U.S. 330 (1953).

When labor requirements in certain areas of the enterprise are expanding rapidly, for example, traditional promotion ladders may be unable to supply the numbers of internally trained workers required. This may demand the use of previously untapped sources of skills in other mobility clusters and distribute the productivity effects of the adjustment process more widely in the enterprise.

The changes in promotion patterns can involve increases in both the rate of promotion along traditional ladders and a rearrangement of promotion lines. The relative importance of these two points depends upon the previous allocative structure of the internal labor market. Where workers pick up skills required on higher-level jobs before they are actually promoted, there is an excess supply of skilled labor along promotion ladders, and the enterprise will be able to accelerate promotion rates readily. When there is no excess supply of workers, linkages may be developed between existing promotion ladders, or new ladders may be designed. In the automobile industry there is the example of the "temporary skilled craftsmen" promoted from the ranks of production workers. In a chemical plant surveyed, bidding rights were extended on an *ad hoc* basis when the existing bidding area proved insufficient for internal upgrading requirements.

The Less Highly Constrained Instruments

The instruments termed here "less highly constrained"—subcontracting, overtime, job vacancies, recruitment procedures, hiring standards, screening procedures and training—are those which the enterprise normally thinks of as constituting the means of adjustment between internal labor and the external labor market. Decisions affecting these instruments are almost exclusively dominated by this concern. They each constitute a means of obtaining a manpower balance within the internal labor market, and the major factor determining selection among them is their relative costs and effectiveness.

Job Vacancies, Subcontracting, and Overtime

In some respects, subcontracting, overtime, and job vacancies are the least constrained of all the methods of adjustment. Subcontracting and overtime costs are readily estimated; job vacancy costs are not. Job vacancies often mean that work is simply postponed, covered by other employees expending extra effort or working overtime, or performed in a manner which may increase the probability of machine downtime and defective output. Job vacancies are also the residual solution and occur when no adjustment action is taken or when such actions are not successful. The efficiency of subcontracting as an adjustment device is limited by the likelihood that subcontractors will also be experiencing labor short-ages. Overtime is, of course, limited in obvious ways. There are certain cases when these instruments are constrained by union contracts and are less available as means of adjustment.[9]

Recruitment Procedures

Recruitment procedures are also relatively unconstrained. The kinds of recruitment adjustments which occur in a tightening labor market were outlined earlier. Recruitment procedures move in a tightening labor mar-ket, as one would expect, toward groups previously isolated from job in-formation by geographic, linguistic, and cultural barriers. They thus operate to increase the equality of employment opportunity—although the magnitude of this effect is debatable. Presumably, as labor markets loosen, some of the recruitment decisions will be reversed.

One aspect of recruitment decisions which the earlier discussion did not mention, but which employers are extremely conscious of, is the role of recruitment procedures as a screening device. Any given type of recruit-ment procedure tends to produce candidates with certain common attributes. "Word-of-mouth" recruitment tends to provide applicants similar to those already employed; recruitment through civil rights agen-cies yields blacks, and so forth. Employers often make both recruitment and hiring decisions on this basis. This introduces an element of conser-vativeness into adjustments in recruitment procedures, since the perfor-mance qualities of candidate groups attracted by. new procedures are unknown.

In a very tight labor market no recruitment procedures are very effec-tive. It is often necessary to match the recruitment expenditures of labor market competitors in order to avoid more severe scarcities, but this will not overcome the labor shortage. The enterprise is, therefore, forced to place primary reliance upon adjustments in hiring standards, screening procedures, and training. Because they bear the major burden of adjust-ment and because they are constrained in ways which are important for public and private manpower policies, these instruments are discussed in some detail. Although all three adjustments are interrelated, it is con-venient to discuss hiring standards and screening procedures together and then move to a discussion of training.

Hiring Standards and Screening Procedures

The content of the entry-job vacancies, and the jobs related to them through upgrading sequences, influence the characteristics that workers

[9] See "How Issues of Subcontracting and Plant Removal Are Handled: By the Courts (Robert F. Koretz); By the National Labor Relations Board (William Feldesman); By Arbitrators (Saul Wallen)," *Industrial and Labor Relations Re-view*, January 1966, pp. 239-272.

must possess to be hired, at least in the short run. These characteristics relate to the worker's ability to perform a job, to acquire new skills and abilities, and to adapt to the social environment and behavioral norms of the plant. The employer initially establishes preferred hiring standards based upon these characteristics. Some standards, such as the ability to perceive color, may be absolute prerequisites, but many, especially skill and ability factors, are flexible to the extent that the level of job performance does not fall to zero when they are lowered. Within the limits established by job content and training costs, management can exercise discretion over the kind of worker it is willing to hire. The discretion is often extended further by modifications in training procedures.

While the concept of a hiring standard is clear in theory, it is not readily applied in practice. The only true measure of a worker's effectiveness is job performance, and it is seldom feasible to assess performance prior to employment. Many of the circumstances which promote internal labor markets tend to make the problems of prior assessment especially difficult. Jobs in internal labor markets tend to be enterprise specific and, therefore, performance in other establishments is not a reliable predictor. The worker is frequently hired into a line of progression, and the employer is more interested in his ability to learn other job skills than in his immediate performance. Moreover, because internal labor markets arise where turnover is costly, the probability that an employee will eventually quit becomes a significant dimension of hiring standards. Turnover costs also make it expensive to give applicants a trial period on the job.

For these reasons, hiring standards are seldom applied directly. Instead, managers develop screening procedures to predict job performance, and it is these procedures that determine whether a candidate is hired or not. Common screening devices include educational attainment, personal interviews, work histories, references, criminal records, security checks, and test scores. The cost of these devices varies: the utilization of a worker's level of educational attainment is quite inexpensive; elaborate testing and lengthy personal interviews are more costly.

Screening is almost always probabilistic. The variables upon which it is based are chosen because they correlate or, are believed to correlate, with job performance. Occasionally, the correlation is statistically valid, but most often it derives from the collective experience and prejudices of the plant management and has never been scientifically verified. In either case, the causal relationship between screening variables and job performance is not necessarily well defined. In fact, only in rare instances are managers able to articulate a plausible relationship between job performance and the screening procedures they employ.

Because screening rests upon statistical probabilities, the hiring process is subject to the two types of statistical estimation errors: the Type I error of *rejecting a qualified candidate* and the Type II error of *accepting a candidate who is unqualified.* For any given screening device, there is a trade-off between the two types of errors, and one can be reduced at the expense of an increase in the other. The two types of errors can only be reduced simultaneously by the introduction of more powerful, and generally more costly, screening techniques.

The cost to the firm of accepting a worker who is poorly qualified depends upon the skill content of the entry job, the present and future skill content of the jobs in the related mobility cluster, and the probability of the worker being promoted. Enterprises with a high proportion of low-skilled jobs and stable or declining employment are therefore least sensitive to such costs. The cost of rejecting a qualified worker, on the other hand, is measured by the expense of recruiting another worker who is similarly qualified, and who also embodies the criteria expressed in the selection procedures.

In most enterprise markets, the pressure to minimize Type II errors is greater than the pressure to minimize errors of the Type I variety. This is attributable, in part, to the cost of turnover which tends to accompany internal markets, but limitations upon the employers' freedom to discharge workers also appears to be important. In enterprises organized by trade unions, the right of discharge is limited by the collective agreement. While it is not impossible to fire an incompetent worker, the procedure is frequently time-consuming and expensive. Union contracts almost universally allow an initial probationary period during which a new employee is not protected by the agreement and the employer is free to discharge without showing cause. The length of probation varies among enterprises: periods of 30 to 90 days are fairly typical, but some run as long as six months. The length of the probation period tends to vary with the cost of Type II error.

Nonunion enterprises do not face quite the same discharge problem. But many nonunion employers place similar restrictions on discharge in order to avoid the kinds of employee grievances which might encourage union organization. In both union and nonunion shops, moreover, the cost of discharge is raised by the social community which tends to form at the workplace. Once an employee develops friendships within the enterprise, his discharge can undermine the morale of the work force and generate resentment against management.

The costs of Type I and Type II errors are affected asymmetrically by the business cycle. As the market tightens, and the enterprise has increasing difficulty attracting candidates, the cost of rejecting workers who actually meet its hiring standards is increased. Because of the pervasive fear of accepting unqualified workers, this tends most often to lead to the introduction of more sophisticated screening devices rather than a simple reduction in the levels of the existing criteria.

For example, a high school degree is commonly used as a proxy to measure reliability and ability to learn when external markets are loose, presumably because it involves little cost and produces a small Type II error. The lowering of the educational requirements by one or two years as the market tightens would shift the distribution toward lower Type I errors, but at some cost in Type II errors. But educational requirements are seldom varied in this way. For example, a machine tool manufacturing firm substituted I.Q. and mechanical aptitude tests when the market tightened in 1965 and dropped the high school requirements which had been its main hiring criteria in the late 1950's and early 1960's. Similarly, an apparel company experiencing rising training costs and higher turnover among new hires, began to screen out slow learners with sophisticated tests involving simulated work tasks.

A good deal of what appears to be a general reduction in hiring standards in a tightening labor market is, in reality, simply a change in screening procedures. But real reductions in hiring standards do occur. Typical changes in the tightening labor market of the mid-1960's involved reductions in educational requirements and acceptable test scores, less stringent work history requirements, and the like. Reductions in hiring standards are generally accompanied by increasing training and higher average unit costs generated by rising scrap rates, reduced labor productivity, damaged machinery, additional supervisory burdens, and the like. Often standards are waived on an *ad hoc* basis according to the difficulties which unfilled jobs pose for meeting production targets.

The reduction of hiring standards in the internal labor market is constrained by the permanence of employment and the promotion rights which it confers. Because employment is permanent, the effects of lowered standards are not reversible: poor employees cannot be replaced by better-qualified workers when they become available, and the cost impact of poor workers tends to cumulate as they become eligible for promotion to more difficult jobs. Even in the mid-'60s, some managers were still preoccupied by the adverse impact upon efficiency of poorly qualified workers hired in the tight markets of the World War II and Korean periods.

The irreversibility of the effects of reduced hiring standards leads many employers to prefer to meet labor shortages through apparently costly short-term expedients. Subcontracting is frequently introduced for this purpose. In other cases, employers only accept less-qualified workers if they can find some means of circumventing the permanent employment obligation. Temporary help services are one means of doing so. Workers supplied by these services are screened on the job and occasionally are hired permanently. One midwestern machine tool company actually had its own "captive" temporary help service. Another means of avoiding permanent obligations is to discharge employees at the end of the probationary period and hire replacements. Finally, when standards are lowered, some employers attempt to minimize the permanent effects by concentrating on groups with exceptionally high rates of voluntary attrition and whose ambition and capacity for promotion is limited. Thus, some manufacturing firms in the mid-1960's favored hiring married women with working husbands.

Training

A reduction in hiring standards is often accompanied by training procedures designed to reduce its long-run impact upon plant productivity. Most employers appear to favor training as a long-run remedy to labor scarcities, and it is also a prominent means of adjustment to technological change. Recognizing the limitations of out-plant vocational training for enterprise-specific skills, they are generally willing to provide the required in-plant training. Some employers are even prepared to train in general skills such as English, shop math, drafting, and typing, if the need is sufficiently great, and if there is reasonable expectation of recapturing the educational investment during a "payoff period" of employment.

In analyzing adjustments through training, it is useful to distinguish three kinds of worker attributes which are, or can be, developed within the enterprise: (1) basic skills, (2) speed and precision in job performance, and (3) behavioral traits.

Basic skills. The layman—and indeed most management personnel—generally associates the term "training" with basic skills. The term, which is largely self-explanatory, includes such things as verbal and mathematical literacy, blueprint reading, carpentry, machining, core-making, and the like. The skill may be narrow or broad; specific to the enterprise or general. Most basic skills can be taught either in a classroom or on the job. As has been noted, however, when skills are provided in the enterprise, on-the-job training predominates.

Speed and precision. The speed and precision of job performance involve the ways in which a skill, or set of skills, is utilized in a work situation. They are generally developed through practice and repetition on the job once the basic skill has been acquired. Some training of this type is necessary for almost all jobs. In manufacturing plants, the training process is commonly called "learning to make standard." It can be described by a *learning curve* showing output as a function of length of time on the job. At the point where the learning curve levels off, the worker is said to be trained. Actual learning curves have been measured in only a few enterprises—in airplane manufacturing during World War II, in electronics assembly, and in apparel—usually for purposes of monitoring training. But the concept of a learning curve appears to characterize all on-the-job training, even for semiskilled jobs where the basic skill content is negligible.

Behavioral traits. The third group of attributes capable of development in the enterprise are behavioral traits such as punctuality, attendance, the ability to accept supervision, and compatibility with fellow workers. These attributes have not traditionally been taught within the enterprise, and management is accustomed to treating them as determined by external social processes. In the past, work procedures have been accommodated to a labor force with certain behavioral traits, and candidates not possessing these traits have been excluded. In recent years, however, there has been a certain amount of interest, particularly among the "progressively" managed enterprises, in the possibility of changing behavioral traits of employees. The initial concern has been with leadership and managerial training for supervisory employees and with motivating incumbent employees to be more productive.[10] In the last several years pressure to combat racial discrimination in employment has expanded the scope of interest to include attitudinal training for both management and workers. Concomitant interest in hiring the "disadvantaged" has produced a concern with the development of the behavioral traits of regular attendance, punctuality, and the ability to accept supervisory direction, a lack of which is thought to be the primary barrier to the employment of disadvantaged workers.

The most publicized techniques for the development of such traits are sensitivity training and role playing. These are widely employed for leadership training and to combat racial prejudice, but are also used in programs designed for disadvantaged workers.[11] Such training may be termed formal in the sense that it is analogous to formal classroom instruction in basic skills.

There is a strong counter-theory, however, that behavioral traits are best developed by managerial insistence upon strict adherence to explicit standards. Many managers feel that the application of strong, progressive discipline for behavior in violation of these standards is the only effective technique for dealing with the difficulties caused by disadvantage and racial prejudice. Some maintain that it will also produce the group cohesion and direction sought in leadership training. Techniques of this kind are analogous to training on the job.

---

[10] See Douglas McGregor, *The Human Side of Enterprise* (New York: McGraw-Hill Co., 1960) and Paul Pigors and Charles A. Myers, *Personnel Administration,* 6th ed. (New York: McGraw-Hill Co., 1969).
[11] See Peter B. Doeringer (ed.), *Programs to Employ the Disadvantaged* (Englewood Cliffs, N. J.: Prentice-Hall, Inc., 1969).

On-the-job training for behavioral traits and training in speed and precision (which is always on the job) pose one special managerial problem. Both processes have a potential for permanently lowering the work norms of the enterprise. This potential derives from three characteristics of the customary law which sanctions these norms. One is the basic dependence of the law upon precedent and past practice. The second is the principle of horizontal equity (equal treatment of equals). The third is that when different standards of performance arise in a plant, only the practice most favored by the internal labor force is likely to survive.

Most of the production norms at which training in speed and accuracy are aimed and many of the behavioral norms of the enterprise are resented by the internal labor force. Workers typically would prefer slower work speeds and less stringent quality requirements. In many cases, as individuals, they would also like a more tolerant managerial attitude toward lateness and absenteeism. And both workers and managers would prefer to relate to each other in the work situation in the manner most natural to the personalities which they bring to the workplace rather than conform to some standards which have been imposed upon them.

When management hires workers who do not conform to traditional behavioral norms, or when management tolerates performance which is subnormal as part of the training process, this often signals the incumbent labor force that the norms could be permanently reduced. If, for example, standard output had been traditionally reached after six weeks on the job, and new workers cannot make standard after eight, there is a danger that incumbent workers may begin to reduce their output as well. If workers are traditionally fired for unexcused absences, and such absences are permitted to special groups of new hires, incumbent workers may also begin to expect such treatment.

The problem is most acute when training in production or behavioral norms is first introduced. In enterprises which have engaged in such training before, there is usually a precedent to distinguish training procedures from concessions in work rules. Thus, behavioral training, because it is relatively new, is more of a threat to enterprise performance standards than is training in speed and precision.[12]

There is a variety of ways of minimizing the tendency of training concessions to become permanent norms. When there is a union contract, the negotiation of the program with the union is often sufficient to gain labor force acceptance of its privileged status. Job titles such as "assistant" or "trainee" are sometimes used to distinguish groups facing different norms. Differing wage rates, even if the same titles are utilized, may also

---

[12] This problem, as it affects the employment of the disadvantaged, is further discussed in Chapter 8.

suffice in making this distinction. Finally, the trainees can be isolated from the rest of the plant labor force. Vestibule training is sometimes used for this purpose and some companies have even developed separate "feeder" plants, partly to prevent the performance of norms in their regular operations from being corrupted by new hires.[13]

Vestibule training programs also permit closer contact between new hires and supervision. These programs provide an introduction to the workplace in an environment where supervisors are more concerned with training and worker adjustment than with meeting production schedules. Moreover, where learning rates and earnings are related under "payment-by-results" systems, accelerating the training process yields direct economic motivations for the employee.

Training for labor scarcities. Most of the training in basic skills which occurs in a tightening labor market is on the job and exhibits the characteristics of on-the-job training discussed earlier. There appears, however, to be somewhat greater reliance upon formal training procedures in a tight labor market than in a loose one. This reflects the economies of scale available through large formal training programs and the inherent limitations in training capacity on the job. In tight labor markets, enterprises also extend training into basic skills which lend themselves to classroom instruction and which are sufficiently general to use the standard techniques developed for the classroom. In loose markets, such skills can usually be obtained externally.

Much of what is called formal training in the enterprises surveyed, however, proved to be no more than formalized on-the-job training, which did not change the basic character of the training process. Formalizing the training creates a greater managerial awareness that such training is occurring and of the costs which it imposes. One way in which on-the-job training is formalized is by adopting a systematic process of exposing the trainee to the variety of skills he is likely to need when working on his own. In one plant, for example, trainees learning machine repair were rotated through various production departments. In another enterprise, one with a plantwide maintenance department, the maintenance foreman assigned trainees according to a formal training schedule listing the sequence of operations to which they were to be exposed.

Vestibule training, as noted, is sometimes no more than a means of isolating the work norms applied to the trainees, but it is often also introduced to reduce the cost or increase the effectiveness of the skill training process. Vestibule training ranges from orientation to work rules, to classroom instruction in general skills, to simulations of the work

---

[13] See Jack Chernick and Georgina Smith, "Employing the Disadvantaged," in Doeringer (ed.), *Programs to Employ the Disadvantaged, op. cit.,* pp. 14-22.

environment. Several electronics programs taught the fundamentals of soldering, spot welding, or cable making; a shipbuilding company established a vestibule welding program; and two apparel companies taught machine sewing in a separate training area.

Vestibule training is not a panacea for limited on-the-job training capacity. Vestibule programs which are substitutes for on-the-job training require supervisory skills, equipment, and raw materials from the plant floor which are likely to be in scarce supply.[14] Moreover, it is difficult to reproduce the breadth of work experience encountered on the job. Nevertheless, there are indications that vestibule programs can be substituted for on-the-job training when the numbers of trainees are large, and the job content relatively standardized.

In one apparel plant, for example, line supervision provided the instruction, and actual production tasks were performed in the program. Initially trainees learned to operate their machines by sewing on paper and scrap material. Then the jobs for which they were being trained were divided into simple steps, much like the process of work simplification. Production speed and quality were then developed for these simple tasks. Gradually, the tasks were assembled into more complex jobs until the trainee was performing a complete assignment at full production speed. Trained workers were then transferred to the plant floor along with their training machines.

Formal training programs can also be used to prepare workers for upgrading. In steel, machine tool, and screw machine plants, for example, formal apprenticeship programs have been expanded or reactivated in order to accelerate the development of skilled journeymen or line foremen. More immediate skill needs were sometimes met through special training programs which combined on-the-job training with formal classroom instruction. These programs resemble apprenticeship training since they explicitly pair trainees with skilled mechanics in the training process.

When enterprises rely upon classroom training, it is often designed to facilitate learning on the job and, by itself, is of little value. One good example is a program in an electronics plant operated by an equipment vendor for his customers' personnel. Although primarily designed to overcome a shortage created by a change in technology, it is typical of the type of formal classroom program introduced in a tightening labor market. The program consisted of a two-week course in higher mathematics, electronic theory, and equipment maintenance. The material was oriented toward the vendor's equipment, but a good part of it was at

[14] For example, data collected by Charles R. Walker *et al., The Foreman on the Assembly Line* (Cambridge, Mass.: Harvard University Press, 1956), p. 84, suggest that during loose labor markets foremen spend almost 5 per cent of their time on training-related activities in automobile assembly plants.

college, or even graduate school, level. The vendor recognized that much of the material was above his students' capabilities, but he expected them to emerge from the course with enough vocabulary to describe equipment difficulties to his employees and receive verbal repair instructions over the phone. Much of the material which the students did not understand initially would become clear on the job.

Vendor-designed programs involve certain problems not likely to arise when the enterprise initiates its own training programs. The vendor, for example, is compelled to accept the students which his customer assigns to the program. With no control over the prior preparation of the trainees, it is difficult to adjust the training curriculum accordingly. The basic features of the program, however—a sophisticated curriculum taught in a brief period and designed to supply a framework for further training on the job—are common to in-plant classrooms as well.

Occasionally employers turn to out-plant training institutions such as vocational schools for skill development. Usually they were less interested in the basic or general vocational education than with instruction specific to their enterprise-skill requirements. Respondents from a number of plants mentioned programs conducted through their school systems which were designed to meet their particular skill requirements. In one case involving basic training for literacy, the program was clearly a short-run response to an immediate labor shortage. Most other programs were more permanent, instituted to create a small but regularly available supply of graduates possessing the required skills.

These programs took a variety of forms. Two of them, designed to supply craftsmen skilled in electronic maintenance, were revisions of the high school vocational program and supplanted a training program previously conducted in the plant. In several other cases programs were developed in local community colleges to train technicians in the plant's somewhat specialized technology.

It is characteristic of all these programs that they were initiated by the enterprise, rather than the school systems, and were so dependent on it that they appeared to be an extension of its internal training activities. As indicated above, these connections generally grew stronger and more frequent as labor scarcities became more acute. Occasionally the enterprise supplied the specialized equipment required, as well as the necessary teachers, and it often developed the curriculum.

In general, there was much less formal classroom training than one might expect. It appeared to be the preferred training technique only for the orientation of large groups of new employees to enterprise rules and procedures. Instruction in specific jobs, even in periods of rapidly expanding employment, was given on the job whenever possible — and the companies studied went to great lengths to insure that it was possible.

Moreover, in contrast to on-the-job training, formal classroom training costs appear as budget items and are likely to become the target of cost reduction activities once the training crisis is past.

While the visibility of costs may affect the form of a training program, costs were never an explicit factor in deciding whether the training was to be undertaken, or where it was to be conducted. This might be explained by the costs being minimal. A more likely explanation, however, is that the adjustment costs are manifested in subtle ways that escape detection until they cause a discontinuity in the production process. In most cases, enterprise programs were developed in direct response to labor shortages which interfered with production goals. Cost seemed to matter little in comparison to the concern with production bottlenecks.

Internal training, however, cannot always be relied upon to overcome these bottlenecks. Especially where training occurs on the job in the process of production, it can interfere with production. During periods of rapid employment expansion, on-the-job training facilities may become limited, and inventories of pretrained workers exhausted. Because on-the-job training requires the same supervisory inputs, materials, and equipment as production, large-scale training can lead to serious drains on productive capacity. Although estimates varied, most of the employers surveyed were convinced that there were limits to the rate at which new employees could be absorbed.

Summary

It has been argued in this chapter that the internal labor market of the enterprise operates through a series of adjustment instruments to reconcile imbalances between the supply of labor on the external market and the labor requirements of the internal market.

There are two types of adjustment instruments available to the enterprise internal labor markets: those that are highly constrained and those over which management can exercise considerable discretion. The highly constrained instruments are often the focus of custom at the workplace and are part of decision processes largely unrelated to the resolution of labor market imbalances. These instruments are: the compensation structure, the job structure, the internal allocative structure, and written managerial procedures. The less constrained instruments—hiring standards, screening procedures, training, recruitment procedures, subcontracting, job vacancies, and overtime—are the principal instruments of labor force adjustment. Selection among these instruments approximates their relative costs and benefits.

This view suggests that there are limits to the rate and volume of labor force adaptations which the internal labor market can provide at any point in time, and emphasizes the costs of the adjustment process. It also indicates that sufficiently powerful adjustment instruments are available to most internal labor markets to permit them to achieve a viable balance with the external labor market. The process of technological change and adjustments in job content have been largely ignored in this discussion, however, and will be considered in the next chapter.

Appendix to Chapter 5

Quantitative Measures of the Internal Adjustment Process

In Chapter 5 it was argued that the particular adjustment strategy adopted by an enterprise would reflect both the flexibility of the various instruments and the relative costs and benefits. It is, however, by no means easy to estimate adjustment costs in any precise fashion or to allocate them to specific labor instruments.

The costs of variations in hiring standards are perhaps the most difficult to estimate. Reduced hiring standards are reflected in lower labor productivity, equipment downtime, repair costs, higher costs of supervision, and so forth. The costs, in other words, are indirect and spread over a number of variables. Estimation is further complicated by other factors that impinge upon these variables, making it difficult to identify the independent effect of hiring standards. Experiments that might make it possible to separate the influence of hiring standards are inhibited by the rules and customs restricting management's freedom to assign or to discharge workers once they have entered the enterprise and passed probation. Hiring standards will thus affect the costs not only of the job for which the worker is hired, but also the costs of other jobs to which he may later be promoted. While it is not impossible to estimate these costs, it is exceedingly difficult to do so.

Any attempt to arrive at the cost of training encounter similar problems. Only where training takes place in formal classroom programs can its costs be readily identified. Much training, however, takes place on the job, and its costs, like those of reduced hiring standards, are reflected only indirectly in higher unit production costs. Indeed, in many respects the period of on-the-job training is much like a temporary reduction in hiring standards.

Among the instruments of adjustment, only compensation and recruitment costs are readily measurable because they appear explicitly in operating budgets. Even where some adjustment costs are identifiable, the mix of instruments varies considerably among enterprises, making it difficult to develop an index of cyclical changes in adjustment costs at either the enterprise or industry levels.[1]

In this Appendix some quantitative materials pertaining to the costs of the internal adjustment process are presented.

Recruiting and Hiring Costs

None of the enterprises surveyed estimated its hiring costs or changes in these hiring costs beyond the gross information contained in personnel department budgets. Several studies of hiring costs have been made, and the resulting estimates are shown in Table 3.

On-the-Job Training

On-the-job training, it has been argued, is one of the more significant instruments of manpower adjustment. Conceptually, this suggests that individual learning curves would provide a basis for measuring the adjustment process within enterprises. Calculating the difference between actual efficiency and 100 per cent efficiency of individual workers, and then summing these differences across all workers in the enterprise would provide an estimate of the costs of informal training.

A simple model approximating this process would assume the general form:[2]

$$OMH = f(A, U, T)$$

where

OMH = Output per man-hour
A = Accession or new hire rate
U = Utilization rate of plant and equipment
T = State of technology

---

[1] Caution must be exercised in interpreting individual measures. Often such measures do not move consistently over time and there is a tendency for the more significant or visible elements of cost to be reduced through cost-cutting efforts.

[2] Such a model is related to recent attempts to explain short-run changes in factor productivity and short-run behavior of production functions. The major difference is that the effect of new hires and promotions upon labor productivity, through on-the-job training, is explicitly incorporated into the model. See James S. Duesenberry, *et al., The Brookings Quarterly Econometric Model of the United States* (Chicago:

TABLE 3.   Estimates of Hiring and Training Costs

		AVERAGE HIRING COSTS	AVERAGE TRAINING COSTS	AVERAGE HIRING AND TRAINING COSTS
All occupations	[1]	$ 65.00[a]	$ 74.00[b]	n.a.
	[1]	118.00[c]	71.00[d]	n.a.
	[1]	145.00[d]	79.00[d]	n.a.
	[2]	n.a.	369.00[e]	n.a.
	[3]	n.a.	n.a.	$200.00[g]
	[4]	22.66	n.a.	208.20[f]
	[5]	43.27	n.a.	245.69[h]
Professional, managerial	[1]	168.00[a]	119.00[b]	n.a.
and technical	[1]	837.00[c]	268.00[d]	n.a.
	[1]	907.00[c]	116.00[d]	n.a.
	[6]	990.00[g]	n.a.	n.a.
Skilled labor	[6]	149.00[g]	n.a.	n.a.
Unskilled labor	[6]	117.00[g]	n.a.	n.a.
Secretary	[6]	172.00[g]	n.a.	n.a.
Clerk	[6]	145.00[g]	n.a.	n.a.
Other occupations	[1]	36.00[a]	66.00[b]	n.a.
	[1]	55.00[c]	59.00[d]	n.a.
	[1]	49.00[c]	43.00[d]	n.a.

SOURCES:
[1] John G. Meyers, "Hiring Costs: Some Survey Findings," *The Conference Board Record,* January 1967, p. 34. Data are for June 1965, November 1965, and February 1966.

[2] Edwin F. Estle, "The Extent of Private Industrial Training in New England," *New England Business Review,* February 1964.

[3] Charles C. Holt *et al., Planning Production, Inventories, and Work Force* (1960), cited in Meyers, "Hiring Costs," as adjusted to 1965 prices.

[4] Walter Y. Oi, "Labor as a Quasi-Fixed Factor," *Journal of Political Economy,* December 1962, cited in Meyers "Hiring Costs." as adjusted to 1965 prices.

[5] Merchants and Manufacturers Association (of Los Angeles), *Labor Turnover: Causes, Costs, and Methods of Control* (1959) cited in Meyers, "Hiring Costs." Adjusted to 1965 prices.

[6] Bureau of National Affairs, Survey No. 86 "Recruiting Practices," *Personnel Policies Forum,* March 1969.

[a] Average of 16 employers.   [e] Average of 210 employers.
[b] Average of 15 employers.   [f] Single employer data.
[c] Average of 14 employers.   [g] Sample size unknown.
[d] Average of 13 employers.   [h] Average of 24 employers.

Rand McNally Co., 1965), and Lester C. Thurow and L. D. Taylor, "The Interaction between the Actual and the Potential Rates of Growth," *Review of Economics and Statistics,* vol. XLVIII, no. 4 (November 1966), pp. 351-360.

Unfortunately, few enterprises develop the data on individual worker productivity needed for testing such a model.[3] Several proxy measures were collected during this study, however, which illustrate some of the effects of labor force adjustment upon production efficiency. In piece-rate industries, such as apparel, for example, many establishments collect data on "make-up" payments, wages paid to individual workers equal to the differential between their hourly piece-rate earnings and the minimum wage or guaranteed rate on the job. For each employee, "make-up" declines over time according to his learning curve. In Equation 1, monthly data on the make-up rate in one men's apparel plant studied is regressed on monthly hiring rates for the period January 1966–May 1967.[4]

$$(1) \quad M_t = 2.3189 + .5360H_t** \qquad R^2 = .1686 \qquad\qquad d.f. = 16$$
$$ (3.08) \quad\;\; (2.98)$$

where M_t = make-up for learners as a percent of total wage bill in month t

H_t = hiring rate per 100 employees in month t

This equation indicated an increase of 1 per cent in the monthly hiring rate and is associated with about a ½ per cent increase in make-up costs. Evaluated at the means, on-the-job training of new hires accounted for 16 per cent of the monthly make-up rate.

A second variant of the general model, shown in Equation 2, was applied to quarterly data available for the steel industry.

$$(2) \quad \frac{OMH_t}{OMH_{t-1}} = a + b_1 H_t + b_2 \frac{X_t}{X_{t-1}} + b_3 C_t + u_t$$

Where,

OMH_t = Index of output per man-hour in time t

H_t = Hiring rate per 100 employees in time t

X_t = Index of output in time t

C_t = Capacity utilization rate in time t

For the period 1958 to 1967, the following results were obtained.[5]

$$\frac{OMH_t}{OMH_{t-1}} = .46 - .035H_t** + .52 \; \frac{X_t**}{X_{t-1}} + .005 \; C_t$$
$$\phantom{\frac{OMH_t}{OMH_{t-1}} =} (2.51) \;\; (3.19) \qquad (17.87) \qquad (1.56)$$
$$\phantom{\frac{OMH_t}{OMH_{t-1}} =} R^2 = .9188 \qquad\qquad d.f. = 33$$

[3] See John W. Kendrick and Daniel Creamer, *Measuring Company Productivity,* (New York: National Industrial Conference Board, 1961).

[4] Given the data available, Equation 1 produced the best "fit." Experimentation with various lag structures for hiring rates did not improve the statistical results. Substituting net changes in employment for hiring rates as a test of the sensitivity of training costs to very short-term turnover produced the anticipated reduction in the explanatory power of the model. The t values are shown in parentheses. ** = significant at the 1% level.

[5] t values are shown in parentheses. ** = significant at the 1% level. (Source: Unpublished data, U.S. Department of Labor, Bureau of Labor Statistics.)

The same equation in logarithmic form provided a somewhat improved fit, although the significance of the training proxy H_t fell substantially.

Additional quantitative evidence of the labor force adjustment process comes from the literature on "learning by doing." Studies in the airframe industry, shipbuilding, ironmaking, and electronics all suggest that repeated performance of similar jobs reduces unit labor costs.[6] A number of studies have attempted to relate changes in output per man-hour to variables such as time, the length of production runs, and the number of production cycles.[7] In general, these studies have found a secular decline in unit man-hour requirements as production tasks are repeated and have concluded that factors other than technological change affect short-term production costs and must be incorporated into dynamic production functions. These factors include "learning by doing," improvements in technical knowledge, changes in utilization rates, and minor innovations.

The type and quality of the data available in the examples presented above do not permit precise testing of the thesis that adjustments to labor market imbalances are readily accomplished within internal labor markets. Nor do they provide statistically reliable measures of the magnitude of various adjustment costs when they are incurred. Nevertheless, they present evidence which is consistent with the operation of the internal labor market as described in this chapter.

[6] One study of an iron manufacturer in Sweden, for example, indicated that a continual increase in output per man-hour occurred over a 15-year period despite the fact that the product mix and the production process remained relatively stable. A long-run learning curve was postulated as the explanation for this phenomenon, although such "learning by doing" should be defined to include informal innovations in work methods. See Kenneth Arrow, "The Implications of Learning by Doing," *Review of Economic Studies,* vol. XXIX, no. 80 (June 1962), pp. 155-173.

[7] See, for example, Armen S. Alchian, "Reliability of Progress Curves in Airframe Production, *Econometrica,* vol. XXXI (October 1963), pp. 679-693 and Werner Z. Hirsh, "Manufacturing Progress Functions," *Review of Economics and Statistics,* vol. XXXIV (May 1952), pp. 143-155.

Chapter 6
Technological Change and Adjustments in Job Content

The ability to control unemployment under strong government stimulus to aggregate demand has allayed the fears of structural unemployment prevalent in the late 1950's and early 1960's.[1] Nonetheless, these fears—particularly as they were related to technological change and automation—retain a certain plausibility. In theory, structural imbalances in the labor market should be forestalled by variations in relative wages and the adjustments in the composition of labor demand and supply which the wage variations induce. Innovations in technology, however, are not subject to this discipline; and it is perfectly consistent with the conventional theory for innovations to generate a set of jobs which the labor force is incapable of manning.

In the preceding chapter it was shown that processes of labor force adjustment occur within the internal labor market through instruments operating primarily upon the characteristics of the labor supply. In this chapter the relationship between the labor market and the job content of the enterprise will be examined. In the concluding section, the implications of this relationship for aggregate labor market policies will be appraised.

[1] The greater part of this chapter first appeared in Michael J. Piore, "The Impact of the Labor Market on the Design and Selection of Productive Techniques Within the Manufacturing Plant," *Quarterly Journal of Economics,* vol. LXXXII, no. 4 (November 1968), pp. 602-620.

The Determination of Job Content

The process of job generation within an enterprise may be divided into three stages: (1) the search for areas in which changes in productive technique might be introduced, (2) the design and construction of the capital equipment, and (3) the design of jobs required to man the equipment. The stages roughly correspond to the divisions in time and in the distribution of responsibility within the enterprise. Any part of the process of technological change may be performed within the enterprise or purchased from outside institutions. Although a wide variety of combinations of internal and external participation was encountered in the study, two patterns predominate: that in which the whole process took place within the enterprise and that in which standard equipment was purchased from a vendor. The character of the process can be presented most easily by developing the wholly internal pattern, characteristic of large, multiple enterprises, as the basic model and then introducing outside participation as a variation upon the internal pattern.

The Search

In large enterprises the responsibility for selecting points in the productive process where innovations might be introduced rested with line management and with the engineers assigned to the operating departments.[2] Once a point had been selected, the innovation was frequently designed and constructed by corporate engineers. But, in the search, the latter served primarily as consultants to the operating personnel.

The key role of the operating personnel in search activity may be attributed to the nature of technology. A good part of the technology of work exists only as an operating process. It is not formally described, and its scientific rationale is imperfectly understood. Manufacturing technologies are frequently developed experimentally, through trial and error. Apparently some design problems are in advance of theoretical understanding.[3] Others are either too specialized or too trivial to command theoretical interest, or can be solved more expediently through trial

---

[2] A number of minor innovations are suggested, and frequently designed and introduced as well, by production and maintenance personnel. Together innovations by production and maintenance workers may account for a significant portion of productivity increases. But in the enterprises visited for this study they were frequently designed to increase yields under incentive plans or short-cut standard repair procedures; they were, therefore, hidden from management and not reported in the interviews. See Stanley B. Mathewson, *Restrictions of Output Among Unorganized Workers* (New York: Viking Press, 1931), pp. 110-114; Frederick G. Lesieur (ed.), *The Scanlon Plan* (Cambridge, Mass.: The Technology Press of M.I.T., 1958); and Sumner H. Slichter, James J. Healy, and E. Robert Livernash, *The Impact of Collective Bargaining on Management* (Washington: The Brookings Institution, 1960), pp. 355-361.

[3] The classic example of this phenomenon is the development of coking for coal

and error.[4] Even equipment initially built to formal specifications is subject to a variety of modifications once in operation, many of which are thought too minor to be formally recorded. Over time the minor changes accumulate, and the equipment moves a considerable distance from the recorded design.

Because so much of the existing technology is not formally described, attempts to improve it typically begin with a study of the process in operation. This appeared to be true of both chemical and mechanical processes. One chemical engineer commented: "I spent two weeks in the plant trying to separate the essentials of the process from the witchcraft. I know I didn't completely succeed, but I was afraid to go further. And they told me that process was automated!" In another plant a proposal to move a complex piece of mechanical packaging equipment two feet across the plant floor was rejected for fear that, once disrupted, it would not be operable again at maximum speed.

The necessity of studying the operating process makes line managers uniquely suited to conduct the search, for they are already sufficiently familiar with the process to evaluate its potential for improvement. Insofar as the search is conducted by these operating personnel, it appears to be directed by variables which are largely independent of labor market forces. Many innovations are designed to overcome specific operating problems: an equipment breakdown, a deterioration in the quality of the product, changes in the quality of raw material inputs, labor relations difficulties, and the like. Problems of this kind are subject to a number of random influences, but they seem to cluster around both old and new equipment. Old equipment breaks down frequently, while new equipment often has mechanical difficulties until the "bugs" are worked out. New equipment tends to disrupt processes which are physically related to it. In the plants studied, this last effect was a particularly important stimulus to technological change. A number of innovations were designed specifically to improve the speed and accuracy of processes which fed material into new machines or received output from them.[5]

---

in eighteenth-century iron manufacture. See Thomas S. Ashton, *Iron and Steel in the Industrial Revolution* (Manchester, England: Manchester University, 1924), pp. 24-59.

[4] Abbott Payson Usher, *A History of Mechanical Inventions* (New York: McGraw-Hill Co., 1929), pp. 8-31, and Irving H. Siegal, "Scientific Discovery and the Rate of Invention," in National Bureau of Economic Research, *The Rate and Direction of Inventive Activity: Economic and Social Factors* (Princeton: Princeton University Press, 1962), pp. 441-450.

[5] Simon Kuznets notes this effect in explaining the rate of technological advance within an industry. "Technically, a branch of production is a series of separate operations that lead to an invariable sequence from the raw material to the finished product. Once an important process in this chain is revolutionized by an invention, pressure is exerted upon other links of the chain to become more efficient. Any dis-

In addition to solving operating difficulties, the engineers assigned to operating departments were expected to originate cost-saving ideas. The pressure to do so was reinforced by systems of cost control in all of the enterprises studied. These systems divided total production costs into a series of components. Each component was then compared with a cost standard or "bogey," which incorporated a cost reduction target. Higher management regularly investigated costs in excess of standard.

Cost control systems vary widely among enterprises making generalization hazardous. Nevertheless, it appears that cost *targets* are not greatly influenced by labor market forces. In two plants studied, for example, the cost targets were clearly established after the search had taken place; they incorporated innovations which the engineers had already planned to introduce. In other plants a similar effect was produced by negotiating cost standards with the departmental engineers. As a rule, moreover, cost breakdowns were too broad to provide an effective guide for search activity: labor costs were typically divided into direct and indirect labor, and individual labor grades were never separately identified. In all plants, price and wage increases were generally an accepted explanation for costs in excess of standards. The engineers maintained that the cost control procedures generate a generalized pressure for cost reduction, but have little influence upon the kinds of innovations which are made.

Innovations can also be stimulated informally in two other ways. First, while moving around the plant on other business, the engineers can simply spot points in the productive process where innovation seems possible. Innovations originating in this way are also governed by the distribution of operating difficulties, for it is in areas experiencing such difficulties that engineers are most likely to spend enough time observing the productive process to gauge its potentialities for improvement.

Second, the impetus for cost-saving ideas can come from technologies operating elsewhere in the economy. These are reported in trade magazines and catalogues of equipment vendors, or viewed at trade fairs and in other plants or departments where the engineers visit or work. Both the engineers and their companies typically make a deliberate effort to broaden contact with other technologies. This is often cited as one of the reasons for frequent managerial rotation. Some large companies also organized interplant tours for departmental foremen or engineers, and in certain industries, such as automobiles, interfirm visits are common.[6]

---

parity in performance at the different stages precludes full exploitation of the innovation made." Simon Kuznets, *Economic Change: Selected Essays in Business Cycles, National Income, and Economic Growth* (New York: W.W. Norton, 1953), p. 267.

[6] James R. Bright, *Automation and Management* (Boston: Harvard Business School, Division of Research, 1958), p. 91.

Labor Market Influences Upon the Design and Construction
of Equipment

Minor modifications in technique are frequently designed and constructed on the plant floor by the foremen or the departmental engineers. But for major projects, requiring considerable engineering time or involving large expenditures, design procedures are more formal. Projects are typically reviewed by one or more of the three corporate engineering departments (product, process, and industrial engineering), and the approval of higher management is required before construction can begin. Frequently, the innovation is actually designed and constructed by corporate engineers. In obtaining managerial approval and in resolving disagreements among the engineers, formal cost analysis is critical. Consequently, the costs of the final design and various design alternatives are calculated.[7]

The labor market might conceivably influence any of the components of the cost estimate: (1) the operating wage bill, (2) output per unit of operating time, (3) materials consumption and wastage, (4) maintenance and repair costs. None of these component *estimates* however, is very sensitive to variations in labor market conditions. Moreover, they appear to be particularly unresponsive to changes in the relative scarcities of various types of labor.

In all of the plants studied, the operating wage bill was estimated by multiplying the number of production workers by a single standard wage rate. The standard rate was a convention used throughout the engineering departments of the plant or corporation, and many of the engineers had no idea where it came from or how it was derived. Its source could be traced in only one plant. There, the rate had been developed by the personnel department. It represented the average hourly wage and fringe costs for production and maintenance workers in the plant, corrected to include that portion of the costs of hiring, training, and labor turnover which were reflected in the budget of the personnel department. The figure was revised after each negotiated wage increase, but no allowance was made for interim wage variations due to changes in the composition of the plant labor force, the amount of overtime worked, and the like. Nor was an attempt made to anticipate future wage increases.[8]

[7] For a detailed discussion of administrative procedures for investment decisions, see *ibid.,* pp. 88-106; and Walter W. Heller, "The Anatomy of Investment Decisions," *Harvard Business Review,* vol. XXIX, no. 2 (March 1951), pp. 95-103.

[8] While the source of the standard wage rate was impossible to trace in other plants, it appeared to be derived in a similar manner. For example, the engineers reported that changes in the standard seemed to coincide with negotiated wage changes; they assumed that the standard did not anticipate future wage increases. Neither the engineers nor the personnel department had complete estimates of hiring and training costs in any of the plants, so it is unlikely that the standard reflected these costs except as they appeared in the personnel department's budget. The

Output per unit of operating time and material consumption, insofar as these depended upon the labor force, were estimated by the industrial engineers on the basis of standard time and motion data. Learning periods, when included at all, were derived from standard learning curves for similar jobs. Productivity estimates were based, therefore, upon the productivity of an "ideal worker." There was no evidence that the estimates were altered to take into account the particular hiring standards prevailing at the time or likely to prevail in the future. This procedure persisted despite the fact that plant foremen invariably reported that the engineering standards tended to overestimate the capabilities of the average production worker.

Variations in labor market conditions might also influence the cost of maintenance and repair. These costs, however, were regularly estimated only for large projects, and even there they were frequently introduced only as an allowance for machine downtime. Downtime estimates were based upon the time required for a skilled craftsman familiar with the equipment to repair it. They were not corrected for the delays occasioned by the shortage of craftsmen which many plants were experiencing at the time of the interviews. In none of the plants was it standard procedure to estimate the wages of repair craftsmen. When included, craft wages were valued at the same standard rate used in estimating the cost of operating labor.

Taken as a whole, the cost estimates—in the failure to allow for future wage increases, in the utilization of "ideal" productivity standards, and in the incomplete allowance for maintenance costs—appeared to underestimate the actual cost of labor. The estimates certainly did not reflect variations in labor costs produced by changing market conditions, except as these variations were reflected in the average plant wage rate at the time of negotiated wage changes.

The errors in estimated labor cost may have been corrected by a bias against labor-intensive techniques. Virtually without exception, the engineers distrusted hourly labor and admitted a tendency to substitute capital whenever they had discretion to do so. As one engineer explained, "If the cost comparison favored labor, but we were close, I would mechanize anyway." The engineers, however, justified this bias by reference to the work ethic of hourly labor and the human failings of variability and error.[9]

---

standard rates were in excess of the average wage of production workers in the plants, hence either maintenance wages or fringe benefits or both must have been included in the average.

[9] See Thorstein Veblen's distinction between the industrial and pecuniary employment (or aptitude) and among those in industrial employment between the attitudes of workmen and engineers in *The Theory of the Leisure Class* (New York: B.W. Huebsch, 1912), pp. 228-234; and *The Engineers and the Price System*

It did not represent a deliberate attempt to correct for inaccuracies in the standards upon which labor costs were estimated.[10] As noted earlier, few of the engineers knew how these standards were developed.

Perhaps the most startling aspect of the costing procedures was the practice of estimating labor cost on the basis of a single standard wage rate.[11] The failure of the engineers to estimate the precise wage rates on individual jobs implies that they neglect possibilities of substitution among labor grades. Most of the engineers accepted this inference. They claimed that the savings to be gained from alternative manning arrangements were too small relative to the rates of return required for project approval to affect the fate of the project.[12] Their time, they felt, was better spent on other aspects of the design.

This explanation is not entirely satisfactory. Economists have generally attributed the high internal rates of return on enterprise investments either to the risks associated with innovation or to a corporate aversion to outside financing which necessitates a strict rationing of internal funds.[13] Both

---

(New York: B.W. Huebsch, 1921), pp. 52-82. Also see Perlman's discussion of the economic philosophies of manual laborers and businessmen in Selig Perlman, *A Theory of the Labor Movement* (New York: Augustus M. Kelly, 1949), pp. 237-245.

The qualities which the engineers distrust become more prevalent in the plant in a tightening labor market as hiring standards are reduced and discipline is relaxed. The bias may therefore be responsive to variations in market conditions.

[10] It is not clear, moreover, that the costing procedures lead, on balance, to more labor-intensive methods of production than are justified by actual labor costs. If maintenance requirements are related to capital intensity and if errors in the estimated cost of maintenance labor are sufficiently large relative to errors in the estimated cost of operating labor, the costing procedures will favor capital-intensive methods of production.

[11] In half of the plants studied, the standard wage was used throughout the design process. In the remaining plants, jobs were sometimes individually costed as the project was readied for final review. But this procedure was not standard, and, even when followed, the individual rates did not play a part in the actual design process.

[12] All of the firms in the sample used a payout-period approach to evaluate investment proposals. The required payout period varied with the nature of the project, but fell usually between two and three years, implying an annual rate of return upon invested capital of 30 to 50 per cent. Because the payout period neglects returns in later years, the effective rate on some of the projects may have been considerably greater. See Joel Dean, *Capital Budgeting* (New York: Columbia University Press, 1951), pp. 26-27. These rates are generally in line with those reported in the 1963 McGraw-Hill Survey. McGraw-Hill Publishing Co., *Sixteenth Annual Survey of Plans for New Plant and Equipment* (New York: McGraw-Hill Co., 1963), table XII.

[13] See, for example, Dean, *op. cit.*, pp. 26-27; James S. Duesenberry, *Business Cycles and Economic Growth* (New York: McGraw-Hill Co., 1958), pp. 49-112; Heller, *op. cit.*, p. 101.

interpretations of the required rates of return imply that the neglect of alternative manning arrangements indicates costs to the firm as well as to the engineer. A more plausible explanation for the inattention to possibilities of substitution—one that was in fact provided in one of the interviews—is that precise predictions of manning patterns are too expensive and too uncertain to justify the effort which they would require. Several factors suggest that this is the case.

Until new equipment is actually on the plant floor, the jobs it will create are extremely difficult to foresee. The equipment itself merely defines a set of tasks which must be performed. The way in which these tasks are ultimately combined into jobs will depend upon the physical proximity of the equipment to other work performed in the plant.[14] Even when location is known in advance, the number of tasks which an individual employee can successfully manage is not always apparent. In many cases, manning is set experimentally once the equipment is in operation.

The problem of estimating precise labor costs is further compounded by the difficulty of estimating wage rates for newly created jobs. Individual wage rates are set through elaborate job evaluation and time study procedures which involve detailed observation of the job as it is performed on the plant floor. This is not possible until equipment has been constructed and installed. Moreover, in organized plants, rates for new jobs—and often the job designs as well—are subject to union review and, possibly, arbitration.[15] Rate concessions are often required to smooth the process of transition to a new technology, and their character will depend on the nature of the management-employee relations prevailing at the time. Finally, minimum job qualifications can only be guessed at when a technology is first introduced, since only engineers who are patently over-qualified for the job have had any experience operating and maintaining it.

The barriers to consideration of alternative manning inherent in the process of job design and job pricing are compounded by the nature of the equipment design process. The industrial engineer cannot man a piece of equipment until it is designed. Similarly, the manufacturing engineer cannot design equipment until the product design is complete. While there is a certain amount of collaboration among the engineers, and the industrial engineer can frequently suggest changes in the product or in the process which facilitate his own task, the design must eventually be frozen if the project is to be completed. Since the freezing begins with the product design and progresses to the equipment, it is the industrial engineer who is invariably left with the least degree of freedom.

14 See Louis E. Davis and Ralph R. Canter, "Job Design," *The Journal of Industrial Engineering,* vol. VI (January 1955), p. 3.
15 See, for example, Pike and Fisher, Inc., *Steelworkers Handbook of Arbitration Decisions* (Pittsburgh: United Steelworkers, 1960), pp. 63-83, 200-207.

The influence of labor market forces upon the *innovation* process are limited to two types. First there are average labor costs, and forecasts of these costs, which are incorporated into capital accounting procedures. The larger they bulk in total production costs, the more likely is the adoption of labor-saving technological change.

To say that average labor costs affect the rate of technological change, however, does not indicate that innovation is sensitive to *relative* scarcities of labor. Accounting procedures using average wage costs provide a very imperfect vehicle for transmitting relative labor costs into equipment design.

Job Design Given Capital Equipment

As has been noted, jobs cannot be fully designed until the equipment is operating on the plant floor. Hence, any manning specifications which accompany the equipment design are typically adjusted once the equipment has been installed.[16] In theory, at least, further job changes might be made during the later life of the equipment in response to varying market conditions.

Technically there is at this stage a certain latitude in job design. While the basic tasks are defined by the product and the equipment, they can be combined into a variety of jobs. For example, a machine operator may be required to pick up his materials and deliver his output, or the tasks of pick-up and delivery may be separate jobs assigned to other workers. The technical elasticity of job design is augmented when equipment can be rearranged on the plant floor.

It is extremely difficult to determine what actually governs the process of job design. Almost without exception, industrial engineers speak as if it were a purely mechanical process involving minimization of the number of jobs in the plant without reference to the relative costs of different types of labor or the availability of required skills. Their comments gave the impression that two engineers working independently with the same product and equipment and under the same union and management constraints would produce the same manning schedule.[17]

The weak influence of labor market conditions upon job design was attributed to the fact that both the cost of plant space (a constant preoccupation of management even in new plants) and the costs of managing and coordinating production were functions of the total number of workers. The cost of job design, therefore, was dominated by the number of work-

---

[16] These adjustments are made by the industrial engineer, working in cooperation with the line supervision, and are frequently subject to union review.

[17] Louis E. Davis, Ralph R. Canter, and John Hoffman, "Current Job Design Criteria," *Journal of Industrial Engineering,* vol. VI (March-April 1955), pp. 5.-8.

ers which it required, and substitutions designed to overcome skill deficiencies inevitably increased this number.

The weak influence of the labor market may also be attributed to other constraints. Among these are managerial techniques, the payment system, custom, the collective bargaining contract, health and safety standards, and plant work rules. Further constraints are imposed by the principles of industrial engineering.[18] These principles may have more or less objective validity, but they are nonetheless considered to be valid by the engineers.[19]

It is apparent that *formal* design is only one facet of the process of defining jobs for new equipment. A second facet is *experimental* job design. Indeed, the typical manning procedure for new equipment was to overman initially in terms of numbers and skills of workers, then to modify the original pattern gradually once the equipment was in operation by redistributing tasks and combining jobs. The guiding principle in this process, as in formal job design, was minimization of the number of workers. But skill availability probably enters the process indirectly. In experimental job design the manning schedule ultimately adopted will depend upon the capabilities of the workers who participate in the experiment. Jobs, in other words, are tailored to the employees initially assigned to them. Thus job requirements are automatically adjusted to their skills and other attributes. Some adjustment of this kind takes place on old jobs as well. As new operators are assigned to them, the jobs automatically change to conform to the operators' capabilities. Experimental job design is only possible, however, when management is free to change the manning pattern after the equipment is installed. While management retained this freedom in all of the plants observed, it is severely restricted by union rules in some enterprises.

Formal Job Design and Technological Change as Instruments of Labor Force Adjustment

Relative labor scarcities affect the innovation and job design process only when they pose operating problems. When workers cannot acquire

---

[18] See, for example, William Grant Ireson and Eugene L. Grant (eds.), *Handbook of Industrial Engineering* (Englewood Cliffs, N.J.: Prentice-Hall, 1955) particularly the articles by Dale Yoder (pp. 173-282), and William Gomberg (pp. 1121-84) for the constraints imposed by managerial techniques, engineering principles, and trade unions, respectively.

[19] A much wider disagreement is present in the scholarly literature about the optimal job design than was evident in the comments of industrial engineers in the visited plants. See, for example, Eaton H. Conant and Maurice D. Kilbridge, "An Interdisciplinary Analysis of Job Enlargement: Technology, Costs and Behavioral Implications," *Industrial and Labor Relations Review,* vol. 18 (April 1965), pp. 377-395.

necessary skills, when high turnover jeopardizes equipment or quality control, or when job vacancies are holding up production, new equipment or work methods may be introduced to avoid production bottlenecks. These adjustment instruments, however, are utilized only when less constrained instruments, such as reductions in hiring standards and training, are ineffective in resolving the manpower imbalance.

Many employers interviewed did identify innovations which they believed had eased the burden of labor scarcities. But closer examination revealed that most of these innovations were introduced on the basis of standard cost calculations, and their "skill-saving" benefits were discovered only after the equipment was installed.

Longer production runs, a factor indirectly related to tight labor markets, was found to exercise an influence upon job redesign. Long production runs reduce the need for a flexible, broadly trained labor force. Instead, worker specialization, mass production techniques, and the use of specialized machinery became more efficient work procedures. In several electronics companies studied, for example, small-scale production required engineers and technicians to design and debug the equipment as part of the assembly process. When the length of production runs increased, these companies invested in simplified assembly procedures and utilized semiskilled female assemblers assisted by a small number of technicians.

A machine tool company with an elaborate industrial engineering department was operating under two production principles. For "job shop" items, skilled machinists fabricated the parts, with general purpose equipment, working from blueprints. They made their own setups, laid out the work, and selected the appropriate tools. For long runs, however, the industrial engineering department would carefully define production procedures, specifying the material, layouts, tools, and machine speeds for semiskilled operators. Similar principles governed the introduction of special purpose machine tools, jigs, and other skill-saving devices.

A number of minor instances of job redesign were also encountered which could be attributed unambiguously to "bottleneck" factors such as rising scrap rates or unfilled job vacancies. In all instances these bottlenecks arose from high labor turnover and training constraints. In one electronics company the scarcity of electronics technicians prompted the company to install simple testing devices operated by semiskilled workers, thereby releasing technicians for the most highly skilled portion of the job, the repair of faulty systems. In another electronics plant an automatic spot welding machine was introduced after a particular welding operation developed quality control problems. Analysis of the problem by the industrial engineering staff revealed that the job required several weeks of training and that high turnover was impeding the training process. Forced either to reclassify the job into a higher labor grade to reduce turnover or to introduce an automatic machine, the company chose the machine. Also frequently encountered were attempts to conserve scarce skills by postponing some of the less-critical skilled work, such as preventive maintenance.

Companies also considered ways of redesigning jobs so that they could be filled by women, a more readily available source of labor than men. Several apparel companies substituted pneumatic pressing machines for older, foot-operated models so that they could be operated more easily, and two machine tool companies began to recruit women for light drilling and lathe operations. The latter arrangement did not entail job redesign per se, but required a reorientation of foremen's attitudes and the conversion of lavatory facilities.

Implications for Structural Balance

The efficacy of adjustments in productive techniques as a mechanism for achieving structural balance in the labor market may be questioned on several grounds. First, in order to avoid structural imbalance, rather than simply to eliminate imbalances once they appear, the enterprise must anticipate changes in relative wages, and it is not at all clear that it can do so. Second, the elasticity of substitution among types of labor may be limited by fixed capital equipment. To the extent that this is so, existing equipment will inhibit adjustment until it is replaced with equipment whose labor requirements are compatible with the available labor supply. Third, there is considerable evidence that relative wage rates, particularly within a plant, respond imperfectly to market scarcities.[20] Scarcities will then make themselves felt in other components of cost—hiring, training, labor productivity, and the like—but such costs are difficult to isolate and attribute to different types of labor. Finally, one important determinant of productive technique, technological innovation, is exogenous to the neoclassical model. Several theorists have attempted to deduce mechanisms from the accepted neoclassical assumptions which would subject the impact of innovative activity upon factor proportions to market control. But they have thus far been unsuccessful.[21] Very little is known about the way in which

[20] See, for example, Lloyd Ulman, "Labor Mobility and the Industrial Wage Structure in the Postwar United States," *Quarterly Journal of Economics,* vol. LXXXIX (Feb. 1965), pp. 73-97; Guy Routh, *Occupation and Pay in Great Britain 1906-1960* (Cambridge, England: Cambridge University Press, 1965); E. Robert Livernash, "The Internal Wage Structure" in George W. Taylor and Frank C. Pierson (eds.), *New Concepts in Wage Determination* (New York: McGraw-Hill Co., 1957); and G. H. Hildebrand, "External Influences and the Determination of the Internal Wage Structure" in J.L. Meij (ed.), *Internal Wage Structure* (Amsterdam: North Holland Publishing Co., 1963), pp. 260-299.

[21] See, for example, Paul A. Samuelson, "A Theory of Induced Innovation along Kennedy-Weisacker Lines," *Review of Economics and Statistics,* vol. XLVII (No-

the search for innovation is conducted and the extent to which it is influenced by relative labor scarcities.

Succinctly put by one engineer, enterprises "mold men to jobs, not jobs
to men." The procedures used within the enterprise to select productive
techniques do not respond to the relative scarcities of different types of
labor, although they appear to be consistent with the assumption of cost
minimization.[22] Engineers frequently maintained that the cost of tailoring
jobs to the available labor force was simply unwarranted by the gains to be
had from doing so. This implies that, if major structural bottlenecks develop, widening cost differentials between various types of labor will eventually overcome the cost of considering alternative manning arrangements,
and enterprises will be induced to seek out techniques which substitute
surplus labor for the kinds of labor in short supply.[23]

The implication of the internal adjustment instruments for aggregate
economic policy is that the pressure of costs arising from the adjustment
process rather than unemployment is likely to be the more serious aggregate labor market problem. None of the instruments of adjustment is
truly "free." If changes in technology were used to overcome labor scarcities, long-term savings generated by the new productive techniques could
be offset against the short-run costs of the investment. As has been indicated, however, enterprises cannot identify many of the costs of adjustment. Adjustment costs, therefore, are not accurately anticipated and,
when they are incurred, they appear as costs of current output. These
costs can, in turn, be translated into the inflationary pressure which accompanies falling unemployment.

These conclusions must be interpreted cautiously. The failings of the
neoclassical adjustments within the manufacturing plant are not of recent
origin; therefore, they cannot be responsible for any of the structural mal-
adjustments alleged to have arisen in the recent past. The data do suggest that, in attempting to explain that degree of structural balance which
has been achieved, and in assessing the capacity of the economy to effect
such balance in the future, attention must focus upon other adjustment
mechanisms. The important mechanisms may be others suggested by

---

vember 1965), pp. 343-356. This article also incidentally reviews the earlier literature on the subject.

[22] There was some discussion in the interviews of engineers who became so interested in the technical perfection of their designs that they ignored cost consideration. But the managerial personnel who participated in the study were so clearly
preoccupied with costs that any simplistic abrogation of the cost minimization assumption appeared untenable.

[23] On the other hand, the search and design procedures had been institutionalized
They were not subject to periodic review and, hence, had become resistant to change,
Extreme and persistent labor bottlenecks may be required to overcome these institutional barriers. Even the wartime labor shortages do not appear to have produced revisions in design procedures.

neoclassical theory: the selection of productive technique in nonmanufac-turing enterprises, the substitution of capital for labor,[24] shifts in the distribution of product demand among plants and industries, or changes in the composition of the labor force.

[24] The fact that the average plant wage rate did influence design suggests that, as long as the wage structure reflects relative scarcities, some adjustment to these scarcities will be effected through shifts in demand among plants. Plants which are intensive in scarce labor will, for example, have a greater inducement to substitute capital than plants intensive in surplus labor. The use of an average wage rate may, however, lead to paradoxical results. It may explain Malcolm Cohen's finding that, in certain labor markets, a rise in the wage of skilled workers relative to unskilled workers leads to an increase in the employment of the skilled relative to the un-skilled. Malcolm Cohen, "Determinants of the Relative Supply and Demand for Unskilled Workers," unpub. diss., Massachusetts Institute of Technology, 1967.

Chapter 7
Racial Discrimination in Internal Labor Markets

In analyzing the problem of employment discrimination and in developing remedies, internal labor markets play a central role. Such markets, as shown in earlier chapters, are designed intentionally to "discriminate." They do so by selecting workers at the ports of entry and by conferring privileges upon the internal labor force not available to those in the external labor market. Discrimination arises because of the job security and advancement opportunities which exist for the internal work force and because of the economies of developing and retaining a trained work force which the internal market provides to employers. Discrimination in this sense has a clear economic and social rationale for both employers and workers and need not have racial implications.

Racial discrimination, however, does occur through the rules which define internal labor markets and govern their operation. Sometimes the discrimination is an incidental by-product of distinctions made for other purposes—for example, when educational requirements which exclude more blacks than whites are used as a screening device, or when employers in white suburbs recruit workers exclusively from among local residents. In other cases, race is a significant consideration in decisions affecting entry, internal allocation, and wages.

Before 1964 it was common, especially in the South, for race to be an explicit determinant in hiring and promotion patterns. Since 1964 and the passage of Title VII of the Civil Rights Act, written rules no longer make mention of race. Substitute rules, however, are written with race in mind, and informal customs are continued in order to maintain racial employment patterns.

This chapter focuses upon employment discrimination in the internal labor market and the problem of formulating remedies. In the first section, theories of employment discrimination are examined; in the second, various types of internal discrimination are discussed; the third section analyzes the role of unions in effecting discrimination; and the fourth deals with remedial arrangements.

Legal and Economic Concepts of Employment Discrimination

Where discrimination results in the exclusion of racial minorities from certain jobs it can be dealt with through a variety of policy instruments. The equalization of educational opportunity for blacks and whites, skill training, the elimination of residential segregation, and so forth, constitute a class of programs directed at helping racial minorities to improve their competitive position in the labor market *without changing the rules under which labor markets operate*. In contrast, antidiscrimination legislation is a policy instrument which operates *directly* upon the internal labor market by *changing the rules governing the hiring, allocation, and pricing of labor*. A brief discussion of federal antidiscrimination policies will serve to illustrate the complex of problems surrounding the implementation of such policies.

Legal Concepts

The history of governmental efforts in the field of fair employment practices can be traced to the 1940's. A number of states and cities have regulations prohibiting employment discrimination; racial discrimination by trade unions has been clearly illegal since the Supreme Court decision in the Steele case;[1] and the history of executive orders requiring nondiscriminatory employment practices by Federal contractors extends back to the Roosevelt Administration. For a variety of reasons, however, earlier efforts had a very limited effect and provided little experience upon which to base the policies of the 1960's.[2]

The 1960's witnessed the first serious efforts on the part of the Federal government to attack racial discrimination in employment. The major instruments directed toward this end were the Federal Executive Orders prohibiting racial discrimination by Federal contractors and Title VII of

[1] *Steele v. Louisville and N. R. R.*, 323 U.S. 192 (1944).
[2] Michael I. Sovern, *Legal Restraints on Radical Discrimination in Employment* (New York: The Twentieth Century Fund, 1966), pp. 143-175.

the Civil Rights Act of 1964 banning discrimination by employers or unions. The executive orders have been administered by the Department of Labor's Office of Federal Contract Compliance (OFCC), while the machinery for enforcement of Title VII centers in the Equal Employment Opportunity Commission (EEOC), state and local fair employment practices commissions, and the Federal courts.

Title VII typifies the dilemma of translating conceptually simple anti-discrimination policies into operating programs. The legislation and legislative history surrounding it are brief. They suggest that the Congress started with a naive concept of employment discrimination which assumed that internal labor markets were completely segregated and that unambiguous racial rules were used to exclude minority groups from jobs.[3] As a result, Congress enacted legislation to outlaw employment practices based upon race, while at the same time seeking to protect the legitimate interests of employers in developing a qualified labor force and of incumbent employees in maintaining job security.[4] These twin objectives, as shall be seen, frequently come into conflict in the internal labor market, and one objective cannot be protected without interfering with the other.

Economic Concepts

The view that employment discrimination results in racially segregated internal labor markets has also been incorporated into economic models of discrimination. Gary Becker postulates a model, patterned after the pure theory of international trade, in which blacks and whites inhabit separate societies. These societies freely exchange products, but tariff-like preferences for discrimination, imposed by the white society, restrict exchange in factor markets.[5]

More recently, Lester Thurow developed an alternative theory in which whites act as discriminating monopolists.[6] By virtue of this monopoly power, they establish hierarchical employment relationships, having both economic and social dimensions, in which blacks occupy jobs that are inferior to those held by whites. In Thurow's theory, as in Becker's, racial discrimination is to be understood as a product of a rational attempt of whites to maximize their well-being.

Such an analysis of discrimination is particularly congenial to economists. It suggests that the elimination of discrimination will increase com-

---

[3] See, for example, 110 *Cong. Rec.* 6996 (citation from the daily edition).

[4] See the memorandum on Title VII by Senators Clark and Case, 110 *Cong. Rec.* 6992, and Senator Clark's response to Senator Dirksen's memorandum, pp. 6992, 6997.

[5] See Gary S. Becker, *The Economics of Discrimination* (Chicago: University of Chicago Press, 1957).

[6] Lester C. Thurow, *Poverty and Discrimination* (Washington, D. C.: Brookings Institution, 1969).

petition. Such a step is generally thought to move toward a more efficient use of resources and hence a larger national income. For several reasons, however, such an analysis does not provide a correct understanding of the mechanisms of discrimination, and it implies a degree of harmony among the society's various social and economic goals which is misleading.

Internal Labor Markets

Internal labor markets are established, in part, because the work force values the job security and advancement opportunities which they provide. Inherent in this analysis of the internal labor market is an element of monopoly over jobs. But the internal market is not simply a product of employee interests in job monopoly, it is also the product of employer interests in minimizing the fixed costs of recruitment, hiring, and training. Where these costs exist, it is by no means certain that the abolition of racial discrimination in the internal labor market will raise economic efficiency.

Also, the rules governing the internal market seldom develop from a single factor. They generally represent a compromise between the interests of the employer and employees, and are conceived in the context of the totality of factors governing labor allocation and pricing. Hence, it is not generally possible to change the distribution of jobs between the races without affecting the efficiency of recruitment, screening, and training. The elimination of racial discrimination is likely to raise the inefficiency of the labor force adjustment process, at least in the short run, thereby imposing costs upon both the employer and the society. Only where the effect of discrimination has been to create a grossly inefficient internal labor market will there be offsetting benefits to the employer and society.

Third, the attack upon racial discrimination in internal labor markets occurs within an economic and social context in which, as a general rule, discrimination is permissible and in the interest of *both* the employer and the white work force. The inherent equity of an attack upon *racial* discrimination is thus not always as clear to those within the market as it is to outsiders, and efforts to eliminate racial discrimination are often viewed by the employers and employees as an assault upon the instruments which effect labor market adjustment and preserve job security. Given the difficulty of separating the racial impact of internal allocative rules from their other effects, they may indeed be correct. This is partly true in the case of construction unions which proclaim that it is a concern with training and job security, rather than prejudice, that excludes blacks. Similarly, in enterprise internal labor markets, the seniority and job security of blacks and whites in different departments or job classifications may be at stake if internal discrimination is to be eliminated. In almost all cases the full effects of racial discrimination cannot be remedied without costs being imposed upon the incumbent work force in terms of job security and promotion opportunities. This in turn is often perceived as a threat to the entire rule and equity structure of the internal labor market.

The implication of these considerations is that insofar as Congress intended Title VII to bar rules designed to monopolize employment privileges for one race without interfering with rules developed to achieve other legitimate goals, it imposed a difficult, and perhaps inconsistent, task upon the EEOC and the courts. The theory that racial exclusion is an "all or nothing" type of monopoly and that racial employment practices are embodied in single-purpose administrative rules is incorrect. Most rules governing internal labor markets are not designed to effectuate racial monopoly alone, but are part of the total fabric of labor pricing and allocation. Rules which result in the monopolization of jobs on the basis of race cannot be barred in most cases without impinging upon the efficiency of recruitment, hiring, and training or upon the employment expectations of incumbent employees that have been developed under long-standing allocative rules. Because the several goals which Congress sought to effectuate are not compatible, the courts must weigh the costs to society as a whole and to the various groups within it of the changes in the rules which they are being asked to mandate. The analysis which follows is designed to provide an understanding of these costs.

Types of Discriminatory Practices

In practice, racial discrimination can occur through *any* of the eleven instruments of labor force adjustment: recruitment, screening, compensation, and so forth. There are, however, three major categories of instruments—entry, internal allocation, and wages—through which most employment discrimination is effected.

Entry Discrimination

On its face, entry is the least complex form of employment discrimination. Conditions for entry into most internal labor markets are readily defined, and it should, in principle, be relatively easy to determine whether they discriminate unfairly on the basis of race. If they do, it should not be difficult to eliminate the practices. The superficial simplicity of the problem is, however, deceiving. The identification of discrimination and the fashioning of a remedy is complicated by several factors.

As suggested in earlier chapters, in *enterprise markets,* recruitment, screening, and hiring procedures are among the most loosely constrained instruments of manpower adjustment available to management. These instruments have not generally been the subject of review by either Federal agencies or by trade unions and thus, unlike standards for internal promotion or wage determination, have been largely a management pre-rogative. As such, they have only rarely been evaluated against an objec-tive standard and depend for the most part upon the *judgment* of personnel managers and foremen.

Hiring standards. Hiring standards tend to fluctuate with the state of the external labor market and with changing anticipations of future tech-nology. This permits deliberate discrimination to be practiced under the guise of objective procedures to ensure a competent work force. Thus, when overt discrimination is made illegal, those employers seeking to exclude blacks and other minorities can do so by imposing exceedingly high educational and testing standards.[7] These may then be justified by reference to the requirements of jobs at the top of promotion ladders or to forecasts of changing job requirements. If these requirements prove too restrictive in terms of the added recruitment costs, they can be relaxed ostensibly to adjust to a temporarily tight labor market. In the extreme, the company could relax the standards and hire only when no black appli-cants apply. But this is seldom necessary since minorities soon learn where they will not be hired and do not waste time applying. Here, as elsewhere, it is difficult to administer the law to prevent this evasion without curtailing the legitimate use of hiring instruments to adjust the changing market conditions and job structures.

Additional opportunity for discrimination comes through the hiring process itself. Hiring decisions are often made on the basis of both objec-tive criteria, such as education, and in interviews where more subtle cri-teria such as speech and deportment are applied. Even the managers find such standards difficult to specify, and their informality permits racial discrimination to be practiced. The assertion of effective control over these procedures, whether by a government agency or by the enterprise's own management, requires essentially the same type of modification in hir-ing rules that occurs in internal promotion procedures when a union organizes a plant and forces the foreman to operate within the framework of a collective agreement.

Screening criteria. Entry discrimination may also be seen in the *screen-ing criteria* used to implement hiring standards. As indicated in Chapter 5, the only true test of ability for most jobs is performance on the job.

---

[7] The operation of education as a screening device can be discerned in the empirical relationship between education, on the one hand, and unemployment and income on the other. See Harry J. Gilman, "Economic Discrimination and Unemployment," *American Economic Review*, vol. LV, no. 5, part 1 (December 1965), pp. 1077-1096. Stephan Michaelson has demonstrated, however, that the narrowing of educational differences between blacks and whites in recent years has not been accompanied by a corresponding reduction in income differentials. See Stephan Michaelson, "Rational Income Decisions of Negroes and Everybody Else," *Industrial and Labor Relations Review*, vol. XXIII, no. 1 (October 1969), pp.15-28.

The criteria upon which hiring decisions are based are surrogates for such performance, and there is little evidence of a causal relationship between the two. They may be statistically correlated, but such a relationship is seldom empirically validated. Instead, the screening criteria (like hiring standards) are based upon the subjective judgments of line supervision and personnel managers whose perceptions may be distorted by prejudice.[8]

Because hiring standards and screening criteria are not perfectly correlated with job performance, they are subject to two kinds of error: rejecting a qualified candidate and accepting an unqualified one. There is a trade-off between these two errors, and they can only be reduced simultaneously by increasing the costs of screening. As indicated in Chapter 5, internal markets provide job security by making discharges difficult, and the employer, faced with choosing to reduce one error at the expense of the other, will most often reject workers who are actually qualified but whose qualifications are expensive to uncover. In the case of minority groups, inadequate experience in developing suitable screening criteria may, at least initially, raise screening costs and therefore deter their employment.

Some portion of what appears to be racial discrimination is probably generated by these costs. Race is an inexpensive screening criterion. Where two racial populations differ significantly in terms of the proportion of persons possessing certain desired characteristics, the most efficient hiring policy may be simply to reject all members of one racial population.

Congress appears to have been completely unaware of this problem when it passed the Civil Rights Act of 1964. It meant to require that candidates be admitted solely on the basis of ability, and it sought to legislate the hiring of *qualified* candidates. Because of the statistical nature of hiring criteria, any rule which admits *all* qualified workers will inevitably admit some of the unqualified: a rule that excludes the unqualified ones will exclude some qualified as well. While the conflict cannot be eliminated, it can be reduced, but only through screening procedures which impose costs in excess of those to which Congress intended to commit the society in Title VII.

Recruitment. A final aspect of the problem of entry discrimination relates to recruitment procedures. Internal labor markets tend to establish rather stable channels of recruitment. Most important are the incumbent employees who refer friends and relatives to the internal market.[9] Supple-

---

[8] See Ivar Berg, *Education and Jobs: The Great Training Robbery* (New York: Praeger Publishers, 1970).

[9] See Chapter 5. Also see Lloyd G. Reynolds, *The Structure of Labor Markets* (New York: Harper & Bros., 1951); and Harold L. Shepperd and A. Harvey Belitsky, *The Job Hunt* (Baltimore: Johns Hopkins Press, 1966).

mentary channels include community organizations (churches, civic groups, and the like), a select group of educational institutions, various types of employment agencies, and a limited list of advertising media. Depending upon the state of the external labor market, some or all of these channels may be active, but their number is definitely limited.

Reliance upon a narrow set of recruitment channels has advantages to both the employer and to potential employees. For the employer, it acts, in part, as a screening procedure. Candidates recruited in the customary way tend, again as a statistical proposition, to have certain known characteristics. In the case of recruitment through relatives and friends, applicant characteristics tend to resemble those of the incumbent labor force. Similarly, formal recruiting channels yield applicants who, as a group, possess certain predictable traits. Moreover, potential candidates learn to check regularly with established recruiting channels so that a given advertising effort evokes a larger and quicker response in established channels than it does in new ones. Recruitment through established channels has similar advantages to applicants. Friends, relatives, and counsellors can give them a better picture of the prospective employment, and this reduces the costs of trial-and-error job search. This also results in a certain amount of self-screening by the candidate. Those who *expect* not to be hired or not to like the job do not apply.

These benefits encourage any set of recruitment channels to be perpetuated once they are established, and discriminatory recruitment practices will continue to yield racial employment patterns long after discriminatory intent has been removed. To break the existing patterns, employers must establish new channels which reach minority groups, and this may require a prolonged period of investment before the new channels become as efficient as the old. For example, the cheapest source of referrals—incumbent employees—often cannot serve as a source of minority recruits. New recruitment channels, such as black newspapers, even when essentially comparable in cost to white newspapers, may not immediately yield as large a candidate group because the black community will not necessarily respond to this recruitment. Thus, in recruitment, as in hiring and screening, the elimination of racially biased employment patterns may impose additional costs upon the enterprise and upon the society as well.

Internal Allocative Rules

Racial discrimination *within* the internal market is effected in two ways: in the design of mobility clusters and in the criteria which determine movement within or between them. As with entry discrimination, black workers can be denied promotion by restrictive promotion criteria or by limitations upon the posting and bidding arrangements for internal recruitment. Thus, for example, employers in many southern plants have introduced written tests for promotion in an attempt to evade the requirements of Title VII. Some employers have also shifted from a system of posting vacancies to one based upon word of mouth.

There is, however, at least in enterprise markets, an important difference between the rules producing entry discrimination and those resulting in internal discrimination: the former rules are loosely constrained and variable, the latter are more precisely defined. In general, internal allocative rules, being less nebulous than entry rules, cannot be as readily adjusted to mask continuing discrimination.

Where internal discrimination does pose unique problems is in the design of mobility clusters. The patterns of racial discrimination in promotion systems can, for the most part, be divided into three broad categories (see Figures 5-7). The least common type (Figure 5) consists of two functionally identical mobility clusters which are racially distinct: the two contain the same types of jobs, skill requirements, and upgrading opportunities. This is, in essence, the arrangement which existed with respect to the employment of the black and white firemen, and of white railway trainmen and black brakemen on some railroads during the 1940's and 1950's.[10]

A more typical arrangement is shown in Figure 6. Here blacks are restricted to the lower-paying job classifications and mobility clusters. In some establishments classifications for blacks may be unrelated, in terms of on-the-job training, job content, or the focus of work, to other jobs within the market, but there are also examples of apparently efficient training sequences being arbitrarily interrupted to limit the advancement opportunities of persons in the lower-paying job classifications. In one steel company, for example, skill-related lines of progression were divided so that the unskilled jobs were reserved for blacks, and the more skilled jobs for whites.[11] Traditionally blacks were excluded from white progression lines, but arrangements were subsequently negotiated between the company and the union to permit incumbent blacks to transfer into the bottom rung on the white progression ladder. No transfer of competitive seniority rights was permitted, however.

The third type of discriminatory promotion system, shown in Figure 7, restricts blacks to separate units such as labor pools, less desirable production, warehouse, yard departments, or unskilled job classifications which are unrelated to other jobs in terms of promotion. In the extreme case, blacks may be located in a geographically separate production

---

[10] See *Steele v. Louisville and N. R. R., op. cit.,* and *Railway Trainmen v. Howard* [343 N. S. 768] (1952).

[11] See *Whitfield v. U.S. Steelworkers, Local 2708,* 263 F. 2d. 546 cert. denied 360 N. S. 902 (1959) also, *NLRB v. Rubber Workers,* 150 NLRB 312 (1964).

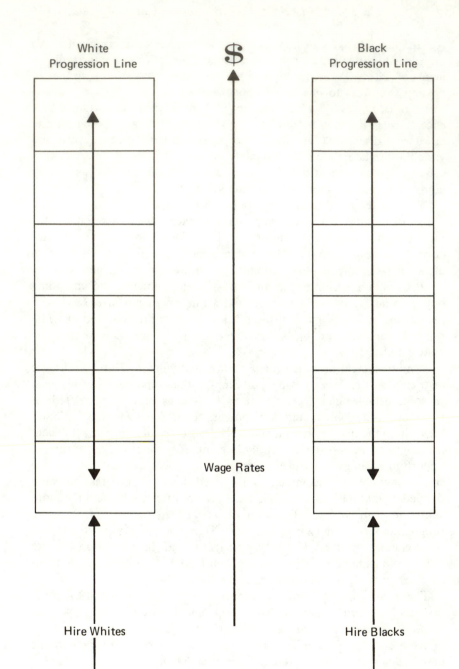

Figure 5. Functionally identical progression lines with racial segregation.

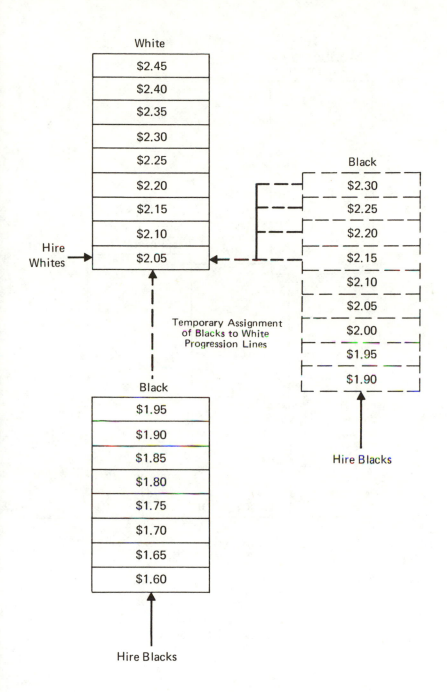

Figure 6. Functionally related progression lines with racial segregation.

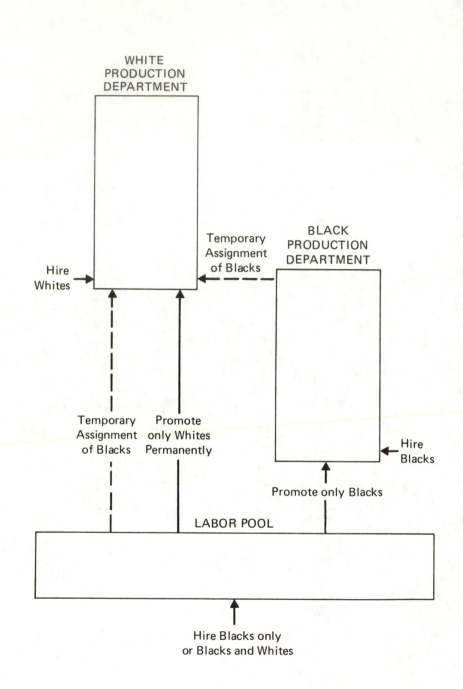

Figure 7. Functionally unrelated promotion units with racial segregation.

facility. Here the functional relationships among black and white mobility clusters are tenuous or nonexistent. While the discrimination may be inferred from the racial composition of the various mobility clusters, discrimination in the design of the promotion system cannot be distinguished from discrimination in hiring or assignment. In some cases the mobility clusters may be reinforced by separate union locals, by NLRB bargaining unit certifications, or by NLRB certifications which have excluded certain groups of workers, such as laborers or janitors, from any bargaining unit.

For example, janitors in a southern telephone company, all of whom were black, were not included in the bargaining unit.[12] In another case a southern paper company was organized into two racially segregated locals. The blacks were employed in the lower-paying jobs, and separate collective agreements were negotiated for the black and white units.[13]

Segregation of promotion units may be formally embodied in local collective bargaining agreements or may exist as part of the uncodified, informal procedure by which workers are assigned to, or allowed to bid for, jobs within the internal labor market. Whether by the design of mobility clusters or through bidding and assignment practices, the net result of these systems has been to reduce the economic opportunities of blacks in the past. This in turn has limited their opportunities to acquire either the requisite in-plant training or the transferable seniority credits to enable them to compete for present and future promotions on an equal basis with incumbent whites.

Wage Discrimination

Determining the extent of wage discrimination is analogous to identifying the impact of unions upon wage rates. Statistical estimation techniques are always hampered by problems of "spillover effects" and collinearity.[14] Most studies of the economic impact of wage discrimination have been limited to comparing the existing income distribution of nonwhites to the hypothetical distribution which would prevail under various assumptions regarding equalizing of white and nonwhite employment opportunities.[15] No studies, however, have attempted to measure the

---

[12] Cited in William B. Gould, "Employment Security, Seniority and Race: The Role of Title VII of the Civil Rights Act of 1964," *Howard Law Journal,* vol. XIII, (Winter 1967), p. 15.

[13] *United States v. Local 189, Papermakers,* U.S. District Court, March 26, 1968, Civil No. 68-205. A similar situation also held in *Syres v. Oil Workers* U.S. Court of Appeals Fifth Circuit No. 15286, June 1955.

[14] See, for example, H. Gregg Lewis, *Unionism and Relative Wages in the United States* (Chicago: University of Chicago Press, 1963).

[15] See, for example, Thurow, *op. cit.*

impact of wage discrimination at the enterprise level. Much of this section must therefore be speculative.

Inherent in the design of discriminatory seniority systems is an element of wage discrimination. Whenever discrimination prevents blacks from advancing into higher-paying, more desirable jobs in production, maintenance, or supervisory mobility clusters, they will continue to remain economically disadvantaged relative to the white employees within any particular internal labor market.

Other forms of wage discrimination also exist. First, to the extent that discrimination within the internal labor market leads to a clear demarcation between black and white jobs in the economy, noncompeting groups of jobs are established which cut across a number of internal labor market units. The result of such a market dichotomy must ultimately be reflected in relative wage rates between these groups unless supply and demand change uniformly in both markets over time.

In theory, this market dichotomy could work in favor of either racial group. There is some evidence, however, of actions by white workers to exploit this dichotomy by systematically seeking to drive black workers from traditionally black jobs in order to expand the demand for white labor. In the railroads, for example, attempts have been made to preempt jobs for white employees by declaring black firemen and black brakemen "unpromotable" or "unassignable."[16] Similarly, in the trowel trades during the depression and in many of the rapidly expanding industrial sectors in the South, such as textiles and cigarettes, the jurisdiction of the white labor force expanded at the expense of the black labor force when job opportunities were scarce or when wages and working conditions were improved.[17]

It is difficult to estimate the extent to which this separation of markets has affected relative wages. Historically, there has been a wider skilled-unskilled wage differential in the South than in any other region of the country. The traditional explanation for this is the relatively greater scarcity of skilled labor in the South, but some portion of this differential is also probably due to the depressing effects of black "spillover" upon the unskilled wage rate.

The internal wage structure can also be discriminatory. First, external labor market discrimination will be incorporated into the wage rates on the jobs which blacks are most likely to occupy because the unskilled wage rate on the external labor market is transmitted to the lower ranges of the enterprise wage structure through community wage surveys and job evaluation plans. Second, jobs which are filled through internal promotion

[16] See *Steele v. Louisville and N. R. R., op. cit.*
[17] See F. Ray Marshall, *The Negro Worker* (New York: Random House, 1967), p. 82.

of blacks may be undervalued through the unequal application of job evaluation criteria. In one southern plant, for example, blacks have traditionally been hired only for a few of the most menial jobs (janitors, for instance) and, although other rates were set through job evaluation plans and community surveys, these jobs have never been evaluated at all, and belong to no labor grade. Their rates are always 10 to 15 cents below the entry wage for other jobs.

There are a number of reasons to believe *a priori* that internal wage equity has not been assiduously maintained in cases where discriminatory promotion systems are also operating. First, it has been customary, especially in the South, to relate wage rates on black jobs to one another, rather than to comparable white jobs. This has led to different wage rates on identical jobs, such as elevator operators or forklift truck drivers, which are common to black and white departments. Second, given prevalent attitudes about the tolerance of blacks for unpleasant work, it would not be surprising if job classifications held by blacks have been undervalued in terms of working conditions. Moreover, if managements have devoted greater efforts to improving working conditions in white jobs than in black jobs, this disparity is likely to have increased over time.

Little evidence is available on this matter, but in at least one cigarette company it was discovered that separate rates were being paid to two different job classifications common to black and white departments. In both cases, machine operations required similar use of tools, responsibility, and skill, but the job classification in the black department was paid less than in the white department. The wage differentials were 3.6 per cent and 13.4 per cent respectively.[18] If it is assumed that job evaluation plans and interpersonal wage comparisons encourage greater consistency of wage structures within mobility clusters than between them, then there is reason to believe that the entire black mobility cluster was underpaid. Conversations with employers and union officials further suggest that problems of wage equity and of wage grievances are generally given much less consideration in black jobs than in white jobs.

Trade Unions

Very little has been said in the preceding sections about trade union responsibility for internal market rules. To the extent that trade unions simply express employees' interests, this omission is not unreasonable. It is consistent with the belief that the rules observed in union shops are similar to the *customary* laws governing nonunion internal markets, and that the major impact of the trade union is not to create rules but to make them visible to the outsider.

[18] See *Quarles v. Phillip Morris, Inc.* 279 F. Supp. 505 (1968).

However appropriate this treatment of trade unions is for analysis elsewhere in the volume, it is less satisfactory in the present context. The attempt to eliminate discrimination by law presupposes an individual or institutional responsibility for that discrimination against which sanctions can be sought, and this creates the practical problems, at some juncture, of assessing responsibility between employer and trade union.

Types of union practices. Unions have actually adopted a variety of positions with respect to employment discrimination. In some cases, most notably the United Mine Workers in the South, unions have opposed existing patterns of discrimination and have gradually accomplished some reduction in the discrimination against minority groups within their jurisdiction.[19] More commonly unions have merely codified existing patterns of discrimination and, by formalizing what previously were discriminatory customs, have fixed these patterns more firmly. While this process tends to deter the elimination of discrimination, it has sometimes protected black employment rights against further encroachment by whites. Finally, some unions have actively extended discrimination by seeking to push blacks out of jobs and replace them with whites.[20]

Perhaps the best way to illustrate the latter two union effects, the codification of customary rules and the displacement of blacks, is by detailed reference to the case of a southern paper mill. This mill was organized by Paper Workers in the late thirties, and in 1966, the black employees were confined by the collective bargaining agreement to the labor pool and to a few short lines of progression containing menial or undesirable jobs in the pulp mill.[21] Before the plant was organized, blacks had apparently worked all over the plant, but usually at laborers' wages. Although the custom was to assign blacks only to menial jobs, this system was abridged in various ways (prior to the union). For example, a white craftsman might occasionally "adopt" a black worker, teach him some parts of the trade, and use him as an assistant to lighten his work load. Or the foreman, in an emergency when nobody else was available, might assign a black worker temporarily to a normally white job and then, if he did well, might reassign him subsequently. Occasionally, the job would go to the black worker on a permanent basis when it became vacant, and some "white" job classifications eventually became "black."

After the plant was organized, the practice of assigning blacks to menial jobs was formally codified in the collective agreement. There was, however, one critical change. Whereas previously the assignment of blacks to jobs occurred informally, and temporary assignment of black workers to

[19] See Marshall, *The Negro Worker, op. cit.,* and F. Ray Marshall, *Labor in the South* (Cambridge, Mass.: Harvard University Press, 1967).
[20] See *Steele v. Louisville and N. R. R., op. cit.*
[21] For a similar case see *Hicks v. Crown-Zellerbach Corp.* 69 L.R.R.M. 2005.

white jobs could sometimes create new precedents for allocative patterns, such "accidental" precedents were not allowed under the formal contract. As a result, the union, in codifying the broad outlines of allocative custom and in policing the agreement, forced conformity with prevailing custom and aborted what might otherwise have been an evolution toward wider black job opportunity. The effect was to push blacks back into menial jobs, not by creating rules, but by writing them down.

While it could be said that, by requiring a codification of prevailing custom, the union is responsible for the discrimination, it is not clear how helpful that observation is in the formulation of a remedy. There is a complex interplay between custom, codification of rules, and the union's expression of white employees' interests, which may confuse the analysis of union responsibility for discriminatory practices.

Craft vs. enterprise markets. In understanding the influence of unions upon employment discrimination it is also useful to bear in mind the distinction between enterprise and craft internal markets. This is particularly important when considering institutional responsibility for remedies.

In enterprise markets the union's role in determining and administering allocative and wage structures tends to be relatively passive. Management plays the active role in initiating decisions, and it is managerial activity which must be reviewed when discriminatory practices are being eliminated. In craft markets the union usually plays the active role, and its administrative practices must be controlled. Thus, for example, in the construction industry the union controls the hiring hall, and it is union activity which therefore must be monitored.

The second difference between enterprise and craft markets is that, in the former, job security is usually achieved through control over internal allocation, while, in the latter, security is effected through control over entry. As a result, discrimination in craft markets tends to manifest itself in racial exclusion, while in enterprise markets it operates through the rules governing compensation and internal movement as well as entry.

Entry standards in craft markets are not generally as responsive to variations in external market conditions as they are in enterprise markets. The security which in enterprise markets is supplied by seniority and limited entry ports is provided in many craft markets by limiting entry criteria, and these are not loosened merely because the external market is temporarily tight. This does not mean that entry procedures are necessarily more formal in craft markets. Indeed they can be quite informal and subjective.

Craft markets appear to rely even more heavily upon relatives and friends for recruitment than do enterprise markets. In part this is explained by the unions' control over entry decisions as a means of generating job security, and the bias this imparts toward the interests of the labor force. Because all members of a single craft are generally paid the same rate, and because underqualified craftsmen can weigh down the group productivity to which the pay rate is linked, there is a countervailing concern with the qualifications of new entrants. But this conflict has, at least historically, been resolved in favor of relatives and friends to a far greater extent than is the case in enterprise markets. In any event, the unfamiliarity with the use of formal recruitment mechanisms which results from this extreme dependence upon relatives and friends may be in part responsible for the difficulties which construction unions report in recruiting minority apprenticeship candidates.

Remedies for Discrimination

Entry Discrimination

As was seen in the earlier sections, racial employment patterns generated by entry discrimination are closely connected to: (1) the informality of the screening and recruitment process, (2) the variations in this process caused by changes in job content and in external market conditions, (3) the statistical nature of screening, and (4) the advantages to employers and workers of reliance upon a limited set of recruitment channels. These characteristics of hiring make certain exclusions on the basis of race economically efficient, quite independent of racial prejudice or the desire of workers to limit entry and monopolize jobs. Moreover, they provide a means of evading legal prohibitions upon racial discrimination which is difficult to eliminate without interfering with nondiscriminatory hiring practices in a way which limits the economic efficiency of the enterprise. In formulating remedies for discrimination, government agencies and the courts must balance the elimination of racially discriminatory employment patterns against economic efficiency.

The analysis embodied in this volume is of little immediate aid in weighing these conflicting social goals. The analysis does imply, however, that the costs of changing hiring standards will vary with the conditions surrounding each internal market and points to a philosophy of case-by-case adjudication rather than to the creation of a set of general rules to apply to all employment situations. It can also provide some indication of interactions between various aspects of industrial relations policies which may not be intuitively obvious and which may be helpful in assessing evidence and in fashioning remedies in individual cases.

Informality of screening procedures. To achieve any degree of control over discrimination occurring through screening procedures will require the formalization, precise definition, and validation of screening criteria.[22]

[22] Formality, for example, creates rigidity in those procedures and can make integration of the internal labor market easier. In a number of cases, building

This is most obvious in the case of screening decisions based upon deportment during employment interviews. Similarly, the evaluation of test scores and educational requirements as predictors of job performance will also be necessary to avoid the substitution of *de facto* for *de jure* discriminatory rules.

Screening criteria and promotion ladders. The extent to which the requirements of higher-level jobs to which entry positions provide access should be permitted to justify excessively high *entry* qualifications depends very much upon the structure of the internal labor market and the rules governing internal movement. Of particular importance is the "shape" of the seniority districts or lines of progression. When districts are pyramidal so that the number of employees at each level of progression is in excess of the number at the level above, higher-level jobs need not necessarily determine entry qualifications inasmuch as nonpromotable employees can be bypassed.[23] Where the progression line is a narrow ladder with one job at each level the requirements of higher-level jobs loom much larger in entry criteria. In all cases, the *rate* of promotion and the proportion of "nonpromotables" already employed will also determine the relationship between screening criteria and the requirements of jobs filled internally.

The weights attached to seniority and ability and the degree to which jobs in the same line are training-related are also relevant in assessing the legitimacy of screening criteria. The strongest case for highly restrictive criteria is in internal markets which give great weight to seniority for internal labor allocation and where jobs in a promotion line are training-related. When promotion districts do not encompass training-related jobs, and the employer is not obligated to promote by seniority, unqualified

---

trades unions have been persuaded to state the conditions and times under which workers can compete for openings in apprenticeship programs. This has provided civil rights organizations with an opportunity to prepare minority group workers to compete for jobs under a fixed set of "rules of the game." In New York City, the Workers' Defense League has been able to recruit and to train black teenagers in a "preapprenticeship" program to enable them to gain entrance to previously all-white programs. In this way, rules which may have been established to exclude blacks can also serve as a device for undermining discrimination. See Edward C. Pinkus, "The Workers' Defense League" in Peter B. Doeringer (ed.), *Programs to Employ the Disadvantaged* (Englewood Cliffs, N.J.:Prentice-Hall, Inc., 1969).

But rigidity also has its costs. When flexibility of one instrument of manpower adjustment is reduced, other, less efficient instruments must be utilized, thereby raising overall adjustment costs.

[23] Some companies with lines of this shape use dual screening criteria: they carefully screen enough candidates to ensure that among the entrants there will be a sufficient number qualified for promotion. The remainder of the candidates are screened less carefully: they have an equal opportunity for promotion if qualified, but the company knows less about their qualifications at the time of hire.

workers can be bypassed without a loss of efficiency, and there is less reason for entry into lower-level jobs to be tied to qualifications of higher-level work.

The anticipation of technological change. It is difficult to evaluate the proposition that screening criteria are related to anticipated technological change, since the skill requirements of technological change are inherently difficult to predict. Nonetheless, it is important to bear in mind the point, emphasized in Chapter 6, that initial estimates of the skill requirements for new technologies are generally adjusted downward over time. As a result, the long-run skill requirements of machinery are generally exaggerated by looking at the requirements when it is introduced. The proposition should also be evaluated against the internal allocative rules. Where the rules give great weight to ability in internal promotion, an employer is not necessarily obligated to man new technologies with incumbent employees, and entry decisions need not be as closely tied to anticipated technological change.

External market conditions. Day-to-day *variations* in screening criteria which systematically result in the exclusion of black candidates cannot be readily separated from the legitimate response of employers to external market conditions. Nonetheless, if such a discriminatory policy is pursued over a period in which there is a flow of black applicants, it should be accompanied by other adjustments in manpower utilization in the enterprise. Not hiring workers on days in which the flow of black applicants is large will either result in job vacancies and uncovered positions, in overmanning as the enterprise attempts to stockpile labor against days on which hiring is deterred, or in erratic subcontracting. This is, at best, circumstantial evidence of discriminatory intent, but it should not be overlooked in assessing the fairness of screening practices.

Quotas and targets. In considering remedies to entry discrimination it should be noted that racial employment quotas are an alternative to formalizing and validating screening procedures or specifying certain recruitment procedures. Quotas have the advantage of specifying a desired set of results without tying the employer to a particular set of remedies which may be particularly inconsistent with efficient resolution of the problem.

The use of quotas and targets is a matter of some controversy and is generally thought to be prohibited by Title VII of the Civil Rights Act which says:

> Nothing in this title shall be interpreted to require any employer
> . . . [or] labor organization . . . to grant preferential treatment to any
> individual or to any group . . . on account of an imbalance which may
> exist with respect to the total number or percentage of persons of any
> race . . . employed by any employer . . . referred by any labor organ-

ization . . . or admitted to . . . any apprenticeship program, in comparison with the total or percentage of persons of such race . . . in any community.[24]

Quotas, however, probably provide the most effective device for ensuring results. Even where not binding, they may be an especially useful management instrument for convincing operating personnel of the need for demonstrating results as opposed to token compliance with remedial procedures. Quotas are a complete substitute for other remedies and render concern with procedural details, such as the validation of testing procedures, unnecessary.

Promotion Systems

As in the case of entry discrimination, remedying discrimination in internal allocation involves conflicts among several interests which Congress failed to recognize in the passage of Title VII. In most enterprise markets, the design of mobility clusters is a "zero sum game" in which gains in promotion opportunities or job security by one group of workers must always be offset by equivalent losses for other groups of workers. There are, in other words, a fixed number of jobs; if blacks get them, whites do not. Moreover, seniority and promotion arrangements are work rules around which internal customs become exceedingly strong, and changes in such customs tend to be viewed as inequitable, independent of any racial consideration.[25] If this conflict is to be avoided, employers must incur the costs of increasing the number, and possibly the wage rates, of the jobs whose distribution is in question.

Discovering the appropriate balance among the costs to the enterprise, the disrupted employment expectations of white workers, and the employment claims of black workers requires normative decisions which cannot be calculated through technical analysis of the internal labor market. Given a set of normative decisions, however, such analysis should help in constructing efficient remedies to implement them.

Types of remedies. The diversity of internal market structures is so great, and the range of potential remedies so numerous that it is difficult to develop general solutions. It may be helpful, however, to point out that the suggestions in recent law journal discussions have tended to polarize around two positions, whereas the actual range of remedies is considerably broader.[26]

At one extreme are those which end discrimination in the hiring of

---

[24] Sec. 703(j) P.L. 83-392, Civil Rights Act of 1964.

[25] See Archibald Cox, "The Duty of Fair Representation," *2 Villanova Law Review* 151, p. 164.

[26] See, for example, "Title VII, Seniority Discrimination and the Incumbent Negro," *Harvard Law Review,* vol. LXXX, no. 6 (April 1967), pp. 1260-1283.

blacks and which offer incumbent black workers access to jobs in previous white mobility clusters in preference to new hires. Under this arrangement, the job security and promotion opportunities of incumbent white employees are completely protected, and discrimination against newly hired blacks is prevented. This is subject to the criticism that it tends to freeze a generation of incumbent black employees into their present mobility clusters, while protecting white promotion expectations that have been acquired under previously discriminatory employment rules.

At the opposite pole is the "freedom now" position. Its proponents argue that past discrimination has deprived Negro employees of their "rightful place" in the job structure of the internal labor market, and that the present effects of past discrimination can only be eliminated by transferring black workers into white mobility clusters as rapidly as possible.[27]

Within this range are an infinite number of combinations of changes in both the scope of the promotion unit and in the rules governing the criteria determining internal mobility. These intermediate remedies have received considerably less discussion in the current literature, but, given the complexity of the interests to be weighed, it is likely that intermediate rather than extreme solutions will ultimately be adopted by government agencies and the courts.

Possible changes in the scope of promotion units include arrangements such as:

1. Dovetailing functionally identical black and white progression lines by merging similar job classifications.
2. Broadening the scope of the promotion unit through the merger of white and black units by job grade, seniority date, or other objective criteria.
3. Removing barriers to transfer between black and white promotion units.
4. Merging less-skilled black and white job classifications to form multidepartment pools or "pans" for the exercise of promotion or transfer rights among the lower-skilled, more easily learned jobs, combined with a narrow promotion unit structure for higher-skilled jobs.

Changes in the rules governing priorities and criteria for determining promotions, transfers, and layoffs include:

1. Modifications in job bidding and posting procedures to give black employees a systematic mechanism for gaining access to previously white job classifications.
2. Allowing black workers to retain partial seniority credits acquired

[27] *Ibid.*

in black promotion districts when transferring into white promotion districts.

3. Modifications in promotion clauses to relax the ability criterion by providing trial periods for promotions, instituting longer training periods to test ability to perform a job, and recognizing an employee's potential for training, as well as his job experience.

4. Establishing programs for upgrading the skills of the lower-paid employees in the plant, to enhance their promotion qualifications within the existing rules system.

Job security. In redesigning seniority districts to end promotion discrimination, it is important to remember that changes which affect promotion opportunities will also affect job security. For example, if black employees are permitted to transfer into previously white promotion districts, but do not retain accumulated seniority rights for purposes of bumping back into their former districts, enhanced promotion opportunity will carry with it costs of foregone job security. Similarly, if racially determined promotion districts are merged, white workers may be able to displace black workers during layoffs. In short, any rearrangement of promotion systems will result in an extraordinarily complex redistribution of benefits, expectations, and preferences for internal mobility among both white and black workers which is difficult to anticipate.

Employer costs. As noted earlier, remedies for discriminatory promotion systems almost always involve additional costs for employers as well as employees. These costs include increases in the average amount of on-the-job training which must be provided when filling internal vacancies, concomitant changes in the costs of other instruments of adjustment, and reduced productivity as a result of morale problems which may accompany alterations in employee expectations. These costs will vary systematically with the type of internal market structure and the type of remedy introduced.

When racial segregation takes the form of identical mobility clusters, or of clusters in which the less-skilled jobs in a skill progression sequence are separated from the more skilled jobs (as in Figures 5 and 6), merging the mobility clusters will permit black workers in the lower-skilled jobs to transfer some of their training to higher-skilled jobs in the sequence. In some cases this may reduce training costs, but it may also be accompanied by an increase in the hiring standards on the least-skilled entry jobs, thereby raising recruiting costs. Similar considerations may apply when blacks have been temporarily assigned to the lower-skilled jobs in the white mobility clusters, regardless of skill progressions.

As skill relationships among segregated mobility clusters diminish (as in Figure 7) the training costs of merging mobility clusters increase. Solutions based upon broadening mobility clusters will permit internal mobility which may bear little relationship to training sequences. In the extreme case, instituting *plantwide* mobility clusters may completely disrupt on-the-job training sequences, and training costs will approach levels which would arise if each job were an entry port. Where training sequences involve many job steps, and skills are dissimilar among the sequences, broadening mobility clusters will involve considerable retraining costs as employees shuttle between training sequences. When the job structure is relatively "flat," however, and skills in various clusters are similar, retraining costs will be comparatively low.

Furthermore, since much of on-the-job training is "automatic," training efficiencies are often a function of the length of time a worker occupies a particular job classification. Stability of employment will therefore also affect the costs of merging mobility clusters. The greater the rate of internal movement, caused either by employment expansion or by instability in demand, the higher will be training and retraining costs. The rate of change of employment is also important to the costs to white employees of various types of remedies. Even the extreme remedy of having black employees displace incumbent white employees, the "freedom now" approach, would have little impact upon the employment expectations of white employees if employment were expanding very rapidly. On the other hand, the impact upon the expectations and economic conditions of white employees would be very great if employment were contracting.

Accommodating conflicts. In many cases, there is a *trade-off* between the costs to the employer and the costs to the incumbent work force of remedial changes in promotion systems. This trade-off can be exploited to facilitate the process whenever one party is more willing than the other to incur additional costs. For example, if the wage rates paid in black and white promotion districts overlap, blacks may be reluctant to transfer into previously white districts whenever a reduction in wages results, especially if they do not retain their previously accumulated rights to job security. This problem can sometimes be resolved if the wage rates of transferring workers are "red-circled"—that is, maintained at their present levels until a comparable rate is attained in the promotion district into which they are transferring.

If solutions are devised which involve additional training costs, or other nonwage labor force adjustment costs incurred by the employer, it becomes possible to utilize various government manpower programs in the remedial process. Thus, an appropriately chosen remedy could conceivably shift most of its costs from the incumbent work force and the employer to the government. Such a shift is not consistent with the philosophy of current equal employment opportunity regulations which see the costs of eliminating discrimination in the internal market as solely a private matter. Nevertheless, some manpower programs appear already used for this purpose, and it may not be inappropriate to extend this practice further.[28] Since Congress appeared not to have appreciated the magnitude of remedy costs in drafting Title VII, the absence of any endorsement of such subsidy arrangements cannot be said to resolve the question. Moreover, it can be argued that racial discrimination in employment is clearly a social, and not a private, problem, and therefore the costs of solving it should be borne by the society, as a whole, through manpower programs and other subsidy arrangements.

Remedying Wage Discrimination

Wage discrimination which is rooted in the operation of an external labor market divided by race cannot be readily eliminated through the enforcement of fair employment legislation alone. It will disappear only if such policies are combined with improvements in education and training of blacks. Wage discrimination occurring through distortions in internal job evaluation, however, can be more readily identified and corrected. There are three types of internal wage discrimination of this sort. First are cases where wage discrimination is *solely* a product of discriminatory hiring and assignment practices. In other words, where the internal wage structure is "fair" in terms of job evaluation practices, but where blacks are confined to lower-wage jobs. Remedies in these cases should focus upon changes in hiring and promotion patterns rather than in the underlying wage structure. In practice, cases of this type are not common. The internal wage structure is usually dictated, in part, by considerations of internal labor allocation, and wage structures in enterprises with discriminatory promotion systems are likely to require a different set of allocative inducements from enterprises where promotion discrimination is not present. Moreover, when revisions are made in promotion and hiring patterns to eliminate discrimination, concomitant revisions in the wage structure may also be necessary. It does little good, for example, to open new promotion opportunities to black workers without providing a wage structure consistent with movement into these opportunities.

A second type of internal wage discrimination involves situations in which an existing job evaluation plan for white jobs has never been applied to black jobs. The remedy here is simply to apply the existing plan to the black jobs. In plants which do not employ formal job evaluation plans, there may either be an informal set of evaluation standards which can be applied to black jobs, or else a formal plan can be imputed from

---

[28] See Peter B. Doeringer and Michael J. Piore, "Equal Employment Opportunity in Boston," *Industrial Relations*, vol. IX, no. 3 (May 1970), and Peter B. Doeringer, (ed.), *Programs to Employ the Disadvantaged, op. cit.*

the existing white wage structure and applied to black jobs in much the same fashion as the steel industry job evaluation plan was developed following World War II.[29]

Finally, there is internal wage discrimination in which the same evaluation procedures are applied to both black and white classifications, but where the weights given to factors which predominate on black jobs are especially low. This type of discrimination is extremely difficult to detect and to cure. In some cases, it may be possible to find a similarly situated enterprise where discrimination has not been practiced, and its wage structure could serve as a benchmark for fashioning a solution.

Impediments to Remedies

Training problems and worker sabotage. Training procedures have not been an explicit instrument of discrimination in the past, but they provide a potent means for frustrating remedies and for perpetuating discrimination. The critical nature of training derives from two factors—the relationship between promotion and training sequences and the importance of on-the-job training. Because many internal mobility patterns presuppose that a worker has learned many aspects of a job before he is actually assigned to it, a failure to have acquired the training or ability to perform the job may serve as a bar to mobility, even where promotion sequences are formally defined. Since most on-the-job training requires the acquiescence of the incumbent work force, white workers may seek to conceal their skills from black workers, thereby denying them access to job opportunities resulting from remedial changes in mobility clusters.

This implies that an effective remedy must ensure that either the employer or the incumbent white employees have responsibility for seeing that training occurs. Establishing this responsibilty may require the creation of formal training programs as substitutes for on-the-job training, the systematic utilization of the less prejudiced white employees in on-the-job training, or the discharge of white employees who refuse to cooperate with the training process. Again these remedies are costly and require a balancing of competing interests within the enterprise, but, as noted above, the availability of government subsidies for training may permit some of these costs to be shifted to the society at large.

The attempt by workers to sabotage remedies by not cooperating with on-the-job training is only one aspect of the broader problem of worker sabotage. Worker resistance can be expressed through much more dramatic means such as slowdowns, strikes, and machine damage. Such behavior is symptomatic of the fact that racial discrimination becomes part of the customary law of the workplace and attempts to change it

[29] See Jack Stieber, *The Steel Industry Wage Structure* (Cambridge, Mass.: Harvard Harvard University Press, 1959).

invite sanctions from the work force. Thus, designing effective remedies requires a program for changing custom as well as for changing hiring, promotion, wage, and training procedures.

In some instances this will require the creation of new customs which the internal work force can accept as equitable. One such arrangement might be to expand the criteria governing promotions to include "training potential," as well as ability and seniority.[30] This wider range might help to divert the attention of the internal work force from immediate qualifications, and from acquired seniority, to a factor which is more neutral with respect to benefiting one group of employees over another.

A second approach is to expand employment opportunities so that the change in customs is accompanied by less threat to the economic security of particular groups within the internal labor force. When racially discriminatory promotion systems occur in multiplant enterprises, for example, it might be possible for corporate management to increase available jobs in the plant by diverting additional production orders, cancelling subcontracts, and even diverting funds for capital expansion to those plants which are attempting to eliminate discrimination. Promotion opportunities could also be expanded by taking some desirable jobs which are normally filled from the external labor market, such as technical, clerical, and maintenance occupations, and staff them instead from the internal work force. Such arrangements to be effective, would have to be accompanied by appropriate training programs.

Where employment opportunities within the internal labor market cannot be expanded, programs might be developed to provide additional general education—basic English, mathematics, and vocational skills—for employees in the lower-paying job classifications. This training could help them qualify for employment outside the confines of their particular internal labor market. Such manpower programs, directed at the external labor market, have succeeded in enterprises facing employment declines due to technological change, and can also be appropriate in a civil rights context.[31]

In changing customs the various roles of unions should not be ignored. First, where the union has codified customary practices, it may be easier to identify the discriminatory rule and to write a remedial rule. Thus, while codification can freeze in discriminatory practices, it may also facilitate their change. Written procedures in nonunion plants have similar effects. Second, unions may organize and focus employer pressure and, in

[30] See *Challenges to Collective Bargaining,* Final Report of the Thirtieth American Assembly (New York: Columbia University Press, 1966).

[31] See, for example, George P. Shultz and Arnold R. Weber, *Strategies for the Displaced Worker Confronting Economic Change* (New York: Harper and Row, 1966).

this sense, may make it more difficult to change rules detrimental to the majority work force. Unions should, therefore, always be made a party to remedial arrangement, even when they do not have direct responsibility for administering work rules.

Finally, there may be changes in custom which neither unions nor managements can *voluntarily* accept, but which the internal labor force will find acceptable if imposed by a third party. Rulings by arbitrators in grievances, for example, permit new interpretations of contract language and past practice which can overturn discriminatory customs. Similarly, the courts can introduce new work rules into internal labor markets which contradict old customs and establish new ones.

Guidelines and General Remedies

In fashioning remedies it should be clear that any solution will have markedly different effects upon the parties depending upon the conditions present in the particular internal labor market. The pattern of employment growth, the configuration of the discriminatory promotion system, future trends in technological change, the seniority distribution of blacks and whites, the dispersion of wage rates in the internal wage structure, and so forth, will all influence the final outcome of any designated plan. These considerations illustrate the complexity of fashioning equitable remedies to promotion discrimination and argue against the view that a simple set of principles can be universally applied. In effectuating the underlying spirit of equal employment opportunity regulations it would not be inconsistent to impose very different remedies from one case to another, indeed consistency may require such differences.

Summary

In this chapter, the concept of the internal labor market has been applied to the analysis of racially discriminatory employment practices and to the development of remedies. A consideration of the factors generating internal labor markets suggests that some discrimination is best understood in terms of the costs to employers of screening, recruitment, and training, whereas other forms of discrimination can be traced to attempts by white workers to enhance their job security and economic opportunity at the expense of black workers.

Title VII of the Civil Rights Act of 1964, regulations of the OFCC, and other equal employment opportunity regulations can best be understood as policy instruments designed to mandate *changes* in the rules which govern internal labor markets as opposed to manpower policies which seek to operate within existing internal market rules to enhance the competitive position of black workers. An understanding of the complex of factors generating internal labor markets, however, suggests that attempts to change discriminatory rules will come in conflict with a variety of other interests and social goals such as efficiency and the protection of job security. Congress, in passing Title VII, failed to appreciate the extent and nature of these conflicts, and it falls to the courts and to government agencies to resolve the difficulties or to effectuate a balance among them. The body of the chapter attempts to evaluate various discriminatory rules and procedures in this light.

In principle, racial discrimination can occur through any of the eleven instruments identified in Chapter 5 as governing the relationship between the internal market and the external labor force. In practice, racial discrimination appears to be effectuated primarily through hiring standards, screening procedures, recruitment procedures, internal allocative rules, and the rules governing wage determination.

Racial discrimination is closely bound to the informality and flexibility of recruitment and hiring procedures. Increasing the formality and the rigidity of these procedures may be required, but this is also likely to curtail the ability of the internal market to adapt efficiently to technological change and changing labor market conditions. Remedying discrimination in hiring is also complicated by the statistical nature of the screening process which makes it difficult to admit more qualified members of a given group without admitting more unqualified members of the group at the same time. Stressing these costs, however, is not to imply that they justify the *status quo,* only that they should be considered in fashioning solutions.

Promotion and wage setting procedures, at least in enterprise markets, are often more formal than recruitment and hiring procedures so that discrimination is more readily identified, and remedies are easier to design. But particularly with respect to promotion, the conflicts among the interests of various groups of workers and between worker and managerial interests are intense. To the extent the society seeks to effectuate some kind of balance among these interests, no single set of remedial rules will suffice.

Finally, it is pointed out that, to a great extent, racially discriminatory practices are customary in nature, and, because of the ability of the majority labor force to enforce custom, their complete elimination may require changes in custom itself. The chapter concludes with some suggestions as to how this might be accomplished.

The body of the chapter does not deal explicitly with trade unions, since much trade union activity must be understood in the context of social groups and customary law. Unions tend to strengthen custom by increasing the amount of group pressure that can be brought to bear in its behalf. They also change the way in which custom evolves over time by committing it to writing. These effects have diverse implications for remedying discriminatory employment practices: some make such practices easier to change and some make them more resistant to change. On balance, given a legal process for reviewing written work rules, the fact that the union commits customary rules to writing is probably of considerable help in eliminating discrimination.

Chapter 8
Low-Income Employment and the Disadvantaged Labor Force

The preceding chapters have concentrated primarily upon internal labor markets and the adjustment processes within medium- and large-size enterprises. These enterprises belong to the most stable and administratively well-organized segment of the economy. The better-educated and skilled workers customarily find employment in such markets. There are, however, a group of low-wage, and often marginal, enterprises and a set of casual, unstructured work opportunities where workers with employment disadvantages tend to find work.[1] The labor market adjustment process for this low-wage employment and its effect upon the disadvantaged is poorly understood. But available evidence suggests that it is less well developed, less effective, and perhaps more detrimental to the work habits of the labor force than the adjustment process in the higher wage labor market. The operation of the low-wage labor market will be examined in this chapter. In the first section, the characteristics of this market are described. The second and third sections present several theories of low-income labor market behavior, and conclusions for policy are offered in the fourth section.

[1] For a similar distinction with respect to enterprises see Robert T. Averitt, *The Dual Economy* (New York: W. W. Norton and Company, Inc., 1968).

The Characteristics of Low-Wage Markets

It is by now well established that disadvantaged workers in our central cities have lower educational attainment, higher unemployment, more part-time work, and less job experience than the average American worker.[2] Moreover, an increasing proportion of the central city labor force is black and receives income from welfare or illicit activities. Various studies have attributed disparities between white and nonwhite labor market experience to differences in education, place of residence, labor force participation rates, and discrimination. They have also shown that the income, employment, and unemployment of nonwhites are more sensitive to economic conditions than those of whites, but that substantial economic disadvantage remains for nonwhites, even at high levels of aggregate demand.[3]

In many cities it appears that these employment and income problems do not reflect absolute barriers to employment so much as a deficiency of high wage or otherwise preferred employment opportunities. For example, a study of the low-wage labor market in Boston showed that employment in hospitals, hotels, warehouses, building maintenance services, industrial sweatshops, and so forth, is readily available to the disadvantaged.[4] But attractive high-wage employment—jobs which constitute, in the current language of manpower programs, "meaningful employment opportunities" —were much less accessible.

Theories of the Low-Income Labor Market

There are several conceptual approaches which can be adopted for analyzing the behavior of low-income labor markets. Although the policy

[2] See, for example, *The Report of the National Advisory Commission on Civil Disorders* (Washington, D.C.: Government Printing Office, 1968), Chs. 6-7.

[3] *Ibid.*, Chs. 6-7. Also, see Harry J. Gilman, "Economic Discrimination and Unemployment," *American Economic Review,* vol. LV, no. 5, part 1 (December 1965), pp. 1077-1096, and Lester C. Thurow, *Poverty and Discrimination* (Washington, D.C.: Brookings Institution, 1969).

[4] See Peter B. Doeringer, *et al., Low Income Labor Markets and Urban Manpower Programs: A Critical Assessment,* report submitted to the Manpower Administration, U. S. Department of Labor, January 1969. For example, a sample of persons seeking employment through ABCD, Boston's community action agency, between September 1966 and April 1968, showed that 79 per cent of those referred to work were offered employment. Moreover, those who were offered jobs had similar socio-economic characteristics to those who were not offered jobs. The employment histories of the workers sampled also suggest that obtaining low-wage employment was not a problem.

National data on nonwhite employment and data gathered in the Department of Labor's Urban Employment Surveys in 1966 are consistent with this view. Both show high rates of *short-term* unemployment relative to *long-run* unemployment.

implications of these theories have much in common, the *emphasis* and the range of the policies are somewhat distinct. Two concepts—the *queue theory* and the *dual labor market theory*—are presented in this section.

The Queue Theory

Stated in its simplest form, the queue theory asserts that workers are ranked according to the relationship between their potential productivity and their wage rates. Given wage and job structures which are rigid, at least in the short run, this theory holds that employers ration the available jobs among workers according to their hiring preferences. The most preferred workers are selected from the queue first, leaving the less preferred to find work in the least desirable jobs on the fringes of the economy or to remain unemployed. Thus the number and the characteristics of the employed are determined by total labor demand, the wage structure of the economy, and relative worker productivities. By definition, therefore, the disadvantaged are located at the rear of the labor queue and have limited access to the most preferred employment opportunities.

According to the postulates of the theory, expanding employment should encourage employers to reduce their hiring standards, to recruit from the disadvantaged labor force, and to provide additional training to raise the productivity of the disadvantaged. These predictions of the queuing process at the enterprise level are supported by the analysis presented in Chapters 3-5. Further evidence is also provided by aggregate studies of the ability of the economy to absorb and upgrade nonwhite workers during the 1960's.[5]

The Dual Labor Market Theory[6]

This theory argues that the labor market is divided into a *primary* and a *secondary* market. Jobs in the primary market possess several of the following characteristics: high wages, good working conditions, employment stability, chances of advancement, equity, and due process in the administration of work rules. Jobs in the secondary market, in contrast, tend to have low wages and fringe benefits, poor working conditions, high labor turnover, little chance of advancement, and often arbitrary and capricious supervision. There are distinctions between workers in the two sectors which parallel those between jobs: workers in the secondary sector, relative to those in the primary sector, exhibit greater turnover, higher

---

[5] See Thurow, *op. cit.*
[6] This theory is developed in Michael J. Piore, "On-the-Job Training in a Dual Labor Market," in Arnold R. Weber, *et al.* (eds.), *Public-Private Manpower Policies* (Madison, Wis.: Industrial Relations Research Association, 1969) and "Manpower Policy," in Samuel Beer *et al.* (eds.), *The State and the Poor* (Boston: Winthrop Publishing Co., 1970), pp. 53-83.

rates of lateness and absenteeism, more insubordination, and engage more freely in petty theft and pilferage.

Disadvantaged workers, the theory asserts, are confined to the secondary market by residence, inadequate skills, poor work histories, and discrimination. Although the interconnections between primary and secondary labor markets are seen as either weak or nonexistent on the supply side, primary employers, through devices like subcontracting and temporary employment, can convert primary employment into secondary employment. The central goal of public policy is to overcome the barriers which confine the disadvantaged to this market.

The high rates of unemployment found in poor neighborhoods and upon which the queue theory focuses are viewed in the dual market theory as frictional, reflective of the relatively high rates of labor turnover in the secondary market. Comments of both employers and workers are indicative of this instability. Employers complain of lateness, absenteeism, and turnover. Workers are especially bitter about arbitrary management, low wages, and job insecurity. As these complaints suggest, the instability appears to be a characteristic of both jobs and workers. Certain of the jobs available to the disadvantaged—jobs in hospitals and hotels, for example—although menial and low-paying, are stable, but turnover among the employees who hold them is relatively high. Other jobs—in nonunion construction, seasonal manufacturing and the like—are very unstable and are not organized to provide continuous employment. Whatever its cause, however, the amount of job changing means that any given level of employment in the secondary sector is associated with a much higher level of frictional unemployment than in the primary sector. In a sense, therefore, high levels of turnover and frictional unemployment may be taken as the salient characteristic of the secondary market.

To a certain extent, the terms *primary* and *secondary* are poorly chosen. They are conventionally associated with the literature on labor force participation in which the term "secondary" is applied to workers such as women and teenagers, who are thought to have a relatively weak attachment to the labor market.[7] But the association with labor force participation which the terms carry is not altogether misleading. "Secondary" workers in the labor force participation literature, because their labor force attachment is low, exhibit high turnover as is characteristic of the secondary labor market. Moreover, because their job attachment is low, they are not interested in chances of advancement and are more tolerant of an unattractive work environment. Thus they tend to be employed in jobs which share many of the characteristics of those available to disad-

---

[7] See, for example, Jacob Mincer, "Labor Force Participation and Unemployment: A Review of the Literature," Robert A. Gordon and Margaret S. Gordon, (eds.) *Prosperity and Unemployment* (New York: Wiley & Sons, 1966).

vantaged workers. This parallel is instructive. It suggests that it is not the existence of secondary employment per se that constitutes the policy problem. It may be quite appropriate for workers for whom the job itself is a secondary aspect of their lives, whose income requirements are limited (as in the case of teenagers without families), or who foresee eventual access to primary employment. It is the permanent and involuntary confinement in the secondary market of workers with major family responsibilities that poses the problem for public policy.

To the extent that the problems of the disadvantaged are characterized by a dual labor market, policy must concern itself not only with the number of jobs relative to the number of workers, but with their distribution between the primary and secondary sectors as well.

Primary Markets and Internal Labor Markets

The queue theory and the dual market theory may be reconciled by emphasizing the association between the primary sector and internal labor markets. The primary sector consists of a series of internal markets of the kind upon which the analysis of the present volume focuses. The process of entry into these "primary" internal markets appears to operate like an employment queue. Prospective employees are ranked in some order related to their productivity, and employers hire along the queue until they have filled their requirements.

In contrast, the secondary labor market consists of three kinds of employment situations. First, some secondary employment is completely unstructured, not belonging to any internal market. Such jobs are the polar opposite of those in internal labor markets and resemble the jobs postulated in competitive theory. Examples are casual laboring jobs in construction, domestic work, and dishwashing in restaurants, Second, other jobs lie in what might be called "secondary" internal labor markets. These markets do possess formal internal structures, but they tend to have many entry ports, short mobility clusters, and the work is generally low paying, unpleasant, or both. Typical of such markets are blue-collar jobs in foundries, stitching and pressing jobs in apparel plants, and menial jobs in hospitals.

Finally, secondary jobs having few, if any, steps of promotion or transfer rights are occasionally found attached to internal labor markets in which the remainder of the jobs are primary. In manufacturing establishments there may be one seniority district composed of such secondary jobs, and entry standards for these jobs are considerably less stringent than for other districts in the plant. In pulp and paper mills, for example, there is the wood yard; in some machine tool companies there are foundry and laboring districts; in light manufacturing there are often temporary packaging lines. Secondary jobs in internal labor markets closely resemble the other two types of secondary jobs described above. Similar enterprises may man these same jobs on a casual basis, without providing incumbent employees any of the privileges of the internal labor market. Other enterprises may subcontract the same work to "secondary" internal labor markets. To the extent that secondary jobs in "primary" internal labor markets are governed by seniority, formal grievance procedures, job evaluation plans, and so forth, this appears to be more the product of the need for consistent internal administrative practices than the result of compelling economic and social forces.

It is characteristic of all three types of secondary employment that the forces promoting internal labor markets appear to be weaker than is the case for primary employment. Entry into secondary employment is less characterized by a queueing process than it is in primary employment. Many employers do not appear to draw distinctions between one secondary worker and another other than on the basis of sex or physical strength, and almost seem to be hiring from an undifferentiated labor pool.[8] Since turnover is high and the right to discharge relatively unrestricted, more careful pre-employment screening is not generally warranted.[9]

For some disadvantaged workers, movement between the secondary and the primary sectors may be described as a queue phenomenon com-

---

[8] Analysis of both population and establishment data collected in Boston, for example, have failed to explain, through quantifiable socio-economic variables, much of the variance in hiring decisions with respect to the disadvantaged. Discussions with employers indicate that this is partially explained by the importance of interviews in measuring less tangible worker qualities. In addition, it appears that fine distinctions are not drawn among workers in the secondary labor market because differentiating degrees of disadvantage is difficult, labor needs are more pressing, and pre-employment screening is less important in secondary internal labor markets.

[9] According to one interpretation, the secondary labor market, and to some degree, labor markets in general can be understood more clearly in terms of two queues—a hiring queue and a job vacancy queue. The hiring queue consists of strata of workers defined by quantifiable variables such as education, age, and test scores, and by subjective information obtained during interviews. The job vacancy queue consists of entry positions ranked informally by workers' evaluations of wages, promotion opportunities, employment security, and working conditions. The precision of ranking along these queues follows a gradient, being well defined in the primary labor market and tapering off into imprecise ranking in the secondary labor market. Once an employment relationship has been established, a second screening operation occurs on the job as employers and workers appraise one another under actual working conditions. If either party is considered to be unsatisfactory by the other during the probationary period of employment, the employment relationship is terminated through quits or discharges, and the labor market adjustment process operates upon the new vacancy. See Peter B. Doeringer, "Manpower Programs for Ghetto Labor Markets," *Proceedings of the 21st Annual Winter Meeting of the Industrial Relations Research Association,* December 1968.

parable to that through which workers enter internal labor markets in the primary sector. When the labor market is loose, many workers in the secondary sector stand at the end of the queue for employment in primary internal labor markets. As the market tightens, primary employers are forced to move down this queue and eventually reach those at the back. However, other workers in the secondary sector, the most seriously disadvantaged, may not be included in the queue for entry to primary employment at all. If primary employees reach the end of the queue and refuse to expand employment further by hiring the most seriously disadvantaged, other instruments of adjustment to market conditions such as subcontracting, technological change and the like may be utilized instead. Some of these instruments, such as subcontracting and the use of "temporary" workers, may then serve to shift the expanding employment opportunities from the primary to the secondary sector.

This view which associates primary employment with internal labor markets, and secondary labor markets with a mixture of internal markets and jobs not belonging to internal markets suggests that the distinction between primary and secondary markets need not imply the strict separation of the two embodied in the concept of a dual labor market. Whether dichotomous or a continuous model of the labor market is appropriate is a matter of both emphasis and empirical judgment. Data from Boston, and broader labor force surveys as well, show that primary and secondary jobs clearly exist in the economy at any point in time and that many disadvantaged workers remain employed in the secondary labor market for long periods.[10] If the labor market mechanisms—as altered by economic growth, education, manpower programs, and pressures for equal employment opportunity—work over time to expand the relative importance of primary employment and to encourage patterns of labor mobility in which disadvantaged workers can readily move into primary jobs, then a theory stressing labor market continuity is most suitable. On the other hand, if the proportion of secondary jobs is large and growing, or if forces are at work which increase barriers to mobility between secondary and primary employment, then a dichotomous theory of the labor market will be most useful.

The Determinants of the Secondary Labor Market

A number of factors operate to distinguish the secondary labor market from the primary market. These are interrelated and interact with each other in complex ways, making it difficult to analyze each factor separately

[10] See Doeringer *et al.*, *Low Income Labor Markets and Urban Manpower Programs: A Critical Assessment, op. cit.*; and Peter M. Blau and Otis D. Duncan, *The American Occupational Structure* (New York: Wiley, 1967).

without doing violence to the simultaneous nature of the processes at work. For example, the characteristics of the secondary labor market most closely related to each other are the relative instability of employment, the comparative instability and the high unemployment rates of the work force, low wages and poor chances of advancement, the paucity of training opportunities, and the arbitrariness in the administration of work rules. It is possible, however, to understand these interactions by starting with any one characteristic of the secondary market and demonstrating how the other market characteristics can be derived from it.

Employment in the secondary labor market fails to provide the kinds of job security, wages, and working conditions required to stabilize the work relationship. This may occur because employers in the secondary sector cannot economically establish internal labor market conditions which are conducive to reducing turnover or because the technical aspects of the jobs are such that the reduction of turnover has little value to the employer. Second, the attitudes and demographic traits of the secondary labor force may be such that workers place little value upon job security in particular enterprises. These two explanations, while examined separately, are not independent. Unstable and undesirable jobs may encourage workers to place low value upon job security, while a work force prone to turnover may make the costs of its reduction prohibitively high. In this section, the implications of the forces determining internal labor markets for the analysis of the secondary labor market are examined.

The Value of the Internal Labor Market to Secondary Employees

There are groups of workers in the labor force whose economic position or phase in their life cycle leads them to place little value upon permanent employment and chances of advancement. Such is the case with certain working mothers who are preoccupied with their families and whose earnings are used as a supplement to the basic wage of the man who heads the household. Many such women expect to quit their jobs to have more children, or when they have accumulated enough funds to finance certain household durables. Moreover, they often seek jobs which will tolerate lateness or absenteeism caused by family emergencies. Another group of workers seeking similar employment are students, whose major activity is school attendance and who seek part-time work to supplement family allowances or school stipends. Some of these youths, in fact, may only be looking for short-duration work during summers, holidays, or simply for a couple of weeks during the term to finance a "heavy weekend." Still another group of workers with slight interest in security or advancement are moonlighters whose major concern is with the characteristics of their main job and who expect only short tenure in this secondary employment. Finally, whenever one job can be readily replaced with another yielding similar rewards, workers generally place less value on job security in particular internal markets and to derive job security from the external labor market.[11] While a portion of the instability which characterizes the secondary labor force can be understood on the basis of demographic characteristics, other factors—the instability of jobs, the influence of "street life," discrimination, and the like—operate on both the supply and demand sides of the market to weaken internal labor markets and to foster the secondary labor market.

The Value of Internal Labor Markets to Secondary Employers

The effect of an unstable work force. If it is assumed initially that the secondary labor market is attributable to worker characteristics, that is that workers can be divided into two groups, a group of stable workers and an unstable group who tend to have high rates of absenteeism and frequently arrive late for work, employers can respond to that labor supply in a variety of ways. Those lucky enough to have the stable workers can simply hire a number of workers equal to the number of work stations. If employers do not differ in their needs for a stable labor force and if the employers must compete with each other in the product market, then enterprises which hire unstable workers will have to make a series of adjustments to operate effectively. Two kinds of adjustment are possible. The company can institute a "shapeup," hiring each day from a gang of workers appearing at the gate a number equal to the number of its work stations. Under this arrangement, productivity per employee will be the same as that in the stable market, and the firm can afford to pay the same daily wage, *provided that the gang is always large enough to fill all available jobs.* Because workers are unstable, however, the gang is likely to vary in size from day to day. The guarantee against job vacancies provided elsewhere by worker stability can only be obtained, therefore, if even on the worst day the shapeup gang is at least as large as the number of jobs. This, in turn, implies that on most days the gang must be larger than the number of jobs, and unemployment among unstable workers will exceed that among stable workers.

The alternative to a "shapeup" policy is "overmanning," insuring that all work stations are covered, despite absenteeism and turnover, by maintaining a labor force substantially larger than the number of work stations. Complete insurance, however, requires that, on the average, there will

[11] This is thought to explain why quit rates rise with employment expansion. See *Wages and Labour Mobility* (Paris: Organization for Economic Cooperation and Development, 1965); and Alan K. Severn, "Upward Labor Mobility: Opportunity or Incentive?" *Quarterly Journal of Economics,* vol. LXXXII, no. 1 (February 1968), pp. 147-151.

be idle employees present. Thus, while productivity *per work station* is equivalent to that in firms hiring stable workers, productivity *per employee* is lower, and to induce firms to hire unstable workers the lower productivity must be compensated by lower wages.

In practice, firms hiring unstable workers will probably tend to pursue a combination of the "shapeup" and "overmanning" policies. Thus, the market with unstable workers will tend to be accompanied by both low wages and higher levels of unemployment.

The other characteristics of the secondary market can also be explained by employee instability. Because the labor force is unstable, the employer has no incentive to invest in training on the job. Indeed, he could not recoup the returns to such investment. Lacking an interest in on-the-job training, the employer is also less interested in building lines of progression which might facilitate such training or capture the training which occurs automatically. The absence of lines of progression reduces promotion opportunities within the enterprise. Indeed, given high turnover and the consequent difficulty of internal training, the employer has an incentive to minimize the skill involved in the work, utiiizing as "unskilled" a technology as he can, and this further reduces training opportunities. Finally, to the extent that the labor force is unstable and turnover is high, cohesive work groups do not develop: custom is, therefore, weak, the work rules tend to be ambiguous, and there is little pressure from the labor force for their fair and equitable administration.

The effect of unstable jobs. The preceding has been developed on the assumption that it is workers who are more or less unstable, but that jobs all possess the same degree of stability. Clearly, that is not the case. Removing this assumption, and attributing all or part of the instability in the secondary labor market to the nature of jobs does not basically change the characteristics associated with it. Unstable work will continue to be found among jobs which, relative to stable employment, involve little training, small chance of advancement, and less equitable work-rule administration. Among the secondary employers who can be understood in this way are those in highly seasonal industries with short employment periods (like the construction business, or industries where demand is generally temporary). In other industries, the job itself may be stable, but the nature of the industry may make turnover relatively inexpensive. Thus it may be possible to understand the secondary character of menial jobs in hospitals by the fact that these jobs are themselves unskilled, and the industry is prevented by licensing requirements and professional attitudes from utilizing any learning that occurs on the job to upgrade low-skilled employees. Thus, either inherently unstable employment or lack of training costs will discourage employers from instituting internal labor structures which will serve to reduce turnover.

Supplementary Influences Upon the Secondary Market

The impact of collective bargaining and trade union organization. While, to a certain extent, the development of internal labor markets may be understood as a free response of employers to the advantages which the internal market provides them, they have in many cases been forced by union pressure to provide greater job security than is otherwise to their advantage. For example, in industries where the labor force has traditionally borne heavy costs of cyclical and seasonal variability in product demand or of labor-saving technological change, rules have been introduced which considerably limit these costs. Some of them—seniority provisions, limitations on layoffs, emphasis upon promotion from within, and union control over jobs—directly created the internal labor market. Others—guaranteed annual wages, formalized work sharing arrangements, grievance procedures to limit arbitrary discharges, supplemental unemployment benefits and termination pay, pension plans, and so forth—have substantially increased the attractiveness of jobs within internal markets.

A side effect of this trend, however, has been the encouragement of some types of secondary employment, such as temporary employment, as a means of providing manning flexibility in the primary enterprise. The costs of economic instability in primary labor markets are therefore transferred to temporary jobs and to smaller nonunion internal labor markets such as job shops, which produce for the residual product market left by the larger enterprises.[12]

Numerous examples of this process can be found. In the cyclical industries, such as steel and automobiles, strong seniority systems have reinforced natural training ladders, and income guarantees have stabilized both income and employment. Small job and specialty shops bear the brunt of the cyclical instability in these industries. In longshoring, employment guarantees, decasualization of work, and automation funds have been the culmination of this process. In some East Coast ports, decasualization has been associated with the formal recognition of a permanent pool of casual workers with little or no attachment to the industry and only residual employment rights. In major nonunion companies such as IBM and Polaroid, employer initiative has carried this logic further by providing virtual guarantees of employment to all incumbent workers.

Grievance procedures and fringe benefits have a similar influence. Any limitation on the employer's use of layoffs or discharges to achieve efficient manning levels creates incentives to stabilize employment and a preference for stable employees. Fringe benefits such as paid vacations and holidays, severance pay, and health and retirement plans that link employer contributions to the size of the labor force, as well as to hours

---

[12] See John Kenneth Galbraith, *The New Industrial State* (Boston, Mass.: Houghton Mifflin Co., 1967), and Averitt, *op. cit.*

worked or wages paid, all discourage primary employers from adapting to absenteeism and turnover by overmanning. The replacement of piece rates by day rates has also operated to raise the costs of turnover, while increasing the incentives which encourage worker stability.

The extent of labor organization, and the concomitant influence of unions on unorganized internal labor markets, is largely determined by the size and stability of the internal labor market. Where markets are small or employment unstable, the costs of labor organization, and of maintaining organizational strength, are high relative to the membership obtained. Rather than attempting to organize the entire product market, unions frequently tolerate a small segment of enterprises paying below union standards. An illustration of this is the residential housing sector which is typically nonunion. These are often secondary employers whose output is too small, or whose efficiency is too low, to jeopardize the union rate. Thus the distinction between primary and secondary employment is similar to the distinction between employment directly or indirectly influenced by union activity, and that which is not.

The impact of labor legislation upon secondary employment. The extent of union organization is influenced by the coverage of the Wagner and Taft-Hartley Acts and by NLRB decisions limiting its own jurisdiction. Enterprises that are formally or informally exempt from these laws —nonprofit hospitals, agriculture, domestic service, and many small establishments—are all part of the secondary labor market. Because of the instability and elasticity of the supply of labor to these enterprises, the absence of NLRB machinery has probably been a more significant obstacle to collective bargaining in the secondary labor market than it would be in the primary market.

The exemptions from the Wagner and Taft-Hartley Acts are symptomatic of broader principles underlying the relationship of Federal labor law to the secondary labor market. For example, unemployment compensation, social security, and minimum wage legislation all exempt parts of the secondary labor market from coverage.

Federal social welfare legislation affects employment stability in a manner similar to that of union contract provisions. The most prominent effects are produced by the ceilings on the tax base of the social security programs and by the experience-rating formulae for unemployment insurance. Where annual earnings of full-time workers exceed the taxable income ceiling, or when an employer can obtain a beneficial experience rate, the employer has an incentive to minimize the number of people on his payroll and to avoid turnover which would raise the total number of workers employed during the year. Employers who are exempt from the coverage of these regulations, who pay annual salaries below the income ceiling, or who have reached the maximum tax rate for unemployment or workmen's compensation insurance face no such incentives for stabilizing employment. More generally, any provision raising employment cost per employee, whether it be recruitment and training costs, private welfare arrangements, or social insurance taxes, will tend to encourage stability of employment by raising the costs of turnover to the employer.

On-the-job learning in the secondary sector. While only low levels of "job skills" are developed in secondary employment, certain modes of behavior and thought are encouraged by such employment. Since this behavior is rewarded in much the same way that conventional skills are rewarded in other work environments, it can become habitual. These modes of behavior are, in other words, *"learned."* When they are antagonistic to employment in the primary sector, they must be "unlearned" if the worker is to transfer successfully out of the secondary market. Thus, for example, the very fact that so many secondary jobs accept lateness or absenteeism and adapt to it tends to encourage unstable, erratic job attachment among workers. Similarly, some secondary employers anticipate that their employees will steal. Rather than attempting to prevent it, employers accept the fact that it occurs, turn their backs, and adjust wages downward accordingly. Where supervision is harsh or abusive, and there is no institutionalized process for resolving grievances, employees often relate to their supervisors in a manner that in primary jobs would be considered insubordinate. Or, again, employers expecting workers to be unskilled purchase either very durable or cheap, second-hand machinery and accept the careless treatment it receives. As a result, the workers who use it become accustomed to treating machinery in this way and can neither understand nor accept the greater respect accorded tools and equipment in primary employments.

To some extent, all workers in the secondary sector "learn" behavioral traits on the job. In this sense, the "disadvantaged" involuntarily confined to such work may not be very different from the student, the working mother, or the moonlighter in the same job. However, the advantaged secondary workers tend to come from environments which foster different behavioral traits and, because of this, weaken the habits which develop at work. For a great many disadvantaged workers, on the other hand, the habits which are developed at the workplace also exist in the home and social environments as well.[13]

Low-income life styles. Leisure time in low-income neighborhoods is frequently dominated by street-corner life, a life style widely prevalent

---

[13] See Herbert Gans, *The Urban Villagers: Group and Class in the Life of Italian-Americans* (New York: Free Press of Glencoe, 1962); Elliot Liebow, *Tally's Corner: A Study of Negro Streetcorner Men* (Boston, Mass.: Little, Brown and Co., 1967); Claude Brown, *Manchild in the Promised Land* (New York: Macmillan Co., 1965); and Malcolm X, *The Autobiography of Malcolm X* (New York: Grove Press, 1964).

among low-income people in general and in the black ghettos in particular. For the individual attached to the street, status and position in the world are defined by his group. His life has reality only in a group context; divorced from the group he is lonely and lost. The goal of group life is constant excitement. Its behavior is episodic; an endless period of "hanging around," punctuated by short adventures undertaken by the group as a whole or by individuals. Life thus tends to be immediate and sensational; past adventures are continually recalled, and the future is not anticipated.

Although cause and effect are again difficult to isolate, the episodic street life and the episodic pattern of work are obviously compatible. Just as the disadvantaged worker relies upon the secondary labor market rather than particular employers for employment security, he relies upon the street rather than the workplace for social satisfaction. Secondary employment lacks the organized social life found in many primary establishments: athletic teams, dances, picnics, and even cafeterias. More important, the constant turnover of the internal labor force in secondary employment precludes the formation of stable friendships at the workplace. Where work is not inherently satisfying, and where there are no social compensations, the tie to the street group is more stable than attachment to a particular work group.[14]

This allegiance of the disadvantaged worker is further heightened by the income-generating activities undertaken within it. Hustling and illicit activities are a favored activity on the street. They are short run and episodic in nature, and their very illegitimacy heightens the sense of adventure which is sought by the group.

The secondary labor market is attuned to street life in a way which primary employment is not. Its limited demands upon the individual permit continued participation on the street; when work schedules interfere with group activity the individual simply skips work. Petty thefts and work disputes become stories of bravado. The piece-rate payment system, found in some secondary jobs, permits the worker to choose his own work pace and, by adjusting compensation to productivity, helps to ensure that poor work habits do not unduly penalize the employer. Primary employment, in contrast, requires the individual to abandon street life and to conform to an ethical code which is not recognized on the street.

Welfare also constitutes a component of the income-generating process in low-income neighborhoods. The payment structure of the welfare system discourages full-time, low-wage work. It is compatible with secondary employment, and, like hustling, is an alternative means of generating income. The public assistance system as presently structured, moreover, encourages people to work on the fringes of the labor market in jobs where

[14] See Daniel Bell, *The End of Ideology* (Glencoe, Ill.: Free Press, 1960), pp. 227-272.

earnings are not reported to official authorities. It involves a personal relationship with the social worker which is much closer to that between worker and supervisor in the secondary sector than the mere formal institutionalized relationship which prevails in primary employments.

Discrimination. Finally, in assessing the development of worker characteristics and their role in the generation of the secondary labor market, special mention should be made of discrimination. Discrimination, on the basis of race but also against low-income people generally, works in two ways. First, to the extent that it leads to concentrations of low-income people and their isolation from members of other social classes, it facilitates the development of a common set of behavioral traits, and acts to perpetuate them. People are deprived of alternative behavioral models; they have no chance of attaching themselves to friends and social settings which reward other traits; they find the same kinds of attitudes at home, at work, and at school, and fail even to develop the "skill" of adapting behavior when moving from one context to another. In this sense, discrimination acts to hold workers in the secondary sector.

Discrimination can also operate to exclude or reject workers who do gain access to primary employment. Line supervision and other incumbent employees who serve as instructors on the job control the rate of learning of the new hire. Without the acceptance of his fellow workers, the black employee may not learn his job and may be the butt of sabotage or harassment as well. Rejection and abuse from the work group can force the disadvantaged worker back to his street group, thus reinforcing his behavioral patterns.

Linkages Between Primary and Secondary Market

The Queue Theory

As discussed earlier, the queue theory places heavy emphasis upon an expansion of aggregate demand as a solution to the problem of disadvantage. Such an expansion will, under this theory, force employers to expand employment along the queue. Individual employers will draw workers both from the ranks of the unemployed and from lower-wage jobs, and, in the aggregate, this should result in both a reduction of unemployment and a decline in the proportion of low-paying jobs.

The very high levels of aggregate demand which the theory implies would be necessary to move the poor into high-paying employment appears, in the American economy, to produce inflation. The attempt to avoid this leads to a second set of policies aimed at raising the productivity of the poor and, hence, shifting them forward in the queue. This is presumably the rationale, under the queue theory, for the array of manpower programs which were developed in the course of the 1960's.

Because the queue theory implies a certain degree of wage rigidity, it also suggests a third set of policies aimed at modifying the wage structure so that it would be profitable to employ the disadvantaged, even at their present level of productivity. This range of policies has not been attempted, although the reasons for this neglect are not obvious. The downward rigidity of wage rates would make it necessary to change the wage structure through upward adjustments. This would contribute to inflation, but not necessarily any more than an equivalent expansion of aggregate demand. The analysis of Chapter 4 suggests that changes in the wage structure within a given internal labor market are exceedingly difficult to achieve, even through upward adjustments. It also indicates certain rigidities in the structure of wages between internal markets, but it implies little difficulty in changing the relative wages on low-paying jobs which lie outside of internal markets.

The Secondary Labor Market

A recognition of the problem of secondary employment suggests a somewhat different approach to policy. It implies that expansion in aggregate demand will not necessarily solve the problem of the disadvantaged. In the extreme version of the dual labor market theory which postulates a complete dichotomy in the labor market, primary employment will stop expanding when it has absorbed the available primary labor force, and further increases in output will be obtained by shifting demand into the secondary sector without any transfer of the secondary work force into the primary sector. Where some secondary workers occupy the queue leading to primary employment, expanding aggregate demand will help to alleviate the labor market problems of the disadvantaged. But more disadvantaged workers may be helped at a lower real cost if direct efforts are made to facilitate the movement of workers out of the secondary sector and if secondary jobs are converted into primary jobs.

For some workers, full employment and growth will be sufficient solutions to labor market disadvantage; for others, manpower and antidiscrimination programs will suffice; but for those that remain confined to secondary employment, the characteristics of this employment will need to be changed if labor market disadvantage is to be reduced. In the remainder of this section, two kinds of policies for the secondary sector are examined; one aimed at the labor force and designed to develop the worker traits required to retain primary employment, and the other aimed at converting what are now secondary jobs into primary employment.

Changes in the Secondary Work Force

The central problem in changing the work force is that the secondary sector is the product of an interaction between workers and jobs. Jobs are adjusted by management to the traits of the labor force hired to perform them. But, at the same time, the characteristics of the work environment develop habits of behavior and thought among the work force. Thus, if secondary workers are placed in primary jobs, they may gradually learn to attend regularly, show up on time, accept prohibitions on pilferage, utilize institutionalized channels for expressing grievances, and acquire the skills necessary to care for equipment. Or the management may gradually adapt to the worker, accept absenteeism and overman to cover it, begin to turn its back on pilferage and adjust wages and prices accordingly, let institutionalized grievance procedures atrophy, purchase second-hand equipment, and the like. In fact, both changes are likely to take place and the end result will be dependent upon which adjusts faster, workers or jobs. The task of public policy is to slow the rate a᷊ which primary jobs adjust to secondary workers and increase the rate at which secondary workers adjust to primary jobs.

In analyzing this problem, it appears useful to rank disadvantaged workers in terms of the ease with which they are able to adapt to the primary workplace. From a programmatic point of view, this should be done on an individual basis. Even program administratives, however, claim to be unable to distinguish among individual applicants on this basis; tests and other simple screening devices are even less successful in doing so. It is, however, possible to define broad socio-demographic groupings of disadvantaged workers in terms of their adaptability to primary employment. The Boston study, summarized in the Appendix of this chapter, and the sociological literature on low-income populations suggest a fivefold classification:

1. Persons with stable, but low-wage work experience. This group consists primarily of adults. Black female workers are disproportionately represented in this group as are recent immigrants from Latin America and the South.
2. Teenagers with little or no previous work experience. Instability is most serious among urban-born blacks within this group.
3. Adults with a work history of chronic turnover and poor work habits.
4. Persons with clearly defined obstacles to employment, including the aged, mothers with young children, students seeking part-time work, alcoholics and addicts, illiterates, and the physically or mentally handicapped.
5. Persons not in the labor force who have sources of income, such as welfare and illicit activities, which are competitive with productive employment.

The group most likely to adjust quickly to primary employment are the adults with stable, but low-wage work experience. A second group with potential for adapting to primary employment are the young just leaving their teens and beginning to marry and form families. In their teens, young men appear to be the most firmly attached to the street life of the slums. Indeed, that life style is characteristic not only of slum youth, but of many outside the slums as well. Most young people, however, make a transition to a more stable pattern of behavior as they mature and begin to marry and have children. A basic problem in the urban slums and ghettos appears to be the frequency, relative to other areas, with which this transition is aborted and adults slip back into an adolescent pattern, adopting it as their permanent life style. This suggests that the critical point in the work history of the slum labor force are the first years of marriage and family formation, and that the manpower policy may be most successful in aiding the movement from secondary to primary employment if it aims at this age group at the time when other forces are aiding the transition.[15]

Other groups require different types of assistance to facilitate their adjustment to the requirements of primary work. Some of these instruments are available in the existing manpower programs. For example, many in the first group need English language instruction and literacy training; those in the fourth group require special health and child care services. For people in the fifth group, the relevant policy, however, is fundamental change in the structure of the public assistance system and in the definition of illicit activity and the environment in which that activity is conducted.

Reforms in the welfare system and in criminal law are seldom considered manpower policies, but, given the problem as defined here, they should be. The basic goal of these "manpower" policies would be to reward behavior and skills similar to those involved in legitimate employment in order to ease the transfer from the secondary to the primary sector. In the area of public assistance, this means a lessening of the penalties on earned income, a depersonalization of the system, and a separation of payments from services.[16]

Finally, in considering policies aimed at facilitating movement into primary employment, special attention should be given to discrimination in schools, housing, and employment. The dual labor market theory is most applicable to blacks in urban slums. These workers seem to be trapped in a world where all of the segments of their life reward a single set of behavioral traits and offer a single set of behavioral models. To attempt to change one component of that setting by opening primary jobs

[15] See Gans, *op. cit.*

[16] See Michael J. Piore, "Income Maintenance and Labor Market Entry: The FAP Proposal and the AFDC Experience," *Proceedings of the Conference on New Labor Market Entrants,* University of Indiana, 1970.

may not be enough, since other aspects of their lives continually pull them back to secondary behavioral traits. The transition to primary employment becomes either impossible or so slow that the employer adapts to them before it is completed. The elimination of segregated housing, schools, and other basic dichotomies in the society may thus be critical to the elimination of the dichotomy in the labor market as it affects black workers.

Adjustments in Secondary Jobs

If a manpower strategy is adopted to free the disadvantaged from the secondary labor market, it is possible that other members of the labor force who find secondary jobs particularly desirable—students, secondary earners with family obligations, and moonlighters—will expand into the secondary sector. Moreover, to the extent that work in the secondary sector has been shifted there because the supply of primary workers is limited, it will shift back as that supply expands. Nonetheless, policies aimed at converting secondary employments to primary employments do appear desirable on two counts.

First, it may be easier to convert the jobs open to the disadvantaged than to widen primary employment opportunities for them. Moreover, since the total volume of primary jobs and the concern with job security in such employment limit the number of available opportunities, an increase in primary jobs for the disadvantaged beyond some point will *require* conversion of secondary into primary employment. Second, as the disadvantaged gain access to primary employment, some displacement of the more advantaged is bound to occur. Such displacement generally creates social tensions. It is also undesirable because it may simply regenerate a new supply of secondary workers who acquire the traits associated with the secondary sector by working with people adjusted to it.

A deliberate policy of converting secondary employment into primary jobs has not been pursued, and, hence, there is no direct evidence of relevance to this strategy. With determination and a good deal of imagination, however, it is probably possible to stabilize most secondary jobs and build into them the kind of career ladders, skill levels, and wage rates which characterize primary employment. Thus, for example, longshoring and unskilled construction work, which were secondary jobs *par excellence* have, since World War II, moved a considerable way toward decasualization. Similarly, in some cities, household and office cleaning firms have emerged which use sophisticated equipment and a regular work force; these services substitute for female day workers once hired through the State Employment Service to help with temporary "spring" cleaning.

While it may not be possible to make primary jobs of *all* secondary jobs, some jobs appear more susceptible to conversion than others. Among these are jobs in stable, low-wage internal markets with formal internal structures but with many entry ports, short mobility clusters, and tolerance for "secondary" behavior on the part of the work force (hospitals and hotels, for example). Similarly, secondary jobs attached to primary internal labor markets (but without the job security, promotion opportunities, wage rates, fringe benefits, and so forth, of the primary internal labor market) are also in this category.

Minimum wage legislation constitutes a direct means of influencing the compensation of jobs in the secondary labor market. Such legislation is normally anathema to economists because of its potential contribution to unemployment and inflation. While the possibility of inflationary effects militates against the use of minimum wages as an aggressive policy toward the secondary labor market, the employment effects of such legislation may be exaggerated. If internal labor markets in the secondary sector customarily adapt to tight labor markets through higher job-vacancy rates, as some labor market data suggest, then minimum wages may reduce overall demand for labor in the secondary market without contributing to unemployment. Should this analysis prove correct, raising the minimum wage may pose lesser conflicts with other goals of economic policy than is normally assumed to be the case. Moreover, the level and coverage minimum wage should be uniform for all employment situations. Otherwise, it is clear that a disproportionate burden of labor force adjustment will be placed upon those jobs in the secondary labor market which are exempt from the full effects of the minimum wage.

Finally, in attempting to affect the character of these jobs, the most successful instruments may be indirect. The probable effects of labor legislation, of social security, and of unemployment compensation were noted earlier. They could be changed to eliminate the features which aggravate the primary-secondary distinction. It may be possible to develop new policy instruments deliberately designed to influence the characteristics of jobs: a tax on labor turnover, for example. Still another instrument which could be used is antidiscrimination legislation; skillfully applied, it might open up career paths out of what are now dead-end secondary jobs in enterprises that also contain more attractive primary employment.

Summary

The disadvantaged customarily find employment in the low-income, secondary labor market. Work in low-wage internal labor markets may be unstable, and therefore ideally suited to a casual labor force. Alternatively, such work may be low skilled or organized so that the costs of worker instability are minimized. Even where such instability is costly, it may be less so than discovering and implementing corrective measures. In short, turnover and absenteeism are tolerated, and perhaps encouraged, in the secondary labor market.

In contrast, high-wage, primary employers seek to avoid the costs of worker instability through selection procedures which exclude the disadvantaged, by internal market structures which encourage stability, and by compensation levels, and industrial relations practices which promote worker satisfaction.

Two theories of the low-income labor market were presented in this chapter, the queue theory and the dual labor market theory. The former stresses increased aggregate demand and manpower training programs as solutions to labor market disadvantage. The latter indicates the possibility of confinement to secondary jobs and the need for policies to eliminate confinement and to improve secondary employment. The data currently available do not uniquely support either a continuous or a discontinuous theory of the labor market. Nevertheless, it would seem that a unified labor market with linkages between primary and secondary employment is most likely to characterize the labor market behavior of the disadvantaged who are white. Despite recent occupational and income gains, racism and discrimination seem to be a continuing and unremitting problem in the society, making the dual labor market concept most appropriate for analyzing the employment problems of racial minorities.

Labor market disadvantage, while often summarized in terms of inadequacies in education and other socio-economic variables, is fundamentally a concept shaped by three factors: (1) the costs of adapting workers with various traits to the performance requirements of particular internal labor markets; (2) the influence of the secondary labor market, welfare, and illicit activities upon work habits; and (3) discrimination. In terms of the labor force adjustment process, low learning ability may be one problem, but tardiness, absenteeism, turnover, and motivation are certainly others. Discrimination, the quality of work available to the disadvantaged, and the style of life in low-income neighborhoods are major causal factors which may overshadow problems of inadequate education and skill.

Quantitative Analysis of Worker Instability in the Low-Income Labor Market

It has been argued that employment instability is the salient feature of the low-income labor market. Instability, however, is not characteristic of all disadvantaged workers, nor are advantaged workers completely free from turnover. For example, national data indicate that two ninths of the deprived household heads worked full time in 1966.[1] Moreover, studies of labor mobility show that turnover affects a high proportion of teenagers and new entrants into the labor force regardless of their socio-economic background.[2]

Data available on low-income workers in Boston indicate that instability, much of it voluntary, varies systematically with the characteristics of both workers and jobs.[3] Cross-classifying the termination rates by age and wage rates, for example, shows that adults tend to be more stable than younger workers, and that turnover rates tend to be lower on better-paying jobs.

[1] Dorothy K. Newman, "Changing Attitudes About the Poor," *Monthly Labor Review*, vol. 92, no. 2 (February 1969), pp. 32-36.

[2] See OECD, *Wages and Labour Mobility* (Paris: Organization for European Cooperation and Development, 1965).

[3] See Peter B. Doeringer *et al.*, *Low Income Labor Markets and Urban Manpower Programs: A Critical Assessment*, report submitted to the Manpower Administration, U. S. Department of Labor, January 1969.

To examine the dimensions of turnover somewhat further a multi-variate model was developed for analyzing the work histories obtained from the Boston manpower study.[4] In the absence of an ideal measure of turnover, the dependent variable employed in the model is length of tenure on previous job. The independent variables are: (1) wage rate of previous job, (2) age, (3) years of education, (4) sex, (5) race, (6) marital status, and (7) birthplace. The general model is specified as follows:

$$T = a + b_1 W + b_2 A + b_3 E + b_4 S + b_5 N + b_6 M + b_7 B + u$$

where

T = Weeks employed on previous job[5]
W = Hourly wage rate of previous job
A = Last two digits of year of birth (beginning with 1900)
E = Years of education
S = Dummy variable for males
N = Dummy variable for nonwhites
M = Dummy variable for married
B = Place of birth[6]

The results of this analysis are shown in Table 4. Equation 1 pertains to the entire sample, equations 2 and 3 to the data grouped by age. While the model has low explanatory power, and is least satisfactory in explaining job tenure among young workers, several variables are significant.

In all three equations, age has a distinct influence upon job tenure. Since the marital status variable is insignificant in all equations, it would appear that other factors associated with age, such as increasing labor market experience, greater job security, pension rights, and so forth, outweigh the financial responsibilities of marriage as factors in determining employment stability for this group. The relatively poorer explanatory power of the model when applied to the sample of young workers suggests that the labor market behavior of young workers is likely to be more random than for older workers.

[4] Ordinary least square techniques were used in estimating the coefficients in the model. The model was applied to a random sample of ABCD's clients during the period September 1967-April 1968, for whom work history data were available.
[5] The relationship between age and *potential* job tenure introduces a bias in favor of the correlation between age and *actual* job tenure. The maximum value of the job tenure variable has been constrained to 99 weeks to reduce the degree to which a small number of older workers with substantial job tenure could influence the significance of the age variable. About 20 per cent of the pooled sample was affected by this constraint.
[6] The index assumes discrete values from 1-8 according to the followin definitions: 1 = Boston, 2 = Other areas in New England, 3 = Mid-Atlantic States, 4 = Southern States, 5 = elsewhere in the United States, 6 = Puerto Rico, 7 = Cuba, 8 = other. There were few instances of persons in category 8.

TABLE 4. Weeks of Tenure on Previous Job — ABCD History Sample September 1967-April 1968 (*t* values in parentheses)

	a	W	A	E	S	N	M	B	d.f.	R^2
EQUATION 1 **POOLED SAMPLE**										
Estimated Coefficient	72.64 (6.08)	4.83 (1.57)	-1.23*** (7.49)	.34 (.47)	-7.34 (1.82)	.64 (.15)	3.34 (.82)	1.22 (1.32)	309[a]	.1955***
EQUATION 2 **YOUNG WORKERS** **(16-25)**										
Estimated Coefficient	54.01 (2.34)	-2.93 (.78)	-.86** (2.23)	1.56** (2.14)	-3.15 (.93)	-7.59* (1.73)	2.68 (.54)	2.14** (2.35)	178	.1030
EQUATION 3 **ADULT WORKERS** **(26-68)**										
Estimated Coefficient	74.98 (4.21)	10.43** (2.33)	-1.06*** (3.61)	-1.19 (1.00)	-12.71** (1.98)	14.14** (2.09)	1.89 (.31)	1.45 (.09)	157	.1310**

[a] Computer program capacity required random reduction in sample size.
* Significant at 10% level.
** Significant at 5% level.
*** Significant at 1% level.

Sex is significant only in equations 1 and 3. Surprisingly, adult females can be expected to have longer job tenure than males. This contradicts the view that females generally have a weaker labor force attachment than males, and probably reflects the importance of the earnings of the female work force in low-income areas. For young workers, however, differences in sex do not influence job tenure, indicating common job shopping behavior, job security, and labor force attachment among young males and females.

The effect of race differs sharply for younger and older workers. Young nonwhite workers average seven weeks less job tenure than their white peers, whereas nonwhite adults can be expected to have fifteen weeks more job tenure than whites. The shorter job tenure of nonwhite youths is customarily attributed to involuntary turnover, but the Boston data indicate that in a prosperous economy much of the turnover is voluntary, and is concentrated among the young.[7]

Birthplace also influences the job tenure of younger workers. Youths born in Puerto Rico, Cuba, and to some extent, the South, many of whom are nonwhite, tend to have greater job tenure than their counterparts born in Boston. This substantiates the impression of several employers that recent immigrants to Boston prove more reliable on the job.

A full explanation of the influence of race and birthplace upon job tenure is beyond the scope and competence of this study. Nevertheless, it could be postulated that factors such as the aspirations of nonwhite youths, the value of job security to recent immigrants to a city, and the possibility of cultural differences in attitudes toward work and job changing are important.[8]

Education level is another variable positively related to job tenure among young workers. Education may contribute directly to habits of stability, or it may improve opportunities for employment in satisfying jobs which discourage turnover. It may also be that the educational system acts as a screening device for distinguishing between stable workers and those prone to "dropping out," be it from school or work.

The wage rate variable is positive and significant only for the sample of adult workers. While it is likely that the influence of wage rates upon

---

[7] See, for example, Samuel Saben, *Occupational Mobility of Employed Workers*, (U. S. Department of Labor: Bureau of Labor Statistics, 1967), Special Labor Force Report no. 84, p. 35 and Lowell E. Gallaway, *Interindustry Labor Mobility in the United States, 1957 to 1960*, U. S. Department of Health, Education, and Welfare, Social Security Administration, Research Report no. 18, 1967, pp. 88-89.

[8] Claude Brown's description of the difference between his parents' and his own attitudes towards ghetto employment opportunities is enlightening in this regard. See *Claude Brown, Manchild in the Promised Land* (New York: Macmillan Co., 1965), pp. 278-282.

younger and older workers is not equivalent when other variables are held constant, statistical problems may also be involved.[9]

[9] For example, job tenure is only an imperfect proxy for turnover rates, so that the two sources of data are not strictly comparable. There are also problems of collinearity. To some extent, the other independent variables in the equation can be used to explain wage rates as well as job tenure. Moreover, there is a problem of simultaneity. Since the causality between wage rates and job tenure presumably works in both directions, the observed coefficient overestimates the true coefficient.

Chapter 9
Summary and Conclusions

The basic purpose of this book is to develop the concept of the internal labor market and to demonstrate some of the ways in which it can be usefully applied to various areas of concern for Federal manpower policy. Part I emphasizes that internal labor markets are the critical units within which decisions are made with respect to employment, wage determination, and training. In seeking to understand the operation of the internal labor market, the principal concern has been with the formal and informal processes governing the employment relationship, and with the various forces which influence them. The availability of workers on the external labor market, the type of technology, the costs of turnover to the employer, the value of the internal labor market to the internal work force, product market considerations, and customs were identified as key factors influencing internal manpower decisions. These decisions, when aggregated, become a major factor determining the structure of wages, the level and composition of employment, and the job content of the economy.

The central theme of the second part of the book is that differences between the skills and abilities of the labor force and the requirements of jobs are reconciled through a series of instruments which are controlled within the internal labor market. These instruments—recruitment procedures, training, compensation, and the like—exist because a number of functions conventionally identified with the competitive labor market have been internalized in the enterprise. These instruments, individually and collectively, constitute a series of labor market adjustment processes by which the internal labor market adapts to changes in both production techniques and labor market conditions.

In this concluding chapter, an attempt is made to bring to bear the analytical apparatus developed in the preceding chapters upon a series of labor issues which have been the concern of government policy. Five problems are considered: (1) efficiency, job security, and equity in the internal market, (2) unemployment and inflation, (3) manpower programs, (4) special programs for the dual labor market, and (5) manpower planning.

Efficiency, Job Security, and Equity

Efficiency. The general presumption of neoclassical theory is that the most efficient economic system is highly competitive. Institutions like the internal market, which insulate workers and jobs from the direct competitive pressures of the external market are thus looked upon with considerable suspicion. A parallel view is shared by many managerial personnel who find at least some of the rules which define and govern the internal market to be burdensome, restrictive, and costly.

The theory developed in Chapter 2 to explain the origins of the internal market and the determinants of internal market structure does not support the presumption of inefficiency. It was argued in that chapter that the internal market was derivative of three factors: value to the labor force of the security and advancement it offers, savings to the employer from the reductions in labor turnover which internalization provides, and efficiency in recruitment, screening, and training of workers. These factors are not generally recognized in the theories from which the efficiency of competition is conventionally derived. Where they are present, however, internal markets may constitute an improvement in the efficiency of the enterprise and perhaps for the economic system as a whole. Whether or not efficiency increases depends upon the degree to which benefits to the work force detract from the technical efficiencies which internal markets provide. Alternatively, the definition of efficiency might be enlarged to include equity at the workplace, in which case the argument for internal markets being efficient institutions is strengthened. Efficiency in the narrow economic sense, however, is conditional upon the net economies in recruitment, screening, and training provided by the internal labor market and by the effectiveness with which the costs of replacing workers are reduced by limiting turnover.

Job security and equity. In many cases, the employers' interest in an efficient internal labor market structure coincides with workers' interests in job security and equitable administration of work rules. When this occurs, the forces determining internal markets reinforce one another, and there is no conflict between efficiency and employee interests. Despite the reduction in competition implied by the internal labor market, efficiency is not impaired.

In other cases, however, the economic efficiency of the internal labor market may be counterbalanced by rules designed to increase the job security or equitable treatment of the internal labor force beyond the point that employers would consider optimal. Indeed, the primary purpose of these rules is often to protect the internal work force when its interests are in conflict with the employer's desire for efficiency.

The extent to which efficiency is disturbed when such conflicts arise depends both upon the ability of the internal market to support inefficiency without being destroyed by more efficient competitors and upon the bargaining strength of the internal work force. Investment in fixed labor costs and reliance upon on-the-job training endow individual workers with bargaining power through the threat to quit or to refuse to participate in the training process. Where such bargaining power is strong, the more likely it is, *ceteris paribus,* that the internal labor market will contain economically inefficient rules.

Even internal markets which were efficient at their inception may become less so over time, regardless of worker pressure. Internal wage and allocative structures are the focus of custom, and custom imparts a rigidity to the internal labor market that inhibits its responsiveness to economic forces. Moreover, the more successful an internal labor market is in enhancing efficiency by reducing turnover, the more stable is the work relationship, and the more likely it is that customs will develop.

Finally, wherever unions are a party to the determination of the rules governing the internal labor market there is an additional probability that conflicts with efficiency will arise. Unions, by solidifying and coordinating the inherent bargaining power of the internal labor force, may increase the weight given to employee interests in the internal labor market. While it is difficult to demonstrate that this bargaining power can be readily translated into wage increases, it is clear that unions have had a substantial impact over the allocative structure of internal labor markets and have contributed to the development of equitable administration of work rules.[1] The growth of union referral systems, the increase in seniority as

[1] For a treatment of the impact of unions on wage rates see H. Gregg Lewis, *Unionism and Relative Wages in the United States* (Chicago: University of Chicago Press, 1963). The impact of unions on work rules and upon efficiency is discussed at length in Sumner H. Slichter, James J. Healy, and E. Robert Livernash, *The Impact of Collective Bargaining on Management* (Washington, D. C.: Brookings Institution, 1960), and in Derek C. Bok and John T. Dunlop, *Labor and the American Community* (New York: Simon and Schuster, 1970), Ch. 10.

an allocative rule, restrictions on layoffs and elaborate grievance procedures all testify to this result. Moreover, even where unions have not exerted any direct influence upon work rules, the codification of such rules, which normally accompanies union organization, reinforces the operation of custom described above.

In summary, internal labor markets can provide a more efficient form of market organization than competitive labor markets whenever fixed labor costs and economies of recruitment, screening, and training are present. This efficiency, however, is subject to being reduced by the opportunity which internal labor markets provide to the internal work force to express its interest in rules which enhance job security and equitable treatment within the market.

Structural Unemployment and Inflation

Structural Unemployment

In the past decade, labor market analysts have evinced two concerns about the process of adjustment between the requirements of jobs and the characteristics of the labor force. The first of these, called the structuralist or the structural imbalance hypothesis, was that adjustment would not occur at all. The second was that it would entail significant price inflation.[2]

The structuralists argued, essentially, that in the late fifties, an important change occurred in the requirements of jobs relative to the composition of the labor force. The change was most often attributed to new technologies and, hence, the argument was frequently associated with automation, although some observers placed greater emphasis on shifting the geographic or age composition of the labor force. The result, however, was the same—the existing work force was simply unable to fill the remaining job vacancies, and, for this reason, unemployment could not be reduced. The corollary was that any attempt to reduce it through aggregate policies would simply generate inflationary pressure without increasing employment. A variety of evidence on both the micro and macro levels was introduced to support this hypothesis. Particular emphasis was placed

[2] For a summary of this debate see: Barbara Bergmann and David E. Kaun, *Structural Unemployment in the United States* (Washington: U. S. Department of Commerce, Economic Development Administration, 1967). See also Edward Kalachek and James Knowles, "Higher Unemployment Rates, 1957–1960, Structural Transformation or Inadequate Demand," Joint Economic Committee, 87th Congress, 86 Session, 1961. Also Charles C. Killingsworth, "Structural Unemployment in the United States," in Jack Stieber (ed.), *Employment Problems of Automation and Advanced Technology* (London: Macmillan Co., 1966), pp. 128-156, and Council of Economic Advisers, *Annual Report* (Washington: 1962) pp. 39-49.

upon an alleged increase in the pace of technological change, especially in manufacturing; upon the increasing education and skill requirements of jobs generally, and especially of new relative to declining technologies; and upon a shift in the age and educational composition of unemployment.

The experience with the tightening labor market over the course of the decade has demonstrated that the fears of the structuralists were misplaced. The society was able to reduce unemployment to levels comparable to those attained in the early postwar period. Observers appear, therefore, to have seriously misinterpreted the data available to them. A recognition of the internal labor market and the process through which it adjusts to external market conditions suggests why such a mistake occurred.

On the microeconomic level, there appears to have been a confusion between the rate of technological change and *job displacement* on the one hand, with the rate of *employment displacement* on the other. The latter is highly sensitive to overall economic conditions, particularly in the blue-collar manufacturing industries such as automobiles and steel, in which fears of structural unemployment were centered. Their sensitivity is, in large measure, attributable to the nature of the internal labor market. In blue-collar manufacturing, the internal market does not provide absolute job security: displaced workers are guaranteed employment only so long as there is a vacancy within the internal market. Hence, they are protected from technological change only if the elimination of their job coincides with a job vacancy created by attrition, an expansion of production, or the like. Such a coincidence is more likely when the market as a whole is expanding. Thus, the same rate of technological change and of job displacement will create more employment displacement in a relatively depressed period, like that of the late 1950's and early 1960's, than in more prosperous times.

The impact of the increased employment displacement from internal markets was no doubt aggravated in the period by the higher overall unemployment rates which made it more difficult for those displaced to find new jobs. Hence, not only did depressed market conditions increase the rate of displacement from internal markets, it probably also acted to increase the adjustment period for the affected workers. These effects, however, are to be distinguished from changes in the rate of technological change or job displacement and could occur quite independently of them.

The structuralists appear also to have misread the micro-economic data. They were impressed by the concentration of unemployment among the low skilled and the poorly educated which they interpreted as a product of the shift in the skill requirements of jobs. In this, they failed to appreciate the way in which the recruiting, screening, and training adjustments which employers make in response to external market conditions affect the composition of unemployment. A loose external market permits employers to utilize the most inexpensive screening devices such as educational levels, age, and race. Therefore, during periods of high unemployment, superficial demographic characteristics are used to define a much higher proportion of the unemployed than during periods of low unemployment. In a tight labor market employers move toward more expensive recruiting techniques that spread labor market information to previously isolated groups, and develop more sophisticated screening procedures. Thus, the demographic categories in which labor force data are collected no longer coincide with employer screening criteria.

This is not to argue that all of the adjustments in hiring practices which led observers to the structural hypothesis in the early 1960's reflected market conditions. There were indeed certain long-run changes in job requirements which undoubtedly would have occurred even in a period of unchanging market conditions. These too, however, must be interpreted in the light of the instruments of adjustment which connect the internal to the external market. When this is done, the implications for structural balance are no longer readily apparent. For example, there has been a long-run increase in the average educational attainment required for hiring. This, however, does not necessarily reflect a change in job content. It may simply be indicative of the fact that education is used as a device to select a group of people who are thought to possess a common set of attitudes and behavioral traits.[3] As educational attainment rises throughout the society, it will be necessary to increase education requirements in order to draw from the same stratum of the labor market. Similarly, in the case of new technologies, it is possibly true that, on the average, jobs associated with new technologies tend to have higher qualifications in terms of formal training and education than the jobs associated with the older technologies which the new jobs replace. This need not, however, indicate a long-term rise in requirements since the qualifications of the new jobs tend to decline over time as they become integrated into the structure of the internal market. For example, the initial supply of workers for a new technology may be drawn from the external market and have high levels of formal training; but, over time, employers typically experiment with new recruiting procedures, screening procedures, and hiring criteria, and a decline in qualifications occurs. At the same time, on-the-job training sequences tend to form around new technologies. Hence, the formal qualifications required for a job tend to go through a life cycle, starting high and gradually declining to the much lower equilibrium level. Any comparison of the newest and the oldest jobs will often

[3] See Ivar Berg, *Education and Jobs: The Great Training Robbery* (New York: Praeger Publishers, 1970).

show a radical shift in education requirements, but the relevant question is whether that shift has increased over time.[4]

The ability of the internal labor market to overcome structural skill imbalances does not imply that technological change poses no problems of unemployment. The internal labor market has certain inherent limitations in providing job security for workers whose jobs are displaced by new technologies. First, the job security must be provided *within* each internal labor market and cannot ordinarily be extended to include other internal markets. Moreover, because employer interests in efficiency favors narrow seniority districts, on-the-job training, and enterprise-specific skills, the potential for job security, in many cases, is further reduced to particular seniority districts. This is in conflict with worker interest in receiving general training which would increase the number of employment opportunities to which they have access should they be displaced by technological change.[5]

Finally, in making a technological change the employer has an incentive to take into account only those costs of worker displacement for which he is responsible under the rules of the internal market. The innovating employer has no financial obligation for workers in other internal markets whose employment is affected by his actions. Nor does he face costs when displacing "temporary" workers from his internal market. This implies that the internal labor market is not a complete substitute for other arrangements, such as unemployment compensation or full employment, which enhance economic security. It also suggests a range of policies aimed at broadening the scope of training, limiting the rights of enterprises to close without warning, and facilitating the transfer of displaced workers.

Adjustment costs. Given the instruments of adjustment within the internal labor market, especially on-the-job training, persistent structural skill imbalances in the economy appear unlikely except where special restrictions upon the adjustment process exist.[6] Most difficulties in labor force adjustment which are encountered seem largely attributable to problems of search and experimentation and to the length of time required to implement the adjustment instruments within the internal labor market. Developing effective techniques for adjustment can be a slow process for the internal labor market as various instruments are tried, and often rejected, until the appropriate mix is discovered. Such an approach introduces lags into the adjustment process which can make it appear initially

[4] Michael J. Piore, "Technological Change and Structural Adjustment in the Labor Market," unpub. diss., Harvard, 1966, pp. 139-147 and pp. 188-189.
[5] See James G. Scoville, "A Theory of Jobs and Training," *Industrial Relations,* October 1969, pp. 36-53.
[6] The view that the internal adjustment process permits society to avoid many

to be working ineffectually, thereby overstating the seriousness of labor market imbalances.

Having argued that much of the evidence used in support of the structural hypothesis failed to appreciate the adjustment processes occurring within internal markets, the findings of Chapter 6 should be emphasized. They suggest that the character of technological change as it affects the requirements of jobs is only weakly controlled by the neoclassical mechanisms of relative wages or, more broadly, labor costs. If the economy has managed to avoid structural bottlenecks, it is due to the adaptability of the labor force and the effectiveness of the instruments through which the employers adjust to the external market conditions. While it is conceivable that absolute structural bottlenecks may still occur, the more likely impact of technological change is to raise the cost of adjustment to it. Ideally, firms should anticipate these costs, and they should be built into the calculations that justify the technical change. But it appears that in fact they are not generally foreseen, even when they are borne by the firm in which the change is introduced. Moreover, as noted above, when the effect of the change is to displace workers from the enterprise in which they are introduced or to displace workers in other competing enterprises, the employer making the change has little or no incentive to anticipate adjustment costs at all. Since technological change is a continuing phenomenon, a certain allowance for adjustment to it is built into the cost structure of the economy. Should adjustment costs rise above that level, however, the effect would be to aggravate the conflict between full employment and price stability.

Inflation

If the concern over structural unemployment with which the nation began the 1960's proved unfounded, the concern with inflation has not. The low levels of unemployment attained in the latter part of the decade have been accompanied by significant wage and price inflation, and the problem of reconciling full employment and price stability—the "Phillips Curve" dilemma—has become the central problem of economic policy in the late 1960's, as it was in the late 1950's.

There has been a trend in the literature on the Phillips Curve to move from explanations based upon market power of unions and companies

---

problems of long-term labor market imbalances does not imply that there are no obstacles to this process, or that conflicts with other economic or social policies do not exist. Where restrictions are placed on certain instruments of the adjustment process, such as licensing requirements, civil service regulations, or negotiated work rules, this process may be frustrated. When the elimination of discrimination is a goal, the incentives of efficiency and the inhibitions of custom at the workplace may work at cross purposes with this objective.

to explanations based upon labor market behavior.[7] Some of these have focused on job search, job vacancies, and labor market flows. Few, however, have considered the internal labor market and the internal adjustment process.

An understanding of the internal labor market does not provide a solution to this policy dilemma, but it does suggest a somewhat different perspective from previous theories. First, one possible source of the inflationary pressure accompanying reductions in unemployment are the adjustments which internal markets make to the external market. As indicated in Chapter 5, the amount of the adjustment, and the associated adjustment costs are likely to rise in tightening labor markets as employment expands, turnover increases, and the average "quality" of job applicants declines. Moreover, these costs are a function not only of the level of unemployment but of the rate of change of unemployment as well. When the internal market is under pressure to fill vacancies quickly or to discover new adjustment techniques, as when the labor market tightens quickly, the more costly adjustment instruments are likely to be brought into play. As with any component of production costs, these costs can be translated into price increases under the appropriate circumstances.[8]

Second, some adjustment instruments appear capable of generating continual cost increases of a kind which would account for observed relationships between the level of unemployment and the rate of inflation. The adjustment instrument most likely to operate in this way is the wage rate. The procedure of setting plant wage levels through a community wage survey makes it likely that wage increases will be followed by other plants in the community, so that the attempt of one firm to adjust to the market in this way will set off a wage spiral among many of the enterprises there. Because internal wage structures are relatively rigid, adjustments in entry wages exert leverage upon the entire wage structure of each enterprise. Since such wage increases will be occurring in a generally prosperous economy, the supply of many kinds of labor is apt to be highly inelastic, and wage adjustments will not only set off a wage spiral but are also likely to have little impact in alleviating the underlying scarcity.

It is thus possible to develop a theory in which the Phillips Curve is generated by a series of uncoordinated actions of individual firms. One firm trying to adjust to a tightening labor market through changes in its

---

[7] For a summary of this literature, see Edmund S. Phelps, *Micro-economic Foundations of Employment and Inflation Theory* (New York: W. W. Norton and Company, Inc., 1970).

[8] This pattern of cost increases postulated is consistent with studies showing that changes in the price level are correlated with both the level and the rate of change of the level of unemployment. See, for example, George L. Perry, *Unemployment, Money Wage Rates, and Inflation* (Cambridge, Mass.: The Technology Press of MIT, 1966).

entry wages would set off a chain reaction in the community spreading through the wage survey mechanism from one plant to another. The changing entry wages would also spread through each enterprise's internal wage structure, and this too would be propagated externally by the community wage survey. By the time the effects of the initial move had been dissipated, the firm would again find itself short of labor and react by initiating a second wage round.

Adjustments through most other internal instruments, however, tend to alleviate the underlying labor scarcity. Thus, in a tight labor market, reductions in hiring standards, changes in screening procedures, and training will all act to increase the supply of labor. Job redesign, job vacancies, and subcontracting all serve to reduce or shift demand. Whether, in the aggregate, such policies can sufficiently reduce labor scarcities and alleviate market pressure depends upon conditions in the sectors of the labor market from which the new supply is drawn or to which the demand is shifted. If the adjustment process is one in which high-wage sectors drain labor from or transfer work to lower-wage firms which face an even tighter market, little will be accomplished. If the result is to equalize the incidence of unemployment and to provide substantial training, the scarcity will be eased.

The public policy goal implicit in the foregoing discussion is that firms should be encouraged to adjust to tightening labor markets through nonwage adjustment instruments, and that these instruments should be directed at sectors of the economy with relative labor surpluses. This could be accomplished through enterprise subsidies for screening, recruitment, and training, or by government programs which performed the same functions at a lower cost than the enterprise.

It should be noted, however, that the same forces which make adjustments to external market conditions through wage changes unattractive to society also make them unattractive to the individual enterprise. Most managers are aware of the tendency for wage adjustments to set off a community wage spiral. Even where they are not deterred by this concern, they are generally discouraged from excessive reliance upon entry wage adjustments by the leverage which they exert upon the internal wage structure of the enterprise.

What is true of wage adjustments is true of other instruments as well; there is an advantage to the firm as well as to the society of drawing labor from and shifting work to those sectors of the labor market where supply is least constrained. This suggests a second explanation of the Phillips Curve, that *primary* internal markets attempt to adjust to labor market shortages through nonwage instruments which shift product and labor demand to the *secondary labor market* where the internal wage structure is less extensive or nonexistent and where there is consequently little deterrent to wage adjustments. This would imply that the key to the Phillips Curve lies in programs directed at the secondary sector, and perhaps in its elimination. An extensive study of adjustments in the low-wage labor market is required to evaluate this hypothesis.

Government-Sponsored Manpower Programs and Labor Force Adjustment

The Adjustment Process

In the preceding section it was argued that government subsidization of the labor force adjustment processes now provided primarily by internal labor markets might reduce inflationary pressures. In the remainder of this chapter, the role of government intervention in the labor market is examined further.

Training. In analyzing government-sponsored training programs a distinction should be made among (1) general training in verbal and mathematical skills, (2) training in occupational skills common to many enterprises, and (3) training in occupational skills specific to a single enterprise or industry. Economic efficiency dictates that training should be provided by the enterprises which utilize it, unless there are external economies or diseconomies associated with the training process.

For training that is general to the economy, or to a number of enterprises, both types of external effects may occur. First, there may be significant economies of scale in training which can be realized through mass training programs. Such programs are only within the training capability of very large enterprises or multi-employer associations. Second, if general training is provided by an individual enterprise, labor turnover may transfer the skills to another enterprise which has not contributed to their financing. For training that is enterprise-specific, however, these external effects are negligible.

The case for governmental programs to provide general verbal and mathematical training is strong. The usefulness of this training is not limited to certain industries, and it readily lends itself to formal programs which can effectively utilize large-scale instruction methods. While enterprises do appear willing to supply some general training when such skills are unavailable on the external market, it is often excessively narrow. Employees, for example, may learn to read only those symbols and to perform only those calculations required by their present jobs. It does not, therefore, enhance labor force adjustment beyond the immediate confines of the enterprise, and it may even hamper further adjustment, should the narrow training encourage learning habits which later impede a worker's ability to acquire additional training.

The analysis of internal labor markets suggests that the responsibility for training in skills and abilities which are enterprise-specific, however, should rest with the enterprise. The structure of the internal labor market makes it difficult for workers outside the enterprise to gain direct access to many jobs utilizing these skills even if trained to perform them. A more important consideration is that training on the job is probably the most efficient method of instruction for most enterprise-specific skills. Where such training is less efficient, institutionalized procedures already exist for transferring the training to equipment vendors or to the local schools.

Considerations of economic efficiency suggest that the enterprise should not only control the process of training in enterprise-specific skills, but should pay for it as well. Specific training by definition, yields few external economies. Hence its costs should properly be absorbed by the enterprise, thus serving as an incentive to economize the scarce resources involved. If the inflationary consequences of enterprise-financed training are significant, however, and the government can absorb the costs in a less inflationary manner, these economic considerations may be outweighed.[9] In addition, government concern with improving employment or income opportunities for minority groups or for the disadvantaged may argue for subsidizing enterprise adjustment costs for these groups, independent of efficiency considerations.

To reduce inflationary pressures of adjustment cost and to encourage the use of adjustment instruments which minimize the conflict with price stability, the government should support enterprise-specific training through a system of subsidies to employers, much like that embodied in the JOBS program. Such subsidization would have the advantage of preserving the existing efficiencies of employer control over training. The major obstacle to such a system is administrative, the training costs being largely indirect and difficult to quantify. This suggests that the government should be less concerned with specifying formal training procedures and should concentrate on results, leaving each enterprise to define its own training strategy.

Training in more general occupational skills—maintenance mechanics, highly skilled machine operations, and the like—presents an intermediate situation between that of general literacy training and specific training. Like literacy training, it tends to be excessively narrow when provided by the enterprise and may, therefore, yield unnecessarily high adjustment costs in the long run. On the other hand, like enterprise-specific training,

---

[9] The additional problem of disturbing competitive cost relationships among firms should be recognized. In highly competitive industries, where labor costs are a high proportion of total costs, the subsidization of training expenses, for example, might provide new enterprises with a critical competitive advantage over established enterprises. A prime illustration of this problem is the concern of the needle trades unions that Federal training funds will be used to finance "runaway" shops.

it can be acquired on the job, and jobs utilizing such training may not be directly accessible from the external labor market. Given these hybrid characteristics, a system of Federal subsidization similar to that for enterprise-specific training, but designed to encourage broader training programs as well to absorb training costs, would be most appropriate.

Recruitment and screening. The same logic applied to the evaluation of governmental training programs can be extended to governmental manpower policies in the field of recruitment and screening. The government should screen and recruit workers with characteristics of general interest to employers, while the cost of recruiting and screening for relatively enterprise-specific characteristics ought to be left to the enterprise, unless there are significant economies of scale.

Again, however other considerations may favor more extensive governmental recruitment and screening. For example, a number of persons currently considered to be disadvantaged may lack access to high-wage employment, not so much because they cannot perform the available work, but because they are difficult, and expensive, to identify under traditional screening procedures. It has been suggested, for example, that a major contribution of the Manpower Development and Training Act (MDTA) institutional training programs has been to screen groups of workers not possessing suitable formal educational qualifications in order to identify a subgroup possessing such qualities as reliability and trainability for which employers use formal educational requirements as a proxy. While this evaluation no doubt understates the contribution of governmental training programs, the programs probably are valuable in this way. To the extent that they are, Federally supported *screening* programs would be a less expensive substitute for training.

Manpower Programs for Low-Income Labor Markets

The distinction between secondary and primary employment suggests two alternative approaches for public policy: (1) programs to accelerate the transition from secondary to primary employment and (2) programs to improve the quality of secondary employment. If linkages between primary and secondary employment exist, then the former programs are likely to be most effective. If there are serious discontinuities between primary and secondary labor markets, the latter policy will be preferable.

Federal manpower policies have followed the former approach, operating under the assumption of the simple queue theory of the labor market. This interpretation points first to aggregate demand policies which expand employment along the queue and, second, to programs of training, orientation to work, and job information which will advance the disadvantaged along the queue. Employment instability, poor work habits, and skill deficiencies are seen as problems of labor supply, to be corrected by modifying worker traits. The process of adapting disadvantaged workers to primary employment involves some or all of the following steps: (1) outreach or recruitment, (2) screening and selection, (3) remedial education and training, (4) placement, (5) orientation to work and to specific job requirements, (6) counselling and supportive services. The particular combination will depend upon the type of disadvantage encountered and the kind of employment involved. Some of the more important steps are discussed below.

Recruitment and labor market information. There is little evidence to suggest that information with respect to secondary employment is insufficient. Disadvantaged workers, at least in urban areas and in periods of high employment, seem well aware of job opportunities. In fact, the high turnover that is characteristic of the secondary labor market probably contributes to a higher overall level of informal labor market information than in the primary market. This information, however, is heavily biased toward secondary jobs, and expanded labor market information about primary employment opportunities may be useful in facilitating transition to the primary labor market, providing other barriers to employment do not exist. Labor market information programs may also be sufficient for assisting the handicapped, and for remedying teenage unemployment by expediting exposure to work while leaving turnover to diminish with age and work experience. Government resources in this area should be directed more at increasing the amount of information on primary jobs, relying upon informal information channels to bear the major responsibility for secondary jobs.

Training. Current programs for improving the competitive position of the disadvantaged through institutional training programs should be viewed with some skepticism. Such programs neglect both the importance of labor force adjustment within the internal labor market and the distinction between primary and secondary employment. They are usually too short and lack the sophisticated curricula necessary to provide a broadly marketable skill. Instead they provide little more than a superficial familiarity with a limited range of equipment, materials, and operating procedures. Even worse, they may instill work habits in the trainees which are inconsistent with enterprise practices and which have to be unlearned. Finally, such programs are often directed at labor scarcities in secondary labor markets rather than at upgrading the disadvantaged into primary employment. As with many labor market information programs, the result is to reinforce the operation of the secondary market rather than to open primary employment.

Orientation to work. The problem of instability and poor work habits among adult workers has generally evaded solution. Some training programs have been able to demonstrate low turnover, especially where the training environment was very attractive or when the training stipend loomed large relative to alternative sources of income.[10] There has been little satisfactory demonstration, however, that this stability has carried over to post-training employment. Moreover, to the extent that turnover can be traced to the quality of work available in the *secondary* labor market, programs for modifying workers' attitudes are misdirected.

Referral to primary jobs does seem to encourage stability, but this poses the basic conflict inherent in the queuing behavior of the primary labor market. Primary employers normally seek to hire advantaged workers and have adopted wage scales and other labor market adjustment instruments which permit them the privilege of selectivity. Successful modifications in selection priorities to hire the disadvantaged are likely to be associated with a longer and more costly labor force adjustment process. Programs to employ and retain disadvantaged workers in primary internal labor markets may therefore involve temporarily overlooking, or treating more leniently, infractions of work rules and the temporary acceptance of production norms which are at variance with customary standards. This, however, establishes dual standards of performance: one for the disadvantaged, and one for the incumbent employee.

Work rules are a compromise between the loose performance standards and less stringent discipline favored by the incumbent work force and management's interest in tighter standards. The incumbent work force in primary internal labor markets normally insists upon uniform application of all rules and penalties, and any deviation from uniformity violates fundamental principles of equity. Since many work rules are defined by precedent, deviations from prevailing standards tend to establish new precedents to be applied uniformly in the future.

The labor force adjustment process within the internal labor market typically involves short-term concessions for the new hire. If additional or longer-term concessions are granted to the disadvantaged worker, there is the ever-present danger that they will be extended to the entire internal work force with implications for efficiency which reach far beyond the disadvantaged employee.

If uniformity of concession is not granted, then problems of backlash may be intensified, especially if similar concessions have been the topic of collective negotiations, or have been denied earlier to incumbent employees. Concessions to the disadvantaged under such circumstances are regarded as special favoritism and in violation of the whole system of equity which primary employees and unions have sought to establish.

[10] See, for example, Peter B. Doeringer *et al., Low Income Labor Markets and Urban Manpower Programs: A Critical Assessment,* Report submitted to the Manpower Administration, U. S. Department of Labor, January 1969.

Typical of the issues at stake is the probationary period. Because work habits are learned, much like any other work skill, it may be necessary to seek an extension of the probationary period if disadvantaged workers are to be retained in primary internal labor markets. Because probationary employees have no access to the grievance procedure, the work rules applied to them do not set precedents for incumbent workers. The probationary period is a signal to incumbent employees that special consideration is to be accorded to the new hire during which time the employer retains the right to summary dismissal. The prevailing probationary period, however, represents a compromise between management's desire to maximize the period in which it is free to deal with workers, unhampered by union limitations, and the union's view of probation as a threat to collective bargaining. Even when both the employer and the union have a strong commitment to hiring disadvantaged workers the issue is difficult to resolve. When the commitment is weak, such programs may become a pawn in larger negotiations.[11]

The recent Federal programs to utilize the labor force adjustment capabilities of the internal labor market to facilitate the employment of the disadvantaged is also an outgrowth of the queue theory. These programs, however, have taken too little cognizance of the problems of poor work habits and their relationship to secondary employment. The resources of the programs have not been concentrated upon opening up new primary employment opportunities or upon overcoming poor work habits by emphasizing upgrading and worker retention.

Special Programs for the Dual Labor Market

The dual labor market concept, in contrast to the queue theory, points to a broad range of policy areas which are not normally thought of as part of manpower policy. For example, racial discrimination, disparities in union organization, and differences in the impact of social insurance taxes operate on the demand side of the market to strengthen the distinction between primary and secondary jobs. Policies directed at modifying these forces will presumably reduce the differences between the two markets and facilitate intermarket labor mobility. On the supply side of the market, some of the proposals for welfare reform along the lines of the negative income tax are conducive to greater accommodation of the secondary labor force to work discipline. Reforms aimed at stabilizing illicit activities and reducing the competition which they pose to legitimate employment should operate in a similar fashion.

[11] See Michael J. Piore, "On-the-job Training in a Dual Labor Market," in Arnold R. Weber, *et al.* (eds.), *Public-Private Manpower Policies* (Madison, Wis.: Industrial Relations Research Association, 1969), pp. 110-113.

The Elimination of Barriers to Primary Employment

Racial discrimination is a significant barrier to the movement of minority groups from secondary to primary employment. The elimination of the effects of racial discrimination is therefore essential to the upgrading of minority groups and the ultimate elimination of income and employment inequality.

Equal access to the full range of jobs in primary internal labor markets is a key element in achieving this goal, but providing such access will often raise the cost of labor force adjustment in the internal market and can impair the job security of the internal labor force as well. The hiring process for internal labor markets is based upon the probabilities of *groups* of workers having certain performance levels on the job. Thus race, education, or aptitude test scores are typically used as statistical screening devices because they are presumed to correlate with worker traits, such as reliability and ability to learn, that are not readily measured. Reducing the racial bias inherent in such screening devices implies either the development of more sophisticated screening procedures or the replacement of screening by a random hiring process. Either option will raise the cost to the employer of acquiring a work force. Similarly, changing recruiting patterns to increase the number of minority group applicants will involve additional costs for the internal market. Where internal discrimination is to be remedied, both the employer and the incumbent work force may experience costs. Employers must retrain workers and perhaps modify internal allocative criteria. Incumbent workers may experience the costs of redistributed job security or promotion opportunities.

In many respects, providing equal employment opportunity is analogous to other types of labor market adjustment which pose costs for the internal labor market. The costs of eliminating entry discrimination are like the cost of adapting to tightening labor markets. Remedying internal discrimination involves adjustments having effects similar to those encountered when adapting to technological change. This suggests that public and private manpower programs can, by relieving cost constraints on both employers and incumbent workers, provide an important adjunct to other efforts to overcome discrimination. For example, there are desirable jobs within the internal labor market in mobility clusters containing maintenance, clerical, and technical work which represent additional promotion opportunities, provided that appropriate training arrangements are established. Filling such jobs internally can expand the number of upgrading slots, thereby facilitating the process of merging seniority ladders and accelerating minority group advancement.

Where employment is declining and additional internal promotion vacancies cannot be made available in great numbers, a more ambitious program could be developed to provide employees in the lower-paying jobs with training in basic English and mathematics, vocational skills, and clerical or technical skills which could then qualify them for a broader range of jobs with other employers in the community.

The pressure of civil rights activities in the employment field has also generated interest among employers and unions to participate in manpower programs. Such programs are valued not only for the trained minority group workers which they yield, but for the tangible evidence of affirmative action which they provide.[12]

Labor Legislation

There is also a range of programs which affect the operation of secondary labor which will be important for those who must continue to fill the poorer jobs in the economy. Improvement in the income-guarantee and work-incentive aspects of the welfare system will make it less risky for workers to leave welfare and enter the secondary labor market. It should also make it easier for disadvantaged workers to invest in the additional job search and to face the additional risk of termination which are involved in obtaining primary employment. Collective bargaining could be encouraged in the secondary labor market through amendments to the Wagner and Taft-Hartley Acts as a means of strengthening internal labor markets in the secondary sector, thereby making secondary work conform more closely to primary work. The coverage of minimum wage legislation could also be extended and made uniform in all employments as the first step in directly improving compensation levels in the secondary labor market.

Public Employment

Proposals for the government to employ the disadvantaged in public works jobs paying the minimum wage are based upon the premise that many of the disadvantaged are otherwise permanently unemployable. Analysis of the secondary labor market, however, suggests that the number of urban "unemployables," for whom sheltered work would be an efficient remedy, is not great during periods of full employment. Public employment programs are likely to expand the demand for low-wage labor in the secondary labor market, which already behaves like a tight labor market, without initiating any corrective mechanisms necessary to overcome instability and to upgrade workers to primary employment. Moreover, a guarantee of work may even aggravate instability on the supply side of the market. Unless such upgrading can be assured, programs directly tied to opening primary employment are preferable.

[12] See Peter B. Doeringer and Michael J. Piore, "Equal Employment Opportunity in Boston," *Industrial Relations,* vol. 9, no. 3 (May 1970).

Training for Casual Labor Markets

A number of persons in low-income neighborhoods, primarily students and women with children, seek part-time employment. These workers, as well as the chronically unstable among the disadvantaged, constitute a casual labor force whose employment needs are best met by intermittent work. Temporary-help agencies provide a ready institution for organizing the casual labor market and for coupling casual employment with intermittent training. Temporary-help agencies have well-established connections with the business community and could develop special training programs to improve the skills of disadvantaged workers who hope to remain permanently in the labor market as well as those with more tenuous attachment. Initially, training could be aimed at low-skilled clerical and laboring jobs. On days when referrals are not available, the disadvantaged could receive training, geared to their own rate of advancement, in lieu of work. The trainees could be referred to increasingly skilled work as their training progressed.

Manpower Planning and Labor Force Adjustment

Finally, whatever types of manpower programs it selects, the government must also identify those sectors towards which they should be directed. To do so, it must both appraise current manpower developments and forecast future trends. The internal labor market and the character of the adjustment process which occurs within it pose serious obstacles to this task.

Manpower data are currently collected in a series of categories that divide the members of the labor force into groups on the basis of socioeconomic characteristics (occupation, educational attainment, industrial attachment, for instance). Manpower problems are then largely identified with imbalances between job requirements and the labor force structure as revealed by the distribution of workers among these categories.

The adjustment process, however, is continually modifying the distinctions among jobs and among workers which are implied by these categories. Required worker characteristics are changed through variations in hiring standards and screening procedures; the on-the-job training process involves both the transformation of the work force, and, in the short run at least, the redesign of jobs. The shifts in job design and required worker characteristics are so continuous as to defy any system of analysis dependent upon discrete categories. Moreover, in the case of technological change, the adjustment process involves innovations in these instruments which are virtually synonymous with discovery, and hence are extremely difficult to predict. Present techniques of manpower planning therefore will inevitably underestimate the capacity of the private sector to effect adjustment.

To some degree, the internal labor market, with its potential for on-the-job training and upgrading, provides manpower flexibility and is an alternative to manpower planning. Overtime, subcontracting, and product inventories serve a similar function. Nevertheless, the limits of this flexibility can be reached during periods of continuing economic expansion.

Planning permits public and private manpower programs to be scheduled to reduce conflicts with resources needed for production. In periods of stable or declining output, for example, excess capacity in capital equipment or in supervisory resources can be utilized for training at little additional cost. Planning can also reduce the costs of adjustment lags by enabling the employer to initiate long-term adjustment programs in advance of labor market imbalances.

It has been argued in this volume that the major governmental concern with labor market adjustment processes should be with manipulating the processes to achieve cost efficiencies and other objectives of national economic policy. Incentives to minimize adjustment costs are already present in the enterprise's desire for profit and in the decentralized mechanisms coordinating plant skill needs with labor market conditions and with training curricula in the educational system. What appears to be lacking are sources of information about alternative modes of adjustment and sufficient incentives to overcome discrimination and to employ the disadvantaged.

Under present arrangements, each enterprise tends to discover on its own the changes in job design, promotion patterns, training techniques, hiring standards, and the like, through which labor force adjustment is effected. Experimentation to hasten the discovery process is inhibited by the difficulties of changing procedures once the labor force becomes accustomed to them and of identifying and controlling adjustment costs. Some sharing of experience occurs through local organizations of personnel managers, various other community institutions, and through industry trade associations.

Although the problems are in many respects analogous to those encountered in selecting new equipment, the channels for communicating information about labor force adjustments are in no way comparable to the trade magazines, exhibitions, and vendors which disseminate information about new equipment. Hence a pooling of information about adjustment techniques through the planning process may be sufficient to hasten the adjustment process and to reduce its costs. Once such systems for pooling information have been developed, the most effective deployment of the relatively small budget which the Federal Government now appears willing to commit to training efforts may well lie in expanding, through the subsidization of experimental programs, the fund of experience with adjustment techniques.

Index

Internal Labor Markets and Manpower Analysis

PETER B. DOERINGER and
MICHAEL J. PIORE,

Originally published in 1971 and now enhanced by a long, reflective introduction by the authors, this reprint will be useful to a wide range of students, scholars, and managers. The new introduction describes recent changes in institutional aspects of the American labor market and assesses the major debate on the origins of those institutions and their significance for the American economic system.

In their new introduction, the authors see a pressing need to construct a new theory of labor markets. They believe that such a theory should be more concerned with distribution and growth than with static efficiency and be better grounded in historical experience. It should depend on group behavior rather than individualistic behavior, and it should stress the importance of institutions as an independent force in the labor market.

Along with such an institutional theory, they would seek new ways of approaching labor market policies with respect to training, fair employment, job creation, productivity improvement, and economic stabilization. Finally, the authors see the need for macroeconomic policy to be conducted with a greater awareness of the labor market institutions whose decision-making such policies are designed to affect.

Peter B. Doeringer is Professor of Economics at Boston University and **Michael J. Piore** is Professor of Economics at MIT.

M. E. Sharpe, Inc. 80 Business Park Drive, Armonk, New York 10504